BUSINESS ADMINISTRATION AND MANAGEMENT

Business Administration and Management

A.K. PHOPHALIA
SARITA SHARMA
G.R. BASOTIA

KANISHKA PUBLISHERS, DISTRIBUTORS
NEW DELHI 110 002

KANISHKA PUBLISHERS, DISTRIBUTORS
4697/5-21A, Ansari Road, Daryaganj
New Delhi -110 002
Phones : 2327 0497, 2328 8285
Fax : 011-2328 8285
E-mail : kanishka_publishing@yahoo.co.in

Edition: 2016

ISBN: 978-81-8457-164-9

PRINTED IN INDIA

Published by Madan Sachdeva for Kanishka Publishers, Distributors, 4697/5-21A, Ansari Road, Daryaganj, New Delhi-110 002, Typeset by Sunshine Graphics, Delhi, and Printed at Rajdhani Printers, Delhi.

Preface

Management and administration of business firms is heading towards a profession. The demand for professional managers is increasing day by day. To achieve professional competence, managers ought to be fully equipped with principles and theories of business management. A comprehensive understanding of principles and techniques of management will increase their decision making ability.

The subject-matter of this book has been adopted from various Indian and foreign books, journals and periodicals. However, the emphasis has been land on Indian management practices based on observations, experiences and research based articles. The idea is to provide all the relevant and up-to-date material at one place so that readers can have an idea about the subject. Though primarily aimed to be a reference book for the students and teachers of colleges and universities, this book will be equally helpful for the practising managers who parsue continuous learning

The author is highly indebted to many eminent authorities of the management whose work have been liberally used in the writing of this book. It is hoped that this book will be useful not only to M.Com. and B.Com. students but also to M.B.A. students. The author is happy to acknowledge his debt and express gratitude to Dr. A.K. Singh, Professor of Management, M.L. Sukhadia University, Udaipur. Who has been a constant source of guidance, encouragement and inspiration.

I crave the indulgence of the readers for any error, omission or commission which may come across in the course of the perusal of the book. I also thanks to M/s. Kanishka Publishers, Distributors, New Delhi, for having worked ceaselessly to bring out the book in time.

Authors

Contents

1

History of Scientific Management

The science of management is as old as human history. In our country during the past few decades, the "managerial revolution" has changed the status of management from amateur to professional. Now management has gained more importance in our industry, trade and commerce. Management compasses fundamental issues relating to human welfare and values. Management is no longer is exclusive domain of the entrepreneur. Social scientists, behaviourists, economists, mathematicians, engineers, scholars, public administrators and so on have significantly contributed to the development of management thought.

Management achieves an objective with the resources available. It functions in practically every phase of human activity, in the home, on the land, in the school, shop, factory, bank, hospital, library, co-operative, labour unions, religious organization, municipality, state, nation and international organization. Although an individual person manages his personal affairs, management usually refers to activities conduced by a group. The social character of management is apparent as soon as one person is employed by another or goods or services are provided for use of others.

Good management, or scientific management, achieves a social objective with the best use of human and material energy and time, and with satisfaction for the participants and the public. It utilizes the resources of nature and of human nature for the benefit of mankind. It applies human intelligence, co-operation and skill, as well as technology to achieve social aims.

In a sense, both management and technology are means, not ends, and can be applied to socially destructive as well as to constructive ends.

The rise of management as a profession, however, has necessarily involved ethical and social considerations. Ends, as well as means, must be taken into account.

An enterprise comes into being to accomplish an objective or a series of objectives which can be attained better by a group of people than by one person alone. An organization is 'a system of co-operative activities of two or more persons'.

People join the enterprise in order to satisfy their needs, desires and aspirations. They will not join unless they believe that the gains from association will outweigh the burdens they assume as members. They may be induced to join through the incentives and gratifications offered; or they may be coerced, as when men were 'impressed' into the navy; or they may be persuaded through appeal to reason, emotion or ideals. The motive or motives with which they join call for the satisfaction of at least some of their needs and desires through the organization. The correlation of individual desires and satisfactions with the existing and emergent aims, methods and results of the enterprise is fundamental to the continuance of the enterprise itself. Hence the importance of the subtle element referred to as morale. 'Morale is the capacity of a group of people to pull together persistently and consistently in pursuit of a common purpose'.

One of the great advantages of a group is that members may be deployed in space and time to make observations, to amplify power and resources, and to maintain a continuity of effort impossible for one person alone. When a number of persons are all engaged in an enterprise, it is normal to divide the activities needed to accomplish the objective into tasks (viewed from the standpoint of the individual) and functions (viewed from the standpoint of the totality) in other words, to develop a structure or 'organization'. Purposes are broken down into intermediate and detailed objectives, so that the functions needed to attain the objectives may be assigned to organizational units, and the detailed tasks to individuals holding positions in those units. Thus there arises a distinction between the structure containing the units and positions and the persons occupying the positions. The work of the units and positions is systematized. Moreover, the wills of the persons must be unified to ensure the continuous unity of effort in the co-operative system.

'Coordination is the orderly arrangement of group effort to provide unity of action in pursuit of a common purpose'. This unity of action requires communication, a constant flow of information between the co-operating individuals so that they may continue to co-operate intelligently in the joint undertaking. Through this flow a system of understandings is developed.

An activity may proceed unchanged for sometime until something in the internal or external system requires an adaptation through either a change of action or a withholding of action. The decision for adaptation takes place at a specific location in time and space. If the activity is to stay correlated, the communication system must convey the new facts, including the adaptation to other points in the system. Each position in the system requires its quota of information. Modification of actions takes place in response to the observations relayed through the communication system. The decision to amend or withhold action is often non-verbal. The observations themselves become cues to action.

Just as differentiation of organs developed in the human individual, so an organization develops special functions, including observation and decision-making for the units and positions which compose it. Making plans and executive decisions becomes a function lodged in position whose occupants have those specialized roles.

Each plan or decision may be considered as a more detailed setting of objectives or methods for their accomplishment within the concrete situation obtaining inside and outside the system at a given time. Plans and decisions are consolidated into policies and procedures which become standards for further activity. The ways of action and though become norms to which people tend to conform.

Plans and decisions connot become effective unless they are communicated, understood and accepted by all those in the system who affected by the change. Willingness to accept patterns for activity is intrinsic to the continuance of the co-operative action.

Thus an order or instruction must be accepted before it carries weight or authority. A usual condition of this acceptance is the belief on the part of each participant that the order is 'authentic' that it comes from a functional and recognized source for directing changes of activity.

Orders which are not understood and accepted are not obeyed. At such time as an individual does not 'go along' with the decisions, he withdraws his contribution of co-operation. In a dictatorship, the price of such withdrawal may be punishment or death but many an individual has preferred dying rather than yielding in situations which went too much against his dispositions or convictions. More commonly, the person does not actively withdraw but contributes only enough activity to scape unpleasant consequences. His contribution is only given in full measure when he works with a will and puts into the joint effort his utmost of skill and energy.

The stability, high productivity and progress of an organization in pursuit of its objectives rest, therefore, on the 'consent of the governed', and still more on the willing and hearty co-operation of its members.

Changes are continually taking place both in the internal system of the organization and in the outside environment. The need for adjustments as well as for continuity requires control and adaptation. Control maintains 'the equilibrium between ends and means, output and effort. It adjusts activities to scure the desired results.

Each organization is a social system within a larger social system, and subject to the laws of the particular situation—economic, physical, legal, sociological, psychological and technical.

A principle and a law of management are two expressions for the same thought. A law is defined as 'a relationship between cause and effect which, so far as the total existing experience goes, has been proved to be valid in all cases....... A law is a statement of fact.

Laws are further defined thus "Uniformities, sequences, and results relative to given courses of action in management are designated as laws. They have somewhat different significance from the laws of the physical sciences, for they deal with different phenomena."

A principle is defined as 'a general proposition sufficiently applicable to the series of phenomena under consideration to provide a guide to action........ A principle is a mechanism of thought'.

In connection with principles of organization, Urwick says, "The principles, however convenient as a shorthand method of thinking, are only guides to action. If they become rules—rigid—they lose their utility. There must be continuous machinery for working out new principles and applying existing principles to cases."

Principles are not necessarily universally true in a social environment as are laws in physics:

1. The principles may be applicable to the great majority of cases, but not to all, and their limitations have not been clearly determined.
2. There is a lack of agreement on the meaning of the words used in expressing the principles, which leads to confusion in thought about them and their application.
3. There are factors not yet covered by general principles which are often or more importance than those already covered.
4. In an individual case various principles must often be balanced against one another, and it may be that there is no general principle which will indicate where the balance should lie ....

'Principles of organization' are those that have been found to work satisfactorily in variety of circumstances. They are in the nature of abstractions from the experience of many organizations and, as such, they are valuable guides in building a new organization or in rearranging an existing one. When it comes to the application of the principles to a particular problem, there are other factors which must be considered, and the principles themselves become merely some of the factors which should be taken into account.

One could look at the problem in algebraic terms: Principle 'a' times, 'x', plus principle 'b' times 'y' plus 'c' times 'z' etc., might give the answer for a particular case. The principles are all considered, but the weights, 'x', 'y' and 'z', have to be determined for the particular case. If 'x' is 5 in one situation and .5 or even –.5 in another, it might appear that the principle which was so important in one case had been disregarded in the others.

The 'laws of the situation' applying to an organization include the statues of the land, and the social attitudes which press in upon it. It cannot escape the impact of a spiral of inflation any more than it can avoid the effect of obsolescence of its machinery or the exhaustion of the mineral reserves in its properties. The enactment of the Industrial Disputes Act, for instance, reflects a change in thinking which has the force of a social fact.

The swiftness and ingenuity of adaptation to new changed forces has much to do with the continuance or success of the enterprise. This applies not only to major adjustments, but also to ordinary vicissitudes of demand and supply, orders for and design of product, labour relations and community opinion.

The capacity for vital and successful adjustment and should growth of the organization demands organs for observation, research, planning, control and decision-making. Means for reaching the desired ends must be carefully chosen. Existing skills and techniques and processes may be used or adapted, or inventions and innovations developed. In the past few decades invention and engineering have immeasurably stepped up the capacities for production. More recently it has been realized that a successful organization requires also the willing and skilful co-operation of the human beings who compose it. The quality of service of the individuals and the temper of the organization may be as significant to the successful achievement of objectives as the technology utilized. Understanding, co-operation and teamwork among members of the organization are essential to good management.

Maintaining and enhancing co-operation is the prime function of leadership. Discrepancies between individual and organizational goals must be reconciled. Members must also secure reasonable satisfactions in return for their contributions to the organization. The leader not only maintains the conditions for co-operation but inspires members with team spirit and helps them move forward to the goal.

Management Thought and Development

The field of management is extremely broad-based. It encompasses fundamental issues relating to human welfare and values. It no longer is the exclusive domain of the entrepreneur of the financier.

Social scientists, behaviourists, economists, mathematicians, engineers, scholars, public administrators and so on have significantly contributed to the development of management thought, its mechanics and functions. In fact, the different approaches to management are not the different schools of management, but rather a kind of intellectual division of labour in studying the problems of management.

When one studies the writings of management scientists, one cannot but be impressed by the insights they provide. A part of the theory of management has been distilled from prolonged first-hand experience, some has been through the process of investigation and verification. Concepts of management serve as set rules or laws of action and conduct. As such, they are also known as principles of management.

However, a theory about management cannot be expected to make possible predictions as exact as could be made in the physical sciences.

The significant element of management theory lies in its integrative process. Management is, therefore, rightly considered as a continuous organisation of people and resources for the attainment of dynamic objectives. Ever since Taylor's contributions to management came to view, it has been proved beyond doubt that management problems and process could be accorded scientific treatment. Today, management is a science of its own class with an inter-disciplinary approach and freely drawing upon economics, mathematics, anthropology, psychology, sociology and so on. Conceptualising management exclusively as an art would not help in formalising and systematising it as an organised body of knowledge.

There was hardly any systematic study of management in the early stages of the Industrial Revolution. It was not until the rise of scientism in the 19th century that theories of management began to take some hold. A number of pioneers applied the scientific method to the solution of business problems but their contributions were relatively unnoticed until Frederick W. Taylor developed what eventually became known as scientific management. Taylor's work marked for the beginning of the modern era of management thought.

The chief appeal of scientific management lay in its logical methodology and its classic simplicity. Taylor popularised his ideas by citing dramatic demonstrations of how the use of scientific management could increase productivity in loading pig iron and in shovelling different kinds of materials into various vehicles. He drew our attention to the need for a scientific approach at factory level in assessing work-load, work-time.

While Taylor's approach to motivation emphasised monetary rewards, another concept invoked the principle that environmental conditions were the prime factors affecting individual productivity. This approach holds that changes in output can be obtained by making changes in working conditions or in the work environment. A series of experiments made by Elton Mayo and his colleagues at Hawthrone expounded a new set of determinants of industrial productivity. The 'Hawthorne Studies' showed that changes in lighting intensities (an environmental factor) on a hand-assembly job had little or no apparent influence on the output of the female workers performing the job. Production increased when lighting intensities increased; gains were also recorded when light levels were lowered. Researchers concluded that productivity was primarily dependent upon non-environmental factors and tentatively identified personal and social relationships in the work group as the variables exerting the greatest effect on output. The studies formed the foundation for many of the personnel-oriented approaches to management that were so wide-spread during the 1940s.

Mayo's views emphasising social and personal relationships as prime forces in motivating output were expanded and developed by his followers. They have now been crystallised into the 'Human Relations' approach. The human relations philosophy views man as a social animal. Taylor's disciples considered man to be primarily an economic being. Contemporary theorists see man as a rational problem-solver and decision-maker; The advocates of human relations approach claim that man is more complex than what Taylor or Mayo envisaged. They believed that the scientific management and human relations approaches fail to understand human motivation. The rational school holds that man is not a thing to be manipulated. Rather he is an entity capable to making adaptations to and evaluations of differing sets of circumstances.

The theory of motivation as applied to work situations has made great strides with the works of authors like Maslow,

Herzberg, W.F. Whyte and Gellerman. The Hawthorne experiments studied factory systems as a social process and exploded the myth that man is a means only. Every man is now conceived as an end in himself. If business is to use man in a co-operative venture, it must be a two-way traffic along with the realisation of mutual goals and needs of employees and management.

Management theories can thus be put under the following classifications: *(a)* Operational School, *(b)* Empirical School, *(c)* Human Behaviour School, *(d)* Social System School, *(e)* Decision Theory School and *(f)* Mathematical School. The current state of management theory has the following five distinct stages.

(i) Theories stating that people are passing followers of direction, not initiators of action. Such formal or traditional theories assume that work can be routinized or broken down by functions. The ideas of F.W. Taylor and some of his disciples fit into this category.

(ii) Theories holding that people have values, attitudes, goals and individual needs. Elton Mayo and other environmentalists fall in this group.

(iii) Theories assuming that social interactions both within and beyond the work situation have an influence on human behaviour. The individual performs a number of roles in his life environment, and he evaluates decisions in terms of their positive or negative effect on the role he plays.

(iv) Theories that explain managerial behaviour in terms of rational mathematical relationships expressed in the forms of models. Managerial activities are simulated in systems of equations or models and the managerial job is to set the limit of the model's responsibilities. Once the model is constructed, the management function becomes automatic. This relatively recent development has evolved since the rise of computer technology.

(v) Theories assuming that successful managerial action can only came from observation of the process of management. The essence of this approach is laid out in sets of principles that provide general guidelines within which managers can exercise individual judgement and skill. The followers of this concept believe that a good theory can only be derived

from observations and modification of successful management practice.

Henri Fayol has referred to six activity areas in every industry. These are: *(a)* Technical, *(b)* Commercial, *(c)* Financial, *(d)* Security, *(e)* Accounting, and *(f)* Managerial. As such, managing is only one part of the totality of business activities. While Taylor was concerned with the operative aspect of management, Fayol was with its administrative aspect. While Taylor worked at the bottom layer of organisation (working as an ordinary worker in a steel factory), Fayol worked for its top layer (being in the top hierarchy of management in a large coal-mining business). However, both conceived management as a process and derived principles for effective work from their practical experience.

Besides formulating activity areas, Fayol contributed 14 principles for good management of which scalar chain, unity of command, unity of direction, discipline, expirit-de-corps, etc., are the more popularly known. L. Urwick contributed to the classification of principles of organisation and management. He mainly emphasised the organisational framework in which management functions. Peter F. Drucker's writings have influenced thinking and application on subjects like decentralisation, managing by objectives, managing for results, etc. According to Drucker, management is a practice rather than a science or a profession, though containing elements of both. The three jobs of management are managing a business, managing managers and managing worker and work. "Managing a business has primacy because the enterprise is an economic institution; but managing managers and managing workers and work have primacy precisely because society is not an economic institution and is, therefore, vitally interested in these two areas of management in which basic social beliefs and aims are being realised."

In management literature, attempts are made to define the general concept of management functions of an industrial undertaking. It is necessary for a manager to visualise management in terms of his own tasks and company environment. E.F.L. Brech sums up the management role as an exercise in deliberative and decisive responsibility, combining four essential elements, viz., planning, motivation, co-ordination and control.

Of these, planning and control tend to be found mostly in the garb of techniques and procedures, often closely interrelated with each other. Motivation, on the other hand, lies largely in personal action and attitude on the part of the manager.

Mary Parker Follet, one of the opponents to formalism, placed more stress on the sociological aspect of the organisation and used the concepts of social science in formulating relations between individuals and the organization. She believes that the subject of management is interesting not because of the profits, but because of the dynamism of the process of management. "Among businessman, I find the greatest vitality of thinking today and I like to do my thinking where it is most alive". The theme of Follet's philosophy centered around conflict in its many forms. The solution to conflict, according to her, lay in integration, a method she preferred to domination or compromise, the two usual methods of solving conflicts. Whereas domination meant the survival of the view of the stronger, compromise meant giving up of something, and, therefore, in either case the settlement was transient. On the other hand, integration meant a revelation of the facts of the situation through analysis, with openness; the purpose of this open analysis being to explore the real needs of the parties. The 'law of the situation', as Follet called it, proposed that when both parties saw the logic of each element of the facts of the situation, the conflict dissolved itself. She has surely left a deep impression on future management thinkers, whether they agree with her views or not. Hers was a simple approach to problems, direct and dynamic.

The Behavioural School of Management movement could be traced to Weber, the German social scientist. The writings of Likert, Simon, Argyris, Bennis, etc., have given a formal shape to this movement. The concepts of leadership, social sensitivity, empathy, etc., have all been moulded to fit into these behaviour influences. The behavioural movement of management is an offshoot of human relations school. Douglas McGregor outlined assumptions of managers in his well-known Theory X and Theory Y. Theory Z assumes that work is inherently distasteful to most people, most people shirk responsibility, are not ambitious, and prefer to be directed; they have little creative ability; they can be motivated largely by providing incentives to meet their primary needs; and they have to be closely controlled and often coerced to achieve organizational objectives. Managers with Theory X assumptions attempt to structure, control and closely supervise employees and believe in the 'carrot and stick' approach for obtaining results. The assumptions of Theory X are based on limited understanding of human motivation and behaviour and they trap a manager in 'self-fulfilling prophecy'. For example, if a manager starts with the assumption that people do not like to assume responsibility, he is not likely to delegate responsibility and in due course, subordinates will become incapable of accepting responsibility. This would fulfil his prophecy.

McGregor has proposed a different set of assumptions on the basis of the emerging findings about human motivation which the calls Theory Y. The assumptions are that work is as natural as play, if the conditions are favourable; self-control is desired by most normal people and is often indispensable in achieving organisational goals; the creative ability is widely distributed among people; people are motivated by higher level needs, such as, social esteem, and self-actualisation needs, in addition to the primary needs; people can be self-directed and creative at work if properly motivated. This set of assumptions would lead to a different style of management in which instead of strict control and close supervision, managers would help their employees to become more mature to exercise self-control by progressively lesser external control. The work can be made more challenging and satisfying and need not be viewed as a necessary evil.

Another movement in the field of management is known as the quantitative approach which started with the work of Neumann and Moregenstern in their Theory of Games. Since then the movement has crystallised around the use of probability theory, linear programming, queueing theory, model building, etc. The use of quantitative techniques in management functioning has become the latest craze in the present times. However, adept practitioners in the field are not many. Perhaps in the remaining years of this century, management thought will be substantially influenced and moulded by mathematicians to an extent which has not happened ever in the past.

2

Management Terminology

The terminology used in the field of management unfortunately is at times ambiguous. The word "management" is often used in referring to the group of managerial personnel of an enterprise. This managerial group includes all those who have supervisory responsibility over others and includes the chief executive of the enterprise, all the way down to the first line supervisor. Frequently, the term "management" is also used as a way of referring to the process of managing, the process of planning, organizing, staffing, guiding, directing, supervising, and controlling. Although it would be desirable to speak of managers whenever reference is made to the people who manage and of management whenever we are referring to the management process, the author will at times be guilty of using these terms interchangeably, as almost all writers in the field of management do, to avoid repetition. Furthermore, sometimes the word "management" is used to connote neither the activity (or the function) nor the personnel who exercise it, but as a substantive describing the subject, the body of knowledge and practice as a whole, the discipline. It is used in this meaning, for instance, when it is said that "in creating the Tennessee Valley Authority, Congress adapted and carefully wrote into law the basic principles and practices of modern management". The same ambiguity exists in the use of the word" administration", which can mean the administrator or the administrative processes.

Administration versus Management

The question arises as to whether or not there is a difference between management and administration. William Newman seems not to distinguish between these terms. He defines administration as "the guidance, leadership, and control of the efforts of a group of individuals towards some common goal". Other authors, however, call our attention to a distinction between administration and management. Administration means the overall determination of policies, the setting of major objectives, the identifying of general purposes, the laying out of the broad programmes, major projects, and so forth. Management, however, means essentially the executive function, the active direction of human efforts, getting things done. One could say that administration, by and large, is more determinative, whereas management, by and large, is essentially executive.

To Ordway Tead the distinction between administration and management lies in the following: "Administration is the process and agency which is responsible for the determination of the aims for which an organization and its management are to strive, which establishes the broad policies under which they are to operate, and which gives general over sight to the continuing effectiveness of the total operation in reaching the objectives sought". And he goes on to say that "Management is the process and agency which directs and guides the operations of an organization in the realizing of established aims."

Now two separate sets of personnel are required, however, to discharge administrative and managerial functions. Each

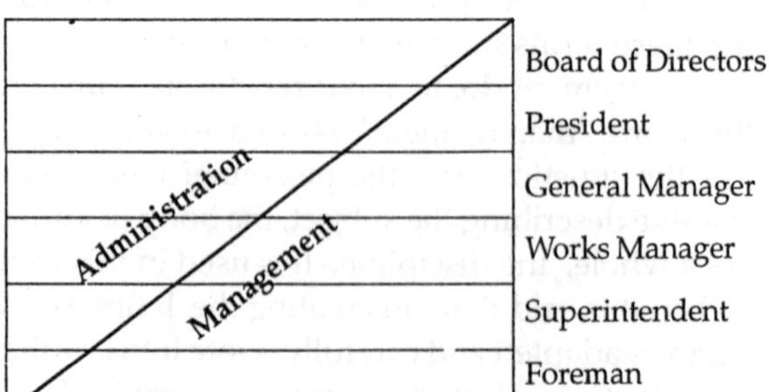

Figure 2.1

manager performs both activities and spends part of his time administrating and part of his time managing. All managers regardless of their level perform the same functions. The higher up in the hierarchy, however, the more time will be spent in administrative activity and the less in management activity in the manager's daily routine, as shown in Figure 2.1. Top management of the enterprise will devote most of its time and efforts to the determination of the objectives, broad policy formulation and so forth, but it cannot possibly avoid spending at least a small amount of time in directing and supervising those immediately under its command.

Administration certainly does not take place by itself, it is not just another function. It is related to the normal business activities such as sales, production, finance, and personnel. We may define a function as follows: "a body of duties closely related in homogeneous character and in operational similarity, which for purposes of execution are naturally and conveniently grouped together as a unified responsibility of a person or department."

Each enterprise has major functions and functions of lesser importance. In a manufacturing enterprise, the production, sales, finance, and personnel would undoubtedly be considered major functions, whereas the purchasing of raw materials would normally be of lesser importance. However, in a department store the purchasing function, the buying of the merchandise to be sold to the consumer, is a major function. The peculiarities and characteristics of each organization must be examined in order to see whether or not a function is a major or minor one. Administration is inherent in the performing of all normal business functions.

Management : Art or Science?

Much has been said and written about the subject of management as an art or a science. If we consider science a discipline in the sense of our natural sciences, it cannot be said that management is a science. In natural science one is able to experiment by keeping all factors constant and varying one at a time. In the natural sciences it is not only possible to define, analyze, and measure phenomena, but it is also possible to repeat the same conditions over and over again, which enables the scientist to experiment and to obtain a proof. This kind of experimentation cannot be accomplished in the area of management since we are dealing with the human element. As long as the human element is involved we cannot speak of scientific experiments in the strict sense of the word.

Taylor, in his Principles of Scientific Management, was thinking of knowledge of two different kinds. When he discussed the best method of making a cut of specified dimensions in a piece of metal of particular size and hardness, he realized it is possible to repeat the same operation over and over again; in this connection he was thinking of scientific management as knowledge found in the physical sciences, where the same conditions can be repeated over and over again and experiments of this nature can be carried on. But when Taylor turned to the human element, he realized that experiment and proof and less possible, and he thought of scientific management in a second way. Human beings are not standardized and experiments cannot be repeated under standardized conditions.

Taylor used the adjective "scientific" in its second sense in his studies of planning, organization, routing and costing. He used the word "scientific" there in its meaning of an organized body of knowledge about a subject "as opposed to mere traditional rules or empirical dexterity." In this case, the word "science" is used in the same sense in which we speak of political science or military science. Undoubtedly, political science and military science are greatly concerned with human beings. Principles of these sciences cannot be subjected to the same kind of experimentation as is customary in the exact sciences. "Yet no one has ever objected to the use of the words science and scientific as applied to these activities, while there is constant disputation and confusion about the application to the activity of management."

The question arises as to whether or not management is an art. Art means the knowing-how, the application, whereas under science one normally understands the knowing-why. Chester I. Barnard, an eminent contributor in the area of management, pointed out that it is the function of the sciences to explain the phenomena, the events, the situations of the past, and that their aim is not to produce specific events, effects, or situations, but explanations which we call knowledge. However, "it is the function of the arts to accomplish concrete ends, effect results, produce situations, that would not come about without the deliberate effort to secure them. These arts must be mastered and applied by those who deal in the concrete". This know-how is indispensable to the manager, and it can only be learned in practice and through experience.

Management contains both elements, those of a science and those of an art. This is not a contradiction in terms, for art and science complement each other and are not mutually exclusive. Consider the example of the physician. There is no doubt that he depends on the sciences for his training and his basic knowledge, but he could not do without the art, the application, the know-how, of practising medicine which he gains from his experience. The same holds true for the manager. He depends on the managerial principles and concepts. In his practical experience in the business life itself, he will learn the art of being a manager. The theory and practice, or the art and the science, are mutually helpful.

Recently, considerable attention has been given to analytical approaches to management, resulting in the emergence of mathematical formulae, business games, operations research, scientific decision-making, and so forth.

The Need for Principles and a Theory

The development of a conceptual framework of the theory of management is essential in the training and teaching of future managers. Henri Fayol decried the absence of management teaching. He wrote that this was due to the absence of theory and without theory no teaching is possible. Fayol went on to say that this lack of teaching would be quite otherwise "were there an accepted theory, that is to say, a collection of principles, rules, methods, procedures, tried and checked by general experience." He appealed to few industriai leaders to set forth their personal views on the general principles which they considered most calculated to promote smooth running, but the majority of managers had neither the time nor the inclination for writing. "It is a case of setting it going, starting general discussion. This is what I am trying to do by publishing this survey." Fayol hoped that from such a discussion a theory would emanate sooner or later. He did not overlook the importance of teaching, but he felt that the question of teaching could be solved only after a body of principles had been established. Fayol was aware, just as we are today, that teaching will no more make good managers out of all students than technical teaching makes excellent technicians out of its trainees. No course on principles of management alone can ever produce a manager. The student will need the clinical experience for refinement and maturity, without which he cannot become a manager.

If we succeed in developing and teaching managerial principles, the job of the manager will be done more effectively and more efficiently. This does not mean that we can give a manager a complete set of principles which will provide the proper answer for each and every situation in which he finds himself. The principles will merely serve as guideposts for his actions, and by following these principles will enable the manager to approach his problems systematically, in a methodological, scientific way. Without principles of management, one could not conceive of a satisfactory method for training future managers. The growing number of enlightened and professionally well-trained managers in top level and junior executive positions has significantly contributed to the high standard of industrialization and high standard of living in the United States.

It has often been said that what works in theory does not always succeed in practice. However, if theory is a body of principles dealing with the subject matter systematically, and if principles are fundamental truths, theory must be practical and applicable; there is then no difference between theory and practice. The theory may not be applicable to a given situation, "but it can hardly be right and applicable and yet be impracticable". The job of a manager will be simplified and his effectiveness and efficiency increased if he understands and properly utilizes the various managerial principles which are at his command. The knowledge of principles and concepts will save the manager considerable labour and energy. Principles and concepts will firmly and securely guide the manager through complicated situations.

Technical Skills versus Managerial Skills

It is necessary to distinguish technical skills from the managerial skills. Most managers at the lower levels of any organization will use technical as well as managerial functions in their daily work. But as these managers advance in the managerial hierarchy they will practice fewer technical skills, and it will become more important for them to apply their managerial skills, to the exclusion of the technical ones. It is clear that the chief executive possesses far fewer technical skills than those whom he employs. But his managerial skills will indicate to him the various technical skills which are needed to provide the solutions. In all probability the chief executive will have enough general knowledge of the special skills so that he is in a position at least to ask pertinent and discerning questions. The chief executive will also know the various relationships among these different skills and how to utilize them. The top executive knows, for example, that a certain problem can best be handled by a statistician and that the legal implications should be taken care of by the legal expert, while the accountant's skill is needed to look at the same problem from a different angle. The manager will call the various skills into action and have these experts apply the tools of their skills to the problem. They undoubtedly possess far more knowledge in their special skills than the chief executive, but he is the one qualified to decide when to call them in and how to coordinate their various functions.

At times the question has been raised as to whether or not the possession of a technical skill is a handicap to a manager as he moves into the top echelons. There are many corporation presidents who were expert accountants, lawyers, engineers, or chemists; and then again, we have others who came into the job out of other managerial positions with a broad executive background, with no one particular speciality. There apparently are a number of shortcomings for the former, and one of them is the amount of time which the executive must have of necessity spent in acquiring and practising his speciality. As a matter of fact, continued practice of a skill for many years will tend to narrow the outlook and actually prevent the individual from having the opportunity to manage.

The manager's skills are unique to him. The executive who has come up the organization ladder through one of the specialities will have to digress beyond his own field of special skill and transform into a "generalist", into a true manager of the enterprise, leaving behind the narrow aspects of the specialist, regardless of his early interest in it. Henri Fayol pointed out that the larger the company the greater must be the managerial capacity of the chief executive and the less specific knowledge he will require. He observed that, as one goes up the scalar chain, "the relative importance of managerial ability increases and that of technical ability declines."

Principle of Universality of Management

The manager uses the same managerial skills and principles in each managerial position. It is of no importance if the enterprise be a business venture, a charitable or fraternal organization, or a government agency. The managerial principles have universal application. A manager well versed in his profession can without much difficulty manage any kind of undertaking. This thought is expressed by what is termed the principle of universality of management.

The validity of this principle was well established during World War II when many business managers left private industry to go into government service. Many of the important war agencies, such as the War Production Board, Office of Defence Transportation, and War Manpower Commission, were staffed on the managerial level by executives who had held key posts in private industry. Though undoubtedly there were a number of executives who did not fit easily into this pattern, and therefore left the government agencies after short service, the overwhelming number of those who did serve proved to be highly successful in government work, though this was entirely different from their previous activities. After a reasonably short time they had their various government agencies functioning with as much efficiency as could reasonably be expected. Many of these managers shifted from one agency to other important posts of other government agencies and were successful in all of them. They applied the same managerial principles and concepts with which they were running their private enterprises to an entirely new situation and function, namely, the activities of the government. They shifted with ease, from the performance of one adminstration function to functions in public adminstration.

The reverse movement took place after World War II when highly skilled organizers and administrators of the armed forces left the military after many years of executive experience and joined private enterprise in managerial positions. They, in turn, after a reasonable time of adjustment, transferred their principles of managing and vast experience to the private business world and, to a great extent, worked out successfully. There, too, of course, were a number who could not make this transition with success. The latter were the exceptions and these probably were not engaged by private industry so much for their managerial ability as for their personal contacts they had made during long years of service in the armed forces. The principles of management are universal. In other words, they are applicable to any kind of enterprise wherever there is the coordinated effort of human beings. The type of enterprise is not significant.

Universality of managerial principles also means that they are transferable. They are transferable from one department to another department regardless of the nature of the function in the other department. A manager's thorough familiarity with managerial principles will facilitate his managing the production end of a manufacturing enterprise, and if he later should be transferred to the selling department, the same managerial principles will prevail there also. At this time it should be stated that universality of managerial principles also means that they can be transferred from one level to another level. All managers perform the same managerial functions regardless of their position in the managerial hierarchy. More about this point will be said later in this chapter.

The Managerial Functions

We can recognize a manager by the functions he performs, and these are managerial in nature. This does not exclude the possibility that from time to time the manager might perform a non-managerial function to fill in or to help out. However, it is not so the other way around. A non-manager does not perform a managerial function. What then are the managerial functions? A manager plans, organizes, staffs, directs and controls. These are the five managerial functions. Some authors in the area of management classify the manager's functions as four managerial types; others have six. The terminology is not always alike, and it might be just as well to use Henri Fayol's original terminology which classifies the functions as planning, organizing, commanding, coordinating and controlling. Of course, the word commanding would be replaced by one with less overtones of an autocratic nature. Coordinating is no longer considered a separate function by most authors as it is maintained that coordination is the essence of management and not a separate function. Coordination takes place in all managerial functions. But, by and large, the functions as outlined by Henri Fayol are as current as those set forth by any of the other writers in the area of management. For our purposes we shall simplify matters and designate the following five as the functions of a manager: Planning, Organizing, Staffing, Directing and Controlling.

Planning

Planning is the function that determines in advance what should be done. It consists of selecting the enterprise objectives, policies, programmes, procedures, and other means of achieving these objectives. In his planning the manager must decide which of alternative plans are to be followed and executed. Planning is intellectual in nature, it is mental work. It is looking ahead and preparing for the future. It is the manager's duty to plan, and this function cannot be delegated to a staff assistant. Such a staff might be helpful in preparing the various plans, but it remains the manager's function to do the planning. There also has been much discussion as to the chronological sequence of planning in relation to the other four managerial functions. Logically, of course, planning must come first. However, it cannot be said that as soon as the other remaining four functions have been performed, the manger would begin his planning function again. In the very beginning of course, nothing can be done without a plan. However, as a manager proceeds in his various functions, he continues to plan, revising his plans and choosing alternates as the need arises. Therefore, it becomes apparent that although planning is a primary function in its inception, the manger persists in his planning as he performs all the other functions.

Organizing

The organizing function means the determination and enumeration of the necessary component activities which are required to achieve the enterprise objectives. It means the grouping of these activities, the assigning of these activities to groups, departments, and so on. When the manager organizes he determines and enumerates the various activities which are required, he assigns these activities, and at the same time he delegates the necessary authority to provide the various functions. He divides and groups the work into individual jobs, and defines the relationships among them. In addition to this, he delegates authority. Authority, as we shall see later, is the key to the managerial job, and the delegation of authority is the key to organization. We cannot speak of a manager unless he has authority, and we cannot speak of creating an organization unless authority is delegated.

Staffing

By staffing we understand management's responsibility to recruit and to make certain that there is enough executive personnel available to fill the various positions needed in the organization. Staffing involves the selection and training of future managers. It also includes the establishing of executive manning tables, tables of replacements and promotions, appraisals, progressions, and rotations, and a wise system of compensation.

Directing

In his function of directing, the manager will guide, teach, coach, and supervise his subordinated, issuing directives for the accomplishment of their activities. It is the manager's job to develop the abilities of his subordinates by effectively directing, teaching and coaching them.

Controlling

The function of control involves those activities that are essential in seeing to it that events proceed as planned. Here again, we can see the importance of planning as primary function of the manager. It would not be possible for him to check as to whether or not the work is proceeding properly if there were no plan against which to check. Under the function of controlling we understand not only the making sure that the objectives are being achieved, but it also includes taking corrective action in the event that there is failure to achieve these objectives.

In the managerial process the manager performs all of these functions continuously. Regardless of his level in the managerial hierarchy, the manager concerns himself with all five functions. As stated above, the term "manager" includes all managers from the president of a corporation down to the supervisor on the firing line. The president of the corporation will obviously spend more time in planning and organizing and less time in staffing, directing, and controlling, whereas the superintendent on the floor probably will devote less time to planning and organizing and more of his time will be spent in directing and controlling. Therefore, time and effort spent on different functions will be determined by the executive's level in the managerial hierarchy, as shown in Figure 2.2. The same five basic functions, however, will be performed by

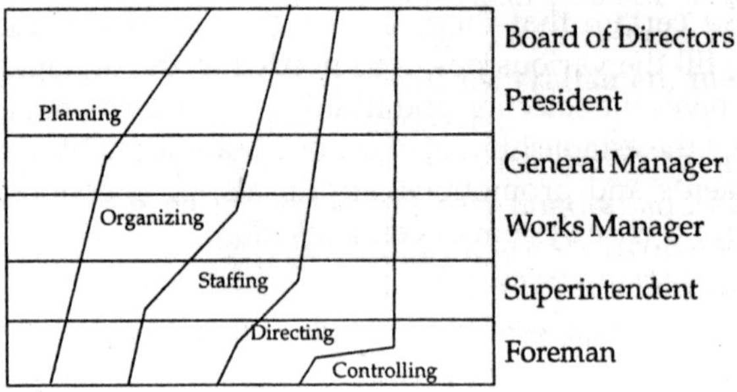

Figure 2.2

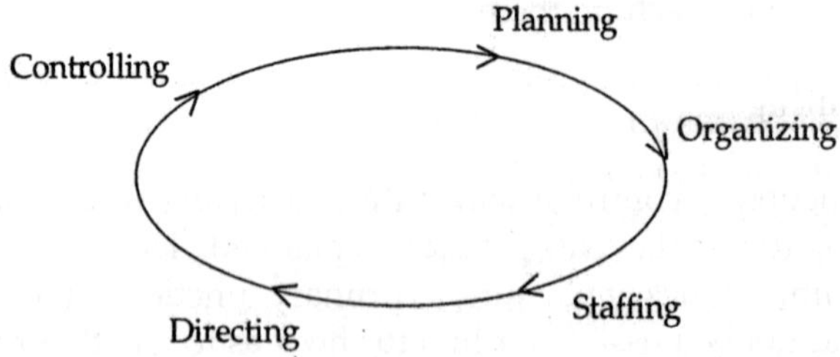

Figure 2.3

every manger regardless of his position in the organization, or in the hierarchy of management. It is helpful to think of these managerial functions as a circular continuous movement.

They flow into each other, as may be seen in Figure 2.3, and at times there is no clear line of demarcation when the one ends and the other one begins. Also, it is not possible for a manager to set aside a certain amount of his time for one or another function, as the efforts spent in one function will vary as conditions change.

Much has been said as to the proper sequence in which these five functions should be considered. Although some writers feel that organizing should be treated first since this is an area in which most conceptual framework of management has been developed, others believe that planning should come first. In this text we shall start out in Part II with the planning function for the reason that no manager can proceed without plans. Planning is the first function. Without plans the manager cannot organize, direct, staff, or control. Therefore, in our conceptual framework the first function which we shall discuss will be the planning function of the manager. But, first, in the remainder of Part I, we will consider the topics of coordination and authority and responsibility.

3

Professionalism in Management

Profession has been defined as a calling requiring specialized knowledge that is backed by long and intensive academic preparation. While this definition may envelope services like medical, legal, teaching and so on, it is doubtful if it could explain the handling of management phenomena so as to make a career in management truly professional in nature. Semantics apart, however, the fact remains that professional careerism is characterised by the technical or the ethical standards of a profession. This underlines the impact of the manager on modern society and its citizens. It can be so great as to require of him the self-discipline and the high standards of public service of a true professional.

Implicit in this is the belief that managing a business is not just a matter of hunch or native ability. Indeed, to a professional manager, management must become a practice rather than a science or even a profession. It is through practice and conscious efforts that managers can bring ethical standards to bear upon their performance. Peter F. Drucker points out that any serious attempt to make management scientific or a profession is bound to lead to attempt to eliminate the unpredictabilities of business life, its risks, its ups and downs, its wasteful competition, the irrational choices of the consumer, and in the process, the economy's freedom and its ability to grow. "No greater damage to our economy or to our society is possible than to attempt to professionalise management by licensing managers or by limiting access to management to people with a special academic degree". We could, therefore, take it that professionalism in management is not essentially identified with acquisition of theoretical knowledge and application of expertise. It must translate into practice the moral, ethical and social standards that are expected of persons in high positions of business administration. A manager has to manage with these objectives in a broader sense and then only management by objectives acquires any relevance for the country's economy.

Management is not just a creature of the economy; it is a creator as well. Therefore, management's function is to make a productive enterprise out of human and material resources. The professional manager has to manage by organising the work so as to make it suitable for human beings. He has also to reckon with another dimensions and that is of time. The manager needs to consider both the present and the long-range future. More than immediate profits, the long range profitability and the survival of the enterprise should be the major concern. A business enterprise is a social institution. If it does not prosper, it is the society that loses.

Hopefully, both professionalism and professional management are fast coming in India's corporate sector. Our managers have to learn to manage in an economy that is dominated by shortages. Therefore, management styles which were nurtured in conditions of plenty will have to be abandoned in order to manage in situations of scarcity. As such, today's management has to *crave* out a culture of its own in order to safeguard consumers' interest, rather than maximise profitability in the environment of scarcity.

Professionalism has to take an integrated, even a non-specialist approach. If deviations from set principles of management are called for in the larger interest of the community, there should be no hesitation in doing so. Management has to draw its inspiration from the ideals of socialism and economic growth for the nation as a whole. The manager should be aware of the social costs of his various actions. His abilities will get reflected in formulating an optimum-mix of various priorities in the short-term and long-term programmes without creating a lopsided growth.

The professional manager feels that although he is normally left out of the overall planning process, yet he cannot overlook the social objectives of planning as he has to manage the scarce resources. These are as important to him as materials management and profitability in the undertaking in which he works. There is no doubt that the professional manager has to work under internal restraints and external constraints. He feels that he can succeed in an atmosphere of reasonable freedom, attractive incentives and warm appreciation of his work. Only then, he feels, he can work with some resemblance of social responsibility. May be, he requires some management training in which he learns the basic ingredients of freedom from interference and the kind of autonomy which he aspires so much.

Nevertheless, the professional manager needs to have the confidence of the planners and the policy-makers who, in their own turn, have to repose full faith in him. The Indian manager has, by now, acquired industrial skills and managerial expertise quite in abundance. The only thing that needs to be taken care of and developed further is a proper approach towards managing the enterprise from the standpoint of bringing about social welfare. This should be the result of his own commitment to the enterprise he serves. Should there by any clash in the interest of the enterprise and the interest of the society, he should owe his allegiance to the latter. In sum, a professional manager owes as much as to the society as he owes to the organisation where he works. It is in this spirit that he can truly demonstrate the ideals of professionalism in his work.

Managerial Responsibility

The managerial system of any concern needs to provide for the decision-making processes at different levels of management, *i.e.*, top, middle and supervisory personnel at the work level. Each of them also requires information control systems for its own specific needs. Thus, an essential link has to be established between decision-making and measurement of results. Alongside, factors necessary to interpret the differentials of potential in the various departments of an enterprise, need to be measured separately. Keeping in view the fact that the strength of a chain is that of its weakest link, some kind of relationship has also to be established between decision-making and measurement of results.

The system of management that attempts to put heavy stress on control and not on responsibility makes the real issue submerged in a mass of irrelevancies. In this context, Pareto's law that "In the series of elements to be controlled, a small fraction, in terms of numbers of elements, always accounts for a large fraction in terms of effects", has an important bearing. It means that the vital few must be separated from the trivial many. In fact, to attempt to control everything is to control nothing. Hence under the law of selectivity, key factors for control have to be selected for designing a management control system.

Today, progressive management techniques are said to widen the application of conventional management tools for evaluating the human component of business. As such, it will now be possible to hold individuals accountable, at various levels of the organization, for the proper performance of their managerial functions. An appropriate designing of the control system can play an important part in making the techniques more effective.

It may be pointed out that an executive can be held responsible provided *(a)* he knows what he is expected to achieve and also that it is achievable, *(b)* he knows what he is actually achieving, and *(c)* it is within his personal control to regulate what is happening. With all these conditions being present simultaneously, it is reasonable to hold the person in question responsible for taking decisions and for implementing them. If all these provisos are not fully answered, it may as well lead to the rise of alibis for failures.

In order to cope with the increasing complexities of modern management, methods must be developed to meet them. There is no longer any justification for slavish adherence to systems which do not fully meet the challenge. The many sided pyramid of management made up of a series of ascending layers represents a different level of management at each layer involving a different type of decision. On each face of the pyramid and hence in each facet of management, a control activity does take place. It is, therefore, necessary to knit the various facets of control together into a 'fully integrated system' which must embrace the whole pyramid, not just individual facets. This is necessary for properly presenting control information for the top management decisions.

This kind of coordination will lead to the establishment of a controller function. It is a function intended as a major aid to management decision-making; to present and, as far as possible, interpret facts in order that management may make decisions and take action thereon. While doing so, it will have to assign responsibilities for various functions. The controller's task begins with the design of the control system to meet management needs. He guides the system designers, system analysts and computer programmers to achieve a control system tailored to management's needs. He selects the key factors, remembers Pareto's law and the control points. He segregates the non-controllable factors so that the controllable aspects emerge out clearly. He relates the corporate plans and decisions to individual accountability at the various levels of management. In this way a team effort is achieved with effective action throughout. The controller himself may not be a specialist in the setting of physical standards but he ensures that the basis used for them meet the needs of the control system. He will work with the various executives to build the agreed standards for departmental plans.

All said and done, it is true that the modern complexities of management have made it increasingly more difficult to identify responsibility with particular executives. For example, at the level of supervision, can it really be said that a foreman is answerable for the performance of his shop when the planning department is in fact sending instructions as to the order in which work should be done, the processes to be used, the times to be offered for bonus purposes, the supply of jigs and tools and a great deal more? Whether it is called planning, production, control, methods engineering, drawing office, production engineering, or by any other names—the supervisor has certainly a dozen excuses for delay because a dozen things have been wished upon him by other people. It is for his immediate superior in the line, called the production manager, to control specialists of these activities. Unless a problem like this is squarely faced, the quite thick layer of junior and middle management when chased for results will, in their turn, reply that they have not the authority to ensure results and cannot, therefore, be fully responsible for them. This then becomes a demoralising and a confusing situation in which the buck is passed on.

The alternative to individual responsibility is to base policy on definable groups—to accept that in the modern specialised system, a single man cannot, in the nature of things, be made responsible for a complex function, except at a very high co-ordinating level. The line manager cannot shout down a designer, metallurgist, chemist, electrical engineer and perhaps one or more highly specialised men who may form a necessary part of his own function. Likewise, the work of people below the line is rather too difficult to be identified and pinpointed separately both for achievements and responsibility. As such, a system of collective responsibility has to be experimented upon. In the scheme of integrated control, the aspect of collective responsibility must be usefully explored for effective implementation. It will then be realised that coordination does not come from authority but that authority is derived out of coordination of responsibility at all levels of management.

4

Setting up a New Business

Customer needs, wants and desires can be satisfied when managerial and other resources such as men, money, materials and machinery are applied to perform the activities necessary to run a business. The resources are applied to creating the product, financing the business operations, providing human resources, processing of information and marketing the product to satisfy consumer demand. The results of the aforesaid activities are supply of goods and services for customers, compensation for owners, managers and employees and meeting expectations of society. If results are not acceptable, management has to modify the activities as well as the resources in order to produce desirable results or achieve the set goals. Management is the allocator, co-ordinator and controller of all resources or inouts and plays the role of entrepreneur or risk-bearer as the managerial group is in effective control of a business enterprise.

Reward of Entrepreneurship

Profit is the reward ror bearing the uncertainty in the business and it is the remuneration for entrepreneurs. Profit is the income minus 'outgo' or 'expenditure.' Profit is one of the important incentives to launch a new enterprise. Without profit a firm cannot expand and grow. When costs exceed income, the firm cannot meet its liabilities for very long period. Often the profits are reinvested into the business and the business can steadily grown through such self-financing.

Business Entrepreneur

An entrepreneur (risk-bearer) is the central figure in the world of business. He is also in charge of organization, management and control of the new enterprise. Broadly speaking, entrepreneurial or managerial decisions play an important role in three branches: (1) Setting up a new project. (2) Form of organization to run the business. (3) Growth of existing business.

Setting up a New Project

Managerial decisions regarding the setting up a new project will have to deal with the following topics:

(1) Determination of objectives: Individuals or organizations must have purposeful economic activities. The first step in the planning of a new project is to define clearly the goals or objectives to be accomplished. Once the goals are known, efforts and activities can be directed to achieve them and reach our destination as per our plans. The entrepreneur must answer a few questions relating to objectives. What product or service shall be provided to customer? What business is to be started? What will be its basic goals? The total objective or goal may be subdivided into subgoals or components for each department and accordingly an organization structure can be created. Such clear-cut statement of purpose will influence the perspective of the organization. Modern business organizations have their basic goals to provide returns to customers, owners, managers, employees and society.

An example of possible impact of an organizational goal can be seen in the objective of Henry Fort to make a car that could be bought by an average family just for $ 400. The result was the phenomenal development of the techniques of the assembly line production, the unprecedented growth of automobile industry and within two generations, an entire nation of the U.S.A., literally on wheels.

(2) Discovery of an idea or invention and its preliminary investigation: In the launching of a new project, the discovery of

an idea or invention and its informal investigation to determine the business potentiality should constitute an important branch of managerial decision. Decision on commercialisation of an idea is the starting point in the launching of a new enterprise.

(3) *Pricing of the product:* Managerial decision on pricing the product is rather complex and crucial. Right price to match competition and invoke greater consumer response is a difficult problem. Nature of the project and elasticity of its demand are closely related to pricing. Again we have to consider the danger of price war as our gain due to lower price may be offset by retaliatory price reduction by rivals in the market. Resale price maintenance was used to prevent unhealthy price competition in retail trade. But it is now considered as a restrictive trade practice under M.R.T.P. Act: Branded goods introduce product differentiation and manufacturer can enjoy better control over prices, demand and channels of distribution through the device of Branding. In modern marketing mix greater emphasis is given on non-price competition. Among these are quality, service, credit, free home delivery, money-back warranty, discounts, advertising and sales promotion devices. These are the marketing techniques for motivating consumers to buy with or without price competition. Of course, pricing must cover costs incurred in the devices of non-price competition, irrespective of their success or failure. In the end, buyer has to pay all expenses on account of non-price competition.

(4) *Marketing of the product:* The managerial decision to enter the market with product or service is based on fact-finding approach. We need marketing research in two branches. 1. Product research. 2. Consumer research. The product must be fitted to consumer demand. Marketing research is a good tool in decision-making process. It is necessary before we enter the market to discover the nature, direction and trend of demand. It is also needed in the formulation of our marketing-mix as well as the evaluation of the effectiveness of our marketing plans and policies, *e.g.*, decisions on product, price, promotion and distribution programmes. Marketing management is expected to recognise and solve all problems in the field of marketing.

(5) *Size of business enterprise:* Managerial decision regarding the size of the plant or firm will depend upon the size of the market to be catered. Technical, managerial, financial and human

resources at our disposal are the crucial factors determining the right size of our business operations. Usually, entry in the market may be on a small or medium-scale. If we have ample capital, adequate human resources and competent top management and if we are to produce a staple product, we may launch our business based on large-scale production so that we can avail the economies of large-scale operations immediately. We must strive to reach the optimum size in order to obtain the lowest cost of production as well as the lowest cost of distribution.

(6) Location: Managerial decision on plant location is most important because location affects the cost-structure as well as profitability of the plant throughout its operating life. Given equivalent managerial talent, a plant with best location will mean quite a different thing from a plant with a bad location. We have first to decide the region of location; secondly, the community inside that region is chosen; and lastly, the specific site is finally selected. Please note that once the plant is errected, it is very difficult to shift it subsequently. Hence, thorough investigation on scientifically collected data is necessary for decision on location. Location factors such as nearness to market, adequate labour, transport facilities, availability of raw materials and power, banking facilities and favourable economic and political climate influence our choice of location. Location can make or mar the future of any enterprise.

(7) Plant and equipment: Manufacturing process governs the character of plant, building, machinery and equipment. It is preferable to purchase new machinery and equipment. We must take advice of expert consultants in procuring our plant or machinery. There are agencies who take full responsibility in procurement and installation of plant or machinery. Sophisticated plant will naturally demand trained and experienced personnel. Otherwise it will not give rich dividend.

(8) Plant layout: Managerial decision on the proper plant layout must be based on the report of a layout specialist. The objective of plant layout is to integrate machines, materials and men (the three pillars of a plant) for most economical (least-cost) production. Wise arrangement of machinery and physical facilities and the best use of space can offer maximum production facilities with necessary convenience and amenities at relatively lower costs.

Notes: (1) Optimum location, optimum size and optimum

layout—all have one chief objective and that is to achieve maximum output with minimum expenditure and waste. The net result will be profit maximisation and cost minimisation. (2) Human considerations must be duly recognised in evolving a good plant layout and man-machine organization. Ease of work gives speed of work. Management decisions must be based on the recognition of human values in Industry. (3) It is the management responsibility to provide and ensure appropriate and congenial work environment with particular reference to physical conditions of work.

(9) Preparation of the product: Once we know that our product has good marketing potential and it can be marketed at the desired price, we need management decisions on all problems of production management which includes production planning and control. Product planning and development, product flow, materials handling, quality control and production research are some of the important problems demanding managerial decisions and actions. These are the responsibilities of production management.

Note: Size, location, layout, plant and equipment, and manufacturing of the product as per consumer demand are the technical problems demanding attention of technical experts, *viz.* technocrats.

(10) Financing business: In our modern world, business and finance are unseparable factors. Finance is the life-blood of business. We need fixed capital or permanent finance for acquiring fixed assets such as land, plant, machinery, equipment, etc. Long term finance is provided mainly through ownership resources and the balance, say, 30 to 40 per cent through borrowed resources. Business also needs working capital for financing current assets and day-to-day expenses. Purchase of raw materials, payment of wages and salaries are the two big elements of working capital. When our return of income on sales is greater than the rate of interest, it is profitable to get short-term loans to buy our supplies and to meet payrolls, *i.e.*, wages and salaries. Usually bulk of the working capital, say, 70 to 80 per cent , is through borrowed resources, *e.g.*, bank loan and/or trade credit. Financial managers are responsible for financial planning and wise use of capital funds. We need managerial decisions on: (1) the amount of long-term

capital needed, (2) the short-term money requirements, (3) the cost of acquiring funds, (4) the estimated return on their use, and a time schedule indicating minimum, average and maximum needs of finance. Financial Plan (pointing out the particulars of outlay, and the particulars of sources of financing the outlay) is very necessary at the time of launching a new enterprise. It is the function of financial management to solve all financial problems and ensure financial liquidity.

(11) Personnel and labour decisions: In all business, we need skills in preparation of products, purchasing of materials, marketing, pricing, financing, employee relations, and over-all management. Large-scale operations demand division of labour and specialised personnel with necessary skills and proficiency. Job analysis, job specifications, selection, remuneration, training, promotion, employee welfare, collective bargaining with labour organization, safety regulations, and such other labour problems are entrusted to personnel management. Business management must have democratic and participative managerial style and it should adopt sound personnel and human relations policies. People are our greatest assets. Morale and motivation constitute a real challenge to the enlightened management. All personnel policies and their administration are the responsibility of personnel management.

(12) Internal organization: Internal organization is the structural framework defining in a precise manner, duties and responsibilities assigned to all personnel in performing allotted functions within the enterprise. It is a means or a tool to exercise typical managerial functions and combine the 5 M's of men, money, materials, machines and management in the enterprise operations to achieve the set objectives. (see Figure 4.1)

(13) Purchasing: At the time of starting the business a number of purchasing decisions are needed, *e.g.*, purchase of materials, supplies, parts, equipment, machinery, real estate, etc. Sound purchasing decisions can reduce our costs appreciably. Sound purchasing policies are needed even for efficient conduct of the business. The main purpose of all purchasing policies and plans is to assure the supply of needed materials in right quantity and quality, at right costs and at the right time and place. Purchasing management is in charge of achieving the purchasing objectives through appropriate purchasing plans, policies, programmes and procedures.

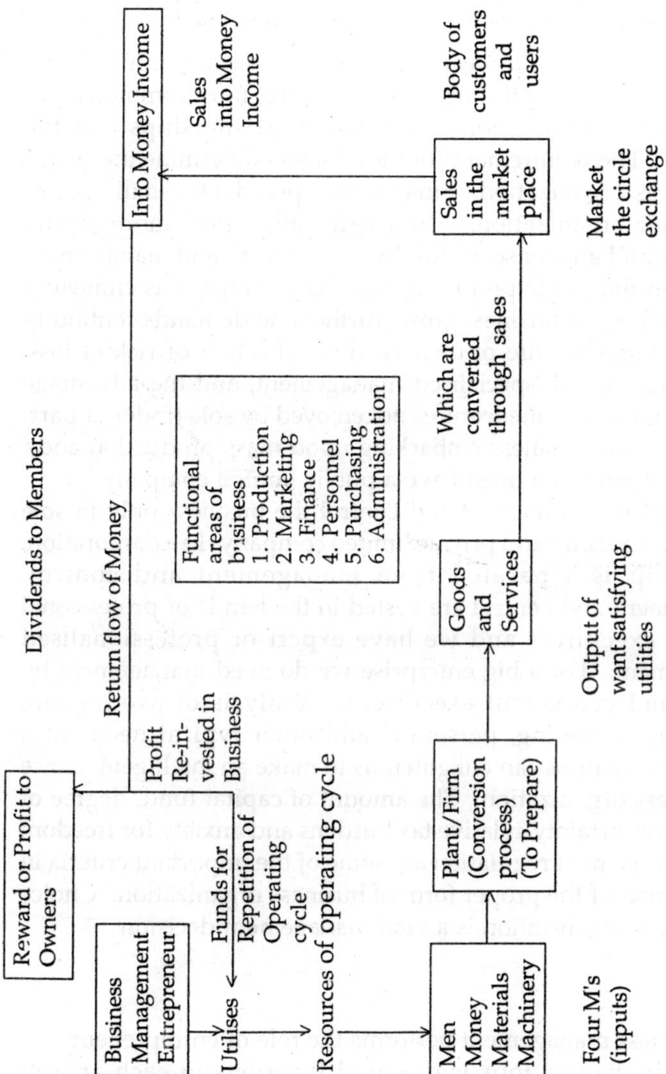

Figure 4.1.

Use of Five M's in Business—Management (Entrepreneur), Men, Money, Materials and Machinery to produce goods and services required in the market to satisfy consumer demand

Note: A commercial enterprise has two basic functions. (1) Purchasing goods for resale and (2) Selling goods to the customers at a reasonable profit. Merchandising or purchasing is very important managerial function in a trading, concern.

(14) Types of business organization: Private enterprise is invariably conducted through one of the three most common types of business organisation—sole trader, partnerships and the company. The requirements of the business determine the choice of business organization. Small-scale operations usually prefer sole trader organization. The partnership offers more capital resources and greater scope for division of work and management skills than the single proprietorship. The company is eminently suitable when the business grows further and demands continuity of life beyond the life of owners, diversification of risk of loss, substantial capital, specialised management, and the advantage of limited liability (the features not enjoyed by sole trader or partnership). Any business embarking upon mass production and/ or mass distribution must have a public limited company.

Owners can manage and control the business only in sole trader, partnership and private limited company. In a corporation, ownership is separated from management and control. Management and control are vested in the hands of professional body of executives and we have expert or professionalised management. For a big enterprise we do need management by expert and competent executives. Analysis of production, financial, marketing, personnel and other typical needs of a particular business can enlighten us to make an intelligent choice of business organization. The amount of capital fund, degree of risk and uncertainty, relative tax burdens and anxiety for freedom from Government regulation are some of the important criteria in the selection of the proper form of business organization. Choice of business organization is a vital management decision.

Notes:

(1) Business management performs the role of entrepreneur.

(2) It discharges four managerial functions in each area of business: (1) Planning, (2) Organizing, (3) Directing and Motivating, (4) Control.

(3) Functional areas of Business are: (1) Production, (2)

Marketing, (3) Finance, (4) Personnel, (5) Purchasing (6) Office Administration.

(4) Entrepreneur is responsible to evolve optimum combination of resources (4M's) in the form of Inputs in order to produce goods and services (output) required in the market to satisfy and serve the needs, wants and desires of consumers and secure normal profit partly to retain in the business for further growth and partly to distribute dividends to owners of the business.

(5) Productivity and satisfaction are the twin goals of any business.

Figure 4.2. **Aims and Objectives of a Corporation**

---

1. To strive to operate at all times in an ethical manner—fair and honest treatment to shareholders, employees, customers, and the general public.
2. To produce a better and better product at a lower and lower price.
3. To provide a fair return on investment in order to ensure continued growth and to satisfy shareholders reasonably.
4. To provide an Environment of challenge and opportunity for every employee of the enterprise.
5. To encourage each person to develop his or her abilities to the fullest and to provide equal and fair employment opportunity for all qualified applicants and equal opportunity for promotion based on merit.
6. To remain a good citizen of our community. To do all in our power to help make our city a pleasant and safe place to live.

5

Business Plans

After deciding the objectives of a business firm, the businessman makes plans which are necessary to achieve this goal. Thus, businessman is ready to translate the goals of business into specific plans. All business plans flow out from the goals of the business organization. In every thing the businessman plans from now on he bears in mind the achievement of the goal.

Therefore, all plans flow from the objective and at the same time have to be made with the objective in mind. There is a considerable number and variety of plans which the manager of business must devise in order to reach these goals, namely, policies, procedures, methods, rules, programmes, projects, budgets, and so on.

In order to clarify the presentation of these various plans one can follow different avenues. They may be classified as to kind, use, origin, or purpose. In considering kinds of plans, one distinguishes among policies, procedures, methods, rules, programmes, projects and budgets. In referring to the use of plans a distinction is made between standing plans or repeat-use plans on one hand, and single-use plans on the other hand. Looking at the origin, one speaks of an "appealed" origin, "imposed" origin, or of policies formulated at the top of the organization. Considering the purpose of the plans, one can conceive of the purpose of correction, one can think that they are there to be operative, or that they are newly created.

All of these plans must be designed to reinforce one another, and they should all be directed toward the same objectives. Major plans are formulated by the stockholders or the board of directors to implement the objectives. These major plans determine the general form of the organization, the functions of the enterprise and the various activities. Each department had then will formulate departmental plans which are ultimately directed towards carrying out the major plan imposed from above. And so on, down the line.

Standing Plans and Single-use Plans

In speaking of a repeat-use or standing plan, reference is made to a plan which is followed each time a given situation is encountered. Repeat plans are used again and again. However, single-use plans are those plans which are used up once the objective is accomplished. They are used only once, and not over and over again. The latter kind includes programmes, projects, and budgets, whereas policies, procedures, methods, and rules fall under the grouping of repeat-use plans.

Policies

Policies are broad guides to thinking. They are general statements which guide or channel the thinking of all personnel charged with decision-making. Although these guides are broad, they do have their definite limitations at either end thus delimiting the area. So long as the subordinate stays within these broad areas he will make an appropriate decision. Policies are not narrow; if they were they would not be broad guides to thinking. However, as broad guides they exist to channel thinking. And, as long as the decision-maker remains within the boundaries, he knows he will make a decision in conformance with the policy. It is obvious that policies will facilitate the job of the executive and of the subordinates.

Major policies are important enough to be made only by the board of directors. The choice of the industry, which is probably one of the most fundamental of company policies, is written into the charter, but it is within the board's prerogative to make policies within these broad limits. For example, the board has decided that it is the policy of the enterprise to seek out the quality market. Within these limits of a quality market every department must make its plans with regards to this major policy imposed by the board which to the purchasing department means that it must buy only good materials from the most dependable sources, to the personnel department means a policy of obtaining workmen to produce only quality products, to the engineering department means close tolerances and fine finishes, to the sales department means emphasis on quality, and to the publicity department means a quality appeal. This basic policy permeates all the various plans. All departments, regardless of where they function, must formulate more specific policies and plans to implement those set by top management.

Flexibility of Policies

The definition of policies as a broad guide to thinking implies that certain amount of flexibility is present. Some policy statements even have such a flexibility built in by adding words such as "whenever possible", "whenever feasible", or "under usual conditions." If such clauses are not built in, then the manner in which the executives apply the policy will determine the degree of flexibility. The subordinate manager must intelligently apply the policy to a given set of circumstances. Such flexibility, of course, must not be carried to extremes and lead to inconsistency. Policies must be administered by the subordinate managers in a consistent manner. Anything else would be contradictory to the basic concept of a policy. It is the purpose of a policy to provide the various subordinate managers with the same guide for thinking. If the policies are clear they will inspire confidence in the plans and goals. If they are not clear then sooner or later widespread dissatisfactions and irritations will develop. If the policies are vague, then the subordinates are bound to be less effective than they should be.

Variety of Business Policies

The areas of policy formulation are as varied as the many activities of the enterprise. One broad group of policies pertains to the managerial functions of planning, organizing, staffing, directing, and controlling, and another broad group is directed toward the functions of the company—the various activities—such as sales, finance, production, personnel relations, and public relations. One can think of the company policy to promote from within (staffing) of the policy that the customer is always right (public relations), of a fixed price policy (sales), of a policy of preventive maintenance of equipment (production), or a policy to adhere to high moral and ethical standards in performing the business activities (planning). There are policies governing the scope of research activities to be undertaken by the enterprise, those which cover distribution and procurement, still others covering the controlling function, and a multitude of other kinds of policies. They all have one characteristic in common: They are broad guides to channel the thinking of decision-makers. As long as they are broad they allow a certain amount of discretion.

Origin of Business Policies

Obviously policies do not come about by chance. They are determined by the managers or at times by outside forces. Policies can emerge in several commonly recognized ways, Generally, distinction is made between originated policies, appealed policies and imposed policies.

The originated policy is no doubt the most significant, and it is the policy that is originated by the managers. To formulate policies is one of the most important functions of top management. Top management is in a position to see the need for the various overall policies which are required to guide the thinking of the subordinates so that the enterprise's objectives can be achieved. It must visualize the policies which are needed for the entire enterprise and are necessarily broad by nature. Once the broad policy has been established by top management, it in turn will become the guide for the various policies covering smaller areas of activities which are originated by the various managers lower down in the managerial hierarchy. Of course, all of these policies will implement the broader policy as originated by top management. This origin of policy formulation, starting with the top management and pursued by the lower managers, is the most important source of policies, and the largest number of policies owe their existence to this origin.

At times policy, instead of originating at the top and flowing downward, may also originate at or near the bottom of an organization and flow upward. "In a sense, policies are sometimes generated at the operating and first-line supervisory levels and imposed upward. If certain matters are not recognised or provided for by the set of policies adopted, or if regularly adopted policies are not enforced, customs may gradually emerge and achieve the generality, permanence, and authority of true policies." The extent to which this source of policy origin contributes will largely depend upon whether or not the enterprise operates under the principles of free and democratic supervision and whether or not subordinates can freely express themselves. Such an origin is less likely to happen in an enterprise which is run along autocratic lines of supervision. It is also conceivable that at times policy has been formulated simultaneously from both directions. In such a case management will incorporate in this policy everything from management's point of view, but at the same time it will give ample thought to what first line supervisory levels or even tne employees largely affected by the policy feel it should contain.

An appealed policy has a different origin. It is most often formulated in order to cope with some exceptional problem. A subordinate manager will appeal to his superior for a decision because he does not know how to decide on a particular problem or because he disagrees and wants the question reviewed and possibly redecided. He leaves it up to his superior who then will make a decision. He has appealed to him in a form similar to that in which appeals are taken to higher courts in our legal system. The decision which is handed down by the superior than sets a policy, and this is known as an appealed policy. Such an appealed policy could also come about in a different manner: A subordinate might not know if it is within his realm of authority or within the frame of the policy to make a certain decision and he therefore appeals to his superior to make the decision for him. Appealed policy decisions are made mostly to solve current problems.

As one can easily see, there is a danger in having too many policies made in this manner. By making individual decisions, the superior managers might not always bear in mind the consistency and congruity of the various decisions. In creating these policies by appeal, there is the danger that they will not be consistent and that there might be discrepancies between one or the other decision. Often these decisions are uncoordinated and confusing. Therefore, whenever a manager finds himself frequently being appealed to in order to make policy decisions then he had better check into the amount and content of policies which have been issued by organization. Apparently too wide an area has been left without coverage, and additional policies are needed to fill in the various areas. Then the first cited source of policies should be made use of and "originated" policies ought to be promulgated.

A third kind of policy origin is what is known as the externally imposed policy. This means policies have been imposed upon the enterprise by external factors such as the government, trade unions, or trade associations. The word "imposed" indicates compliance with a force which cannot be avoided. One can speak of imposed policy formulation when a law has been passed, the conformance of which forces management of an enterprise to translate it into one of the policies of the company. Labour policies resulting from collective bargaining are of an imposed nature. First, there are those responsibilities expressed in the labour laws proper and then those specified in the union contract. Both sources impose certain labour policies upon the enterprise. The same applies to regulations issued by trade associations or other groups in their efforts to eliminate trade abuses and to protect the members from destructive practices and compitition. The problems of the legality of such directives are at times difficult to decide, but questions of this nature are beyond the scope of this text". Any policy imposed in such manner upon the enterprise is what is known as an externally imposed policy.

Policies as Help in Delegation of Authority

Policies are a guide for the thinking of the various subordinates to use in their decisions. One of the purposes of the policy is to sanction in advance the decision to be taken by the subordinate in various situations as long as he follows the broad guidelines. As such, policies are an aid in delegating authority within the organization. After having set the policies for his subordinates, the manager can delegate authority without being unduly concerned, knowing that whatever decision the subordinate makes will be within the boundaries of the policy. In other words, in making the decisions the subordinate would be guided by the same thoughts and probably come up with the same decision the manager would have made himself. Hence, by having the policies it is easier for the superior to delegate more and more authority to his subordinates. On the other hand, having policies is of great help to the subordinate also. He knows full well the guides which exist to channel his thinking. They will facilitate his decision-making and, at the same time, insure uniformity of decisions throughout the entire enterprise. Therefore, the clearer the policies are and the more comprehensive they are, the easier and better will it be for the superior to delegate authority. At the same time it will be easier for the subordinates to perform their decision-making functions.

Written and Unwritten Policies

In view of this, it is essential that the policies be carefully and explicitly stated and communicated so that those in the organization who are to apply them will fully understand them. This is no easy task. It is difficult to find words which will be understood by all people in the same way since different meanings can be attached to words. Although there is no guarantee that even the written word will be properly understood, it seems desirable that the policy be given in a written statement. Hence, policies should be clearly expressed and preferably issued in writing. However, there are not many firms which have written policies since some companies simply never get around to writing their policies, and other companies purposely do not write them.

There are several distinct advantages, however, to having statements of policy in writing. First, when the manager has to force himself to sit down and write out the policies, in the mere process of writing them down he will discover discrepancies, conflicts, and overlapping statements. The mere process of writing these policies will require the manager to think out these policies clearly and consistently. He might discover that whatever he had thought was a policy in reality is not the policy or should not be the policy. It is not an easy task to state policies in black and white, but the benefits derived from written polices are well worth the time, effort, and money spent in doing so. In addition to the advantage the manager has in clarifying his own thoughts while writing down the policies, written policies are of great help to the subordinate manager, aside from helping him make decisions. First of all, he will be able to read them as often as he cares to. Their meaning cannot be changed by word of mouth because, if there is any doubt, the written policy can always be referred to. Furthermore, they are there for anyone to read if he wants to. The chances of misinterpreting them are remote. And if there should be a misunderstanding it can be narrowed down to a few written words. They are accessible for all members of the organization and can be readily sent to all of those who are affected by them. Subordinate managers who are new in the organization can speedily orient and acquaint themselves.

One of the disadvantages in putting policies in writing is that they may become too widely distributed and get into the hands of subordinates who are not concerned with them. It has also been said that once policies have been put in writing management is reluctant to change them though they might have become outdated and outmoded. This in effect, however, is not a disadvantage of the written policy. In such an instance it is the duty of the subordinate to appeal to the superior manager for a revision of the policy in view of recent circumstances. It is conceivable that under the circumstances a manager might be reluctant to start the entire procedure, though he should not be. It has also been stated that for certain confidential matters now written policies might be more advisable.

The advantages of having a written policy for outweigh the disadvantages. But, numerically speaking, there are not many companies which have their policies written out. Many companies have policies which have been handed down by word of mouth. This kind of policy is more flexible and can be adjusted to different circumstances with more ease than written policies. This, of course, might mean that the exact interpretation is not known. The probability of not being definite makes verbally handed down policies not too desirable.

Implied Policies

There are also policies which are stated neither in writing nor verbally. Policies of this type, which actually exist although they are neither stated verbally nor written, are called implied policies. Only by watching the actual behaviour of the various subordinate managers of the organization in specific questions can the presence of an implied policy be ascertained. There are many companies, for example, that state that there is no policy with respect to the upper age limits for hiring employees. However, examination of the ages of those hired during a given year might indicate that no one over fifty years of age was hired. In such a case, there seems to exist an implied policy not to hire persons over fifty years of age. Such an implied policy can often be observed in the area of not hiring members of certain races or religions. Managers at times justify the existence of implied policies by pointing out that policies in that particular area are too difficult to state, or that they do not want to limit the complete freedom of the subordinate managers, or that the nature of the enterprise is too dynamic to set policies in certain areas. Although such explanations are expedient at times, it would be far more desirable if the policy were clearly stated because the interpretations of the implied policies leave large areas to the subordinate managers who, at times, may even misinterpret the real intentions of the enterprise.

Periodic Reviews of Policies

Due to the dynamic nature of business it is probable that policies will become outmoded, or it is conceivable that the purpose for which they were originally created has ceased to exist. Similarly, conditions may be such that the emphasis which once prevailed is no longer the same. It is therefore advisable periodically to review and appraise the policies in order to see whether they are to be modified, changed, or completely abandoned and new ones put in their place. Such a review might uncover current practices which are a complete contradiction of stated policies. It might also show that the various policies lack integration. In all probability a periodic review of the policies will show the necessity for changes and adjustments. To say the least, it is highly undesirable to have policies on the books which have become outdated and which are followed by no one. In such cases, it is left up to the individual subordinate to judge for himself which of the policies are still current and which are not to be observed any longer. Such decisions are not the job of the subordinate, but they are a duty of management. Regardless of how well conceived the policies were when they were originated, in all likelihood the dynamic nature of the enterprise makes a periodic review and adjustment necessary.

Procedures

Procedures, like policies, are also plans, but procedures are more specific. "Procedures, in common with other forms of planning, seek to avoid the chaos of random activity by directing, coordinating, and articulating the operations of an enterprise. They help direct all enterprise activities toward common goals, they help impose consistency acrcss the organization and through time, and they seek economy by enabling management to avoid the costs of recurrent investigations and to delegate authority to subordinates to make decisions within a frame of policies and procedures devised by management." Procedures are a guide to action not a guide to thinking. Policies lay out a broad filed where the area is determined by the objectives and the limits. Procedures, however, show the sequence of definite acts. They show us a path through this area of policy; they give us the chronological sequence of acts to be performed. Procedures specify a route through the broad area of policy, a route which will take us between the guideposts of the policies, finally to the goal. Procedures will show us the way to implement polices. "Policy always sets an objective or delimits an area of action, while procedures fix a path toward the objective or through the area. Sequence is the sine qua non of procedure."

Consider, for example, the department store's policy that the customer is always right. The procedure, however, will specify the various steps which are to be taken before the customer's desires are fulfilled. The procedure might be that the complaining customer has to first see the buyer and then the department manager or the floor walker or someone else and finally end up in the adjustment office. These are the various steps which are to be taken within this broad field of policy, whatever decision these various managers make is within the broad guide of thinking that the customer is right. However, although they might not feel that in his instance the customer is justified in her complaint, since the policy of the store is for the customer to be right, she will be handled accordingly following a pressribed procedure. The procedure of the various managers concerned merely showed the path through this area of policy. As we have noted, procedure is a guide to action, not a guide to thinking.

There is no doubt that procedures have many advantages. The mere process of preparing a procedure necessitates analysis and study of the work being described. Once a procedure is established it assures uniformity of performance. It gives the manger a standard in appraising work done by his subordinates. Inasmuch as a procedure specifies the chronological sequence of how the work is to be done, it decreases the need for further decision making. Procedures make for closer coordination. There is, however, the danger that due to the existence of the procedures, innovation and development of new procedures or new ways of doing the work is stiffed. This real disadvantage can nevertheless be overcome by periodic reviews of the various procedures.

Methods

A method is even more detailed. Whereas a procedure showed us a series of steps to be taken, a method is only concerned with the single operation, with one particular step, and it tells exactly how this particular step is to be performed. Most of the time one speaks of methods as they are concerned with production, and in this connection the method means the best way the job is to be performed.

Rules

A rule is different from a policy, procedure, or method. It is not a policy because it does not give a guide to thinking and it does not leave any discretion to the party involved. It is related to a procedure insofar as it guides actions and states what must or may not be done. However, it is not a procedure because there is no time sequence to a particular action as it is specified by the rule. No smoking, for instance, is a decision which was made by a manager, one rule of the long list of safety rules. There is no time sequence involved with such a rule; it is just no smoking whenever and wherever it is in effect. It is a guide to action, in this instance to inaction, but it is not a procedure because there is no time sequence involved. Not to be confused with this is the company policy referring to safety practices. This might state that it is the company's policy to carry on a continuous educational campaign for safety. The company's safety policy provides the guiding thoughts for safety rules, but the two must be clearly distinguished.

Strategy

It is often difficult to distinguish clearly between policy and strategy for sometimes the two terms are used interchangeably. It is true that a strategy is a policy in the respect that it is a broad guide to thinking, but a strategy is a particular kind of policy. It is a policy which has been formulated by top management for the purpose of interpreting and shading the meaning of other policies. Strategy is an interpretative policy. If a department store in a city had decided as its strategic point of view that it will not be undersold by any competitor, then its strategy is that nobody will undersell it. This strategy of not being undersold is there to interpret and to shade all other policies the department store sets. Or, if one automobile manufacturer has a strategy of trying to sell more passenger cars in a certain price range than any other automobile manufacturer, everything this manufacturer does will be strategically influenced by the basic strategy toward its competitors of not being outrun by them. Another example occurs in a situation where management foresees a major economic recession. The strategy from then on will be to cut inventories, manpower, expenses, and so on, to a minimum.

The author recalls one chief executive whose strategy was to grant voluntarily to his non-unionized office employees the same pay increases, added privileges, and improvements prior to or at least at the same time at which the unionized factory workers gained theirs. All policies pertaining to the remuneration and working conditions of the office force were shaded by this strategic thought. Such a guide to thinking has a strategic effect on all other existing policies, giving them a specific interpretation and meaning. Although it is difficult to draw a clear line, the terms strategy and policy should be used in their proper meanings.

All of the above described plans, namely policies, procedures, methods, rules and strategies, fall within the category of repeat-use—or standing-plans. They will be used again and again as the occasion arises.

Single-use Plans

A single-use or single-purpose plan is one that lays out a course to fit a particular situation. Once the goal is reached, the plan is used up, and it will not be used over and over again. Programme, and budgets are single-use plans.

Programmes

A programme is a complex set of plans for a major undertaking within the over-all enterprise goal. It usually contains various kinds of policies, procedures, budgets, methods, and so on. Once the goal of this programme has been fulfilled, the plan will not be used again. An example of a programme is the expansion programme of a hospital. It calls for the building of a new hospital in the same or possibly another community, and a myriad of plans, policies, procedures, and budgets connected with this new programme will be embodied in the new building programme. Once this building programme has been accomplished, however, whatever plans there were within this programme will not be used again; they have fulfilled their purpose.

Although this does not exclude the existence of minor programmes, most of the time the term programme brings to mind major changes, such as the one cited above or the well-publicized expansion programmes of universities and colleges in the country. Building programmes, for example, are often spoken of in terms of ten or twenty years. Another major programme was carried out some-time ago when the major airlines of the country changed over from piston engines to jet propelled aircraft. This move not only involved the purchase and the financing of the new equipment, but also a multitude of plans concerned with the many other aspects of jet air transportation such as spare parts, proper airfields, additional training for flight and ground crews, and schedule changes. But after the programme had been achieved, and the planes delivered and put into service the programme had fulfilled its purpose, and the plans were not to be used any more. The above-mentioned examples of major programmes illustrate also the vast effort which is necessary in the planning of the various steps involved and the approximate timing of the started objectives.

Projects

A project is considered merely a part of a general programme, a part which can be planned and fulfilled as a distinct project in itself. For instance the preparation of the publicity necessary to acquaint the traveling public with the advantages of jet travel could be called a project. Although intrinsically connected with the major programme, this project can be handled by itself, and once the pamphlets and literature are printed the project is terminated. It was a single-use plan and it is finished.

Budgets

Budgets are usually thought of only in connection with controlling, but this is common misconception. Budgets are also plans, namely, single-use plans. A budget is a plan which expresses the anticipated results in numerical terms. A budget may be stated in time, materials, money, or other units which are necessary to perform work and to obtain specific results. It is a plan expressed in numerical terms, whether in dollars and cents, man hours, tons of coal, kilowatt hours, or units to be produced. Since most values are ultimately convertible to monetary terms, money budgets are used most frequently. A budget is a statement of expected results, and that is why it is often thought of in connection with controls. There is no doubt, or course, that budgets are used in connection with controlling. However, the preparing and making of a budget is planning, and its is the work of every manager.

One of the significant aspects of this managerial process is the activity that precedes the compilation of the figures. The manager should give considerable thought to the objectives to be achieved and the road he will follow before he can develop a budget. This is the only practical method because then it is realistically based on such data as material costs, wage rate, personnel requirements, space requirements, and so on. While budget-making is planning, budget administration, on the other hand, is controlling and will be fully discussed in the chapters on controls. In the present discussion we speak of a budget as a plan.

As a planning device budgets have a number of distinct advantages: the goal is expressed in exact and specific terms, thus enabling the plans of one department to be readily coordinated with those of other departments. Once this plan has been fulfilled it is of no more use; hence budget fall within the area of single-use plans.

Integration of Plans

Considerable care must be taken to see that the multitude of plans of any single enterprise are related to one another and that they are properly integrated. The standing plans must be consistent with each other, and the single-use plans must be integrated with the standing plans, as the former are prepared under the umbrella of the standing plans. It is always advisable to look at any standing plan or single-use plan as a part of the total plan of the enterprise; it must aim toward the achievement of the goal as originally laid out.

The plans must be coordinated from top to bottom, downward, upward and sideward. They all flow from the goals of the enterprise, and they all must contribute towards the achievement of the company goal. A proper balance must be maintained among the various plans of the enterprise, and all of them must be totally integrated since they are interdependent. Over-looking this interdependence could cause much complexity and much difficulty in planning. In order to obtain maximum benefits, then, all plans within the organization must be integrated, they must support each other, and they all must contain a consistency of purpose and intent.

Planning Background

Planning is deciding what is to be done in the future. The manager, however, can only plan against an established background of estimated future facts. Thus, although the future is full of uncertainties, the manager must make certain assumptions about it in order to plan properly. These assumptions are based on forecasts of the future.

Forecasting is an essential element of business, and every conceivable business decision involves some element of forecasting. "The man who starts a business is making an assessment of a future demand for its products. The man who determines a production programme for the next six months or twelve months is usually also basing it on some calculation of future demand. The man who engages staff, and particularly young staff, usually has an eye to future organizational requirements." The use of forecasts is widespread in the operation of all types of business enterprises as well as in governmental agencies, labour organizations, and other organizations such as churches and hospitals. An appraisal of future prospects is inherent to all planning. In fact, the success of a business depends in large measure upon the skill of management in foreseeing and preparing for future conditions.

Every enterprise is affected by and must adjust to three economic climates: the national and international climate, the industry climate, and the climate of the enterprise itself. The business cannot control the first two climates. It can only control the enterprise climate, and in order to do this wisely it must be well informed on industry and nation-wide trends. Although many companies, particularly the smaller ones, still guide their activities according to past experience, intuition, and chance, a more scientific approach to forecasting business conditions is becoming the accepted practice. With each downward fluctuation of business conditions, there is an increasing number of businesses which turn to studied forecasting of the future.

After the depression of the 1930's, businessmen became acutely aware of business cycles, and more and more businesses began regularly to analyze business conditions in order to anticipate future economic trends and to estimate their probable effect on their own operations. In forecasting these various factors a business will gain sufficient time to formulate proper plans to obtain maximum benefits from periods of expanding economy and, on the other hand, to minimize any adverse effects when business activity slackens.

Some companies have had long experience with business forecasting, whereas for other managers it is a relatively recent innovation. These managers have become aware of the difficulty of "bucking the trend" of general business conditions, especially when their companies grow larger. They also have realized the possibility of serious losses when economic factors are not given sufficient weight. Their recent emphasis on the need for forecasting can partially be attributed to the availability of more reliable and detailed information on the nation's economy upon which they can base their forecasts.

Responsibility for Forecasting

The practice of general business forecasting varies among enterprises from the reading of newspapers to the use of trained experts to interpret and analyze current and future business conditions as they relate to the company's operations. In all companies executives are expected to keep abreast of the current developments in business conditions through their reading, contacts, discussions and such. In some, one executive is responsible for the preparation of forecasts, and he normally has at his disposal a staff of specialists who are trained in this kind of work. This staff usually consists of economists and statisticians. Recent research indicates that it is common practice for firms which employ staff forecasters to place them close to top management.

The American Management Association reports that a majority of companies which maintain their own forecasting staffs definitely separate overall economic forecasting from specialized sales forecasting. Firms which have their own forecasting staffs, regardless of whether they are small or large companies, tend to regard their forecasters as "professionals". This is indicated by the title of the person in charge of forecasting, and the term most often used is that of "economist".

If the firm does not employ its own research staff, it is common practice to subscribe to the services of economic consultant firms who provide their clients with analyses and interpretations of business developments and forecasts of future conditions. By retaining outside research services some managers feel that they can obtain expert advice on economic matters and forecasts at a lower cast than if they were to maintain their own staff of specialists. Sometimes a company which has its own research staff will also employ the services of outside research consultants in order to get a reliable check on their own forecasts and to obtain other viewpoints. This, of course, helps to improve the quality of the forecasts.

Forecasts as Planning Premises

In order to plan for the future, the manager needs these planning premises for his own foundation of planning. These forecasts are so-called building stones which will form the foundation on which the manager can do his own planning. In this respect we speak of these forecasts as prerequisites of planning. On the other hand, there are those forecasts which the manager makes relative to his own business, such as a sales forecast; this kind of forecast is considered the result of planning.

Obviously there is a multitude of areas in which forecasts are possible, but a manager seldom requires forecasts in each area for it would be impractical and uneconomical to do so. He normally confines his efforts to those forecasts which his experience tells him are important and decisive for his own planning. The manager selects only those planning premises and makes forecasts only on those which are strategically important and which have material bearing on his business.

Premises which are important to one enterprise might not be of any significance to another, and with time the manager will learn which of the various assumptions have bearing on his planning and which he can neglect. Some assumptions which were important in other years become insignificant and therefore will be eliminated. Others will be added as time goes on. Therefore, in forecasting, the manager must remain fully aware of the shifting behaviour of some of these strategic assumptions. Factors which were of no importance might become very important and forecasts in new areas would be demanded.

The findings of both research projects of the 1957 report of the American Management Association indicate that the type of industry in which the enterprise is engaged influences the amount of effort that is devoted to forecasting. It was also learned that the further company is removed from the ultimate consumer, the more difficult forecasting becomes. For instance, producers of steel and manufacturers of heavy industrial equipment are likely to make wide-spread use of forecasting departments.

Although most planning premises are tangible, the manager must not overlook those which are intangible, such as the company's reputation within the industry, or a possible loss of prestige. While the latter are important, they cannot be quantified.

Nevertheless, they are planning premises the manager must take into consideration. The author knows from experience that though a product may fit well into the profit and production picture of a company, much attention will be paid to the question of how it would affect the prestige of the enterprise. Though not quantifiable, this latter intangible planning premise plays an important role in the firm's final decision.

In reference to the foreseeability of the premises it must be stated that in spite of the thoroughness with which all these planning premises have been selected there will be some which just cannot be foreseen. In the short run it might be possible to predict them, but in the longer run these occurrences cannot be predicted with any degree of exactness. We are particularly referring to premises such as acts of God, wars or strikes in suppliers' plants. We therefore have to distinguish between foreseeable and unforeseeable premises.

Another way to differentiate the various planning premises is to look at them from the controllability point of view. Certain planning assumptions are controllable, others are semi-controllable, and still others are non-controllable.

Under the hearing of controllable planning premises we have policies and programmes, activities which are entirely within the control and the realm of management. The firm's share of the market is an example of semi-controllable premises. This share of the market is a premise which is only partially controllable by management. Management can do its part to obtain as much of the industry's total as possible, but, on the other hand, the activities of the competitors will limit the proportion of the share. In this respect this planning premise is only semi; controllable. There are other premises which are non-controllable, the most important of which is the business cycle. All firms are affected by the business cycle, and there is relatively little a firm can do to stave off its effects. However, acknowledging the business cycle and especially where we are in the cycle can be of great help to the planning of management. Population trends is another important example of the many more additional planning premises which are beyond the control of management.

External and Internal Premises

In examining the multitude of planning premises, we can also distinguish between those planning premises which are external to the enterprise and those which are internal to the enterprise. When we speak of those planning premises which are external to the business enterprise we are primarily referring to the general business climate and to the industry climate, whereas those which are internal to the enterprise are the firm's own climate. We shall first discuss the various premises which are external to the enterprise.

6

Ownership of Business

In modern time there are four main forms in which business activities may be organized. These are:

(i) Sole Proprietorship or Individual
(ii) Partnership Firm
(iii) Joint Stock Company
(iv) Co-operative Society

Above classification is based on the ownership of business and they relate essentially to private business. The forms of organization for the government are:

(i) Departmental Organization
(ii) Government Company
(iii) Joint Venture.

It is important to note that the ownership pattern, nature of liability of owners and size of business concern have a close inter-relationship. Business of a small scale caters to a limited market or deals with small number of customers and has small capital requirements. By virtue of the small scale of operations, the range of management and supervisory problems can easily be handled by the owner himself. Sometimes, face to face relationship with customers is also very important e.g., in small retail stores, while in some cases the personal knowledge or technical skill of the owner is sough to be utilized. For all above reasons a proprietary organization is decided upon by the promoter. Business of relatively larger scale are generally organized as partnership firm. In partnership firm partners wish to pool their capital, expertise, skill and business experience. Thus, partnership firms are enabled to have more funds, operate on a larger scale, have better management through specialisation, pooling of knowledge, experience and decision-making skills. The internal organization can be more elaborate and efficient because every partner can look after some specific activity or certain aspects of business.

If element of risk is relatively greater and the entrepreneur finds some income tax, wealth tax and gift tax advantages in opting Joint Stock Company organization. In those cases, where the capital requirement is largest and risk is comparatively greater, the entrepreneurs prefer limited liability. Thus, the business is generally organized as Joint Stock Company.

SOLE TRADER

Sole trade is the easiest and oldest form of business organization. Organization of the capital and trade is the sole responsibility of one single person. Therefore, the risk is borne by one person only. In every economic system, it is only the single form of organization which is prevailing and has maintained its existence despite the fashion and growing tendency towards the large scale undertakings.

Definition of Sole Tradership

Many a management experts have defined the proprietorship or sole tradership: a few selected definitions are given below:

(a) C.S. Gerstenberg: "Sole trading is that form of business organization which is started and run by one person who bear profits and losses of it."

(b) Prof. Haney: "The individual entrepreneur is the form of business organization at the head of which stands an individual as one who is responsible, who directs its operations and who alone runs the risk of failure."

(c) Stephenson: "A Sole trader is a person who carries on business exclusively by and for himself. The leading feature of this kind of concern is that the individual assumes full responsibility for all the risks connected with the conduct of the business. He is not only the owner of the capital of the undertaking, but is usually the organizer and manager and takes all the profits or responsibility for losses."

(d) Kimball & Kimball: "The individual proprietor is the supreme judge of all matters concerning to his business subject only to the general laws of the land and to such special legislation as may come into effect."

(e) Dr. John A. Shubin: "Under the sole proprietorship form of ownership a single individual organizer has little to invest and operates in his own name."

An analysis of the above definition reveals that the arrangement of the whole capital is done by the person who starts the business. A sole trader, apart from making arrangements of the capital is responsible for the whole profits or losses. A sole trader by his cleverness and labour, his business relations and goodwill, courage, honesty, ability, education and cooperation tries to make his business a success. It should always be remembered that whether, the business is small or big, the gap between the success and failure can be filled up by wisdom only. The businessman is always to keep in mind the maximum "Service first and profit next", so that he can become a successful trader to provide the maximum services to his customers.

Features of Sole Tradership

The analytical study of the different definitions could enable us to find the following important features of a proprietorship firm:

(1) Easy to start and dissolve: The sole tradership firm can be easily started at any time without any typical formalities, similarly, if required at the time of closing the business or dissolving the firm, the trader is not expected to wait for some legal compliances; no doubt he must discharge all his liabilities, otherwise he may have to face the legal repercussions or the suits being instituted by his creditors.

(2) Unlimited liability: The sole trader arranges for the total

capital for his business. The liability of bearing the losses lies with him only. No doubt he alone enjoys the profits also, but the liability towards the total creditors is also to be borne by the single proprietor.

(3) Freedom of occupation: A sole trader can start any type of legal business according to his will (but subject to local rules and regulations). There is no legal binding upon him for starting a business. But it should also be noted that he cannot start any business upon which some legal restrictions are imposed by the Government or he is required to obtain certain types of licences from the different Government authorities.

(4) No legal formalities: Unlike the limited companies, a sole trader is free from any legal formalities to be complied with, in respect of the formation of his firm. Therefore, the time gap is not created due to legal formalities in respect of the establishment of the business.

(5) Sole ownership of capital: Since the arrangement of the total capital is done by the single person, therefore, he owns the total capital, even if it is increased due to additional profits earned by him during the course of business activities.

(6) Sole responsibility for the decisions: Since beginning to the end of the firm, the proprietor is fully responsible for his decisions taken in the business operations, for example, if due to his decisions some losses are caused, it is nobody's concern, but has to be borne by the proprietor.

(7) Sole management: A sole proprietor is not required to follow any laws or bye-laws of the firm, he himself is free in taking suitable decisions to manage the affairs of his business. There is no need of any obligatory consultation with any other person. Therefore, he is expected to be potent enough in taking business decisions to manage the whole show of the business starting from purchasing, selling, finance, production and distribution activities.

(8) Limited scope: Since only a single person is liable to discharge all the duties therefore the scope of expansion of activities cannot be envisaged in the sole proprietor's firm. Although as a matter of practice he can employ as many persons or specialists as his advisers, but in the process of decision-making he is always left alone.

Thus, we find in the above features, that the sole proprietor is fond having his existence in the areas where the extent of business activities is limited, the demand is regular, the capital requirements are limited and competition and risk is limited. The example of such proprietorship firms are—Small vendors, sweet and fruit sellers, retailers, artists, lawyers, doctors, etc. Sole tradership is considered to be a better form of organization in which following characteristics prevail.

(a) *Small trade:* The business activities which require minimum trading operations can be started on sole tradership basis.

(b) *Limited capital:* Since only a single person has to arrange the funds for the business operations, therefore, the business activities which require minimum funds, can only be run on proprietorship basis.

(c) *Limited liability:* The activities in which the business liability is minimum should be run on sole-tradership basis, otherwise, the individual may not face the unlimited liabilities of the business.

(d) *Personal supervision:* The business activities which require more personal involvement and supervision, can be efficiently run on the basis of sole-tradership.

Scope of Sole Tradership in India

There is enough scope for sole tradership in India, because most of the people are largely dependent on agriculture. A large number of small scale business and industrial units are in existence even in villages. Our Gandhian economics and present government's policies are also advocating the expansion of small and cottage industrial sector. Although due to foreign collaboration, we could have a good number of industrial units, but still we observe the simultaneous expansion of sole tradership. In other words, we can say that the expansion of large units have not come in the way of the expanded activities of the sole traders, on the contrary these are increased. Although the small manufacturers who had to face the competition from the mill-made products yet the diversion of their areas or their restrictions of the Government in respect of the industrial activities, sufficient protection is provided to the small scale sole traders. Thus, it should be said that sole trade is not the "Relic of Barbaric Age."

Prof. Honey has also been of the opinion that this form of business will survive in that wide field which required less capital and more personal skill. Economists and politicians cannot forget those qualities of responsibility and self-dependence which are rather more important in business. All these qualities, which require personal involvement are found in Sole Trade Business.

Legal Restrictions on Sole Trade

As we have already seen that there are no legal restrictions on sole traders, therefore, a sole trader can start his business according to his free will. But it should be mentioned that the liability of a sole trader is unlimited. Apart from his business assets his personal property can also be made liable for the payment of his business liabilities. Second important point is that the sole trader should be competent to enter into contract. *i.e.*, he should be a person of sound mind and should not be a minor. Section II of the Indian Contract Act provides:

> "Every person is competent, to contract, who is of the age of majority, according to law, which he is subject to and who is of sound mind, is not disqualified from entering into contract by any law to which he is subject".

According to the previous English Law, windows were not found competent to enter into contract.

An important point should always be kept in mind that a sole trader cannot start any business, which is restrictly by the Government or on which there is a state of monopoly of the Government. In U.S.A. even a sole proprietor is required to pay a regular fee to the Government to commence and continue a business.

Advantages of Sole Tradership

By the above analysis of the features of the proprietorship firm, we find the following advantages of the sole tradership:

(1) Easy to start: The foremost advantage of the sole tradership is its easy start. Otherwise in the case of co-operatives and limited company, the traders are required to wait for their registration and other legal formalities which often take even about

six months time.

(2) Secrecy: The activities of the trader remain secret. His business policies and trade-secrets are not disclosed to others, therefore, he can maximise his profits by maintaining top-most secrecy of his business operations.

(3) Personal contact: A sole trader always keeps (and he is often required to keep) personal contacts with different parties in his business activities. Every customer often comes in his personal contact. Therefore, by his sweet behaviour he can make those persons as his permanent customers. Similarly with other traders also he is required to maintain direct personal contacts, and the business may thus flourish.

(4) Degree of caution: A sole trader is always required to remain cautious and conscious of the business activities, because if his control is left loose, he may be required to suffer any amount of loss, thus even after business hours, he is always found very much busy in the business operations.

(5) Selection and change of business: Sole trader is always free and can enjoy the freedom of selecting the business of his choice, he can also change the business activities according to his requirements and changing circumstances. He is not required to seek permission from anybody else for the purpose.

(6) Economy: Since the total supervision and managerial activities are performed by the proprietor, therefore, the additional expenditure on managerial staff and overhead expenditure are minimised, leading a good deal of savings to the sole-trader.

(7) Self-confidence: Since the sole -trader looks after the total business operations, therefore, he develops a good deal of self-confidence, and often he is found prepared for taking big business (risky) decisions, which may yield him handsome profits.

(8) Harmony in work: A sole trader works alongwith his workers honestly and sincerely. Thus, the workers are also expected to work labouriously which ultimately results in efficiency of the business as a whole.

(9) Loan or credit facilities: Sole proprietorship firm enjoys the advantages of obtaining sufficient credit facilities subject to the goodwill of the owner. Moreover, since the liability of the owner is unlimited, the firms also agree to extend the credit facilities, while for companies often the banks and business houses hesitate to give loan facilities due to their limited liabilities.

(10) Prompt decisions: A sole trader is the king of his own will: for any decisions, he is not required to consult or seek the permission of anybody also. Therefore, the decisions in the firm are taken by him very promptly, thus spontaneous or on the spot decisions in the business often give fruitful results.

(11) Sole-owner: Sole trader is the only owner of the business assets, therefore, he always feels motivated. Working for the firm means working for himself and constant interest is being maintained by him in the business operations.

The above benefits or merits of sole traderships are the important causes of its universal existence. Even in socialist and communist and communist countries, the petty business activities are still run by the sole traders. Similarly, in capitalist countries like U.S.A. U.K., where the large organizations have captured the business operations maximum number of sole traders are found, which are working either independently or as ancillary or auxiliary of the big business activities.

Disadvantages of Sole Tradership

There are many shortcomings and drawbacks, due to which a sole-tradership firm does not assume its important place in the business world. Some of the disadvantages of sole proprietorship business are given below:

(1) Unlimited liability: A sole trader cannot endeavour or take the risky decisions, because at the time of losses not only his business assets are lost, but he will be liable to make good the losses out of his personal property.

(2) Hasty decisions: A person cannot be considered potent enough to take decisions correctly in all the areas, therefore, there may be a good deal of chances that the business decisions taken by the sole trader may be hasty which can cause him sufficient losses.

(3) Limited capital: A person is subject to his own resources, similarly the owner can manage a limited capital out of his savings, borrowings from his relatives and friends, and partly from the banks or financial institutions to the extent of his credit worthiness. Therefore, for big business activities sufficient funds are arranged in the sole trader firm.

(4) Burden of loss: Due to unlimited liability, hasty decisions, limited capital, if some business activities go against his policies, he may be left alone to bear the unlimited risk of the business losses.

(5) Closure of business: As it is easy to start, similarly easily these sole trader firms are closed or face the end of business. Death, illness or otherwise any incapability of the trader may result in closure of the business, always it is not necessary that the heirs will also be able to run the business successfully.

(6) Limited energy: A sole trader cannot extend his work more than his limited physical and mental energy. He can seek the help of his employees, but in the process of decision-making he is left alone. Moreover, it is always not necessary that he may find devoted, trustworthy and sincere employees, therefore, the burden of business operations is increased on his shoulders, and the gradual depreciation in his energy may be the cause of the loss in the business.

(7) Suspicion to the outsiders: Although secrecy was found to be favourable symptom for the sole-trader, but from the point of view of the outsiders, secrecy is proved to be a harmful element. Since the sole trader is not required to publish his accounts and the outside world does not know about his business soundness, he looses the business sympathy from other traders due to his secrecy in the business.

In nut-shell it can be said that sole tradership is full of shortcomings except to the extent it is thought to keep it a small business house. But whenever we think in terms of expansion or increase in the business activities, it is found full of shortcomings. Thus for small operations, the above shortcomings or drawbacks are not proved as hindrance for the sole-trader.

Selection of an Employee or a Partner for Expansion Activities

An instinct of expansion is always found in every human being, a petty trader wants to increase the size of his business, he thinks and goes on making efforts and sometimes and often if he gets success, then a question come before him to control and manage the expanded operations, *i.e.*, whether to select an Employee or to admit a partner?

A sole trader works according to his own energy and resource. Since he extends his business, it may lead to slackness in the organization of his business. Here he is facing the problem of admitting a partner of selecting an employee. Before deciding as to whether an employee would be more helpful or a partner, he would have to give due weightage to the following points·

Benefits in Appointing an Employee

With the extension of the business activities, a sole trader may appoint an employee keeping in view the following benefits:

(1) Independent decisions: An employee is required to carry out the instructions given by his boss, thus the sole trader will enjoy the freedom of taking independent decisions, and the appointed employee will carry out the desired instructions, and the interference shall be minimised.

(2) Complete control: The sole trader can maintain full control over the activities of the business, irrespective of the working of the employee. Because the employee will no doubt help in the business activities, but the control shall be vested in the hands of sole trader.

(3) Appointment of specialists: Sole trader can appoint the specialists according to his needs to conduct the activities of purchase, production, sales, finance, labour supervision, or even for consultation purposes. The desired employees can be appointed according to the requirements and capacity utilisation of these specialists. Thus in the process of decision-making necessary help of these specialists can be obtained without losing the control.

Shortcomings of Appointing an Employee

The followings are the common shortcomings, which may be faced by a sole trader in selecting an employee for his expanded business activities:

(1) Work for salary: A person appointed as an employee is not concerned with the betterment or deterioration of the business activities, nether he is affected by the profits nor losses in the firm, while on the contrary he is more concerned with his salary that

too with regular promotion or increments. Although he may be motivated to work hard, but often the sincerity and integrity is not found in the employees.

(2) *Lack of responsibility:* The employee does not share any responsibility even of the business activities preformed by him, for any irregular or careless act of the employee, the owner will have to suffer. Similarly, employee cannot be held liable for business responsibilities.

(3) *Increased expenses:* If the person so appointed as an employee is not found worthwhile, it will result in the increase in business expenses due to payment of regular and timely salaries.

(4) *Problem of capital will not be solved:* Sole trader cannot solve his problem of the shortage of capital. Although he can expect some loans from his employees, but in exceptional circumstances, therefore, the problem of the shortage of capital is not solved in the tradership organization by appointing an employee.

Benefits of Admitting a Partner

Having found certain shortcomings and lacunas in the appointment of an employee, we find the following benefits in admitting a partner in the sole-trader firm:

(1) *Sharing of liability:* A person admitted as a partner in the firm shall come forward to share the liabilities of the business losses to the extent of the agreement (normally equal partners are admitted thus 50 per cent risks are being shared).

(2) *Investment of capital:* To fulfil the requirements of capital in the business, a sole trader should prefer a partner, who is coming with some capital investment, thus partly the problem of the shortage of funds is also solved by admission of a partner.

(3) *Hard work:* Since the partner admitted in the firm shall be entitled to enjoy the shared profits, therefore, he will work hard, sincerely and devote his full time and attention in the maximisation of profits of the firm.

(4) *Proper advice and management:* Only a partner of the firm can give favourable advice in the management and control of the business. Even in the absence of the trader, the partner will be fully competent to take a suitable and favourable decisions.

Thus, admission of a partner in a sole-trader firm shall be rather beneficial provided the firm needs additional capital and additional hands to manage the affairs of the firm in the absence of the owner.

Shortcomings of Admitting a Partner

A person entering into the firm with capital and who wishes to contribute some advice, shall also be subject to certain shortcomings, which are summarised as under:

(1) Difficulty in obedience: Often partners try to compel the others to obey, while it is never found possible. Moreover, so far the sole trader was in the practice of issuing instructions and his subordinates used to obey only, thus he will be facing a good deal of problems in dealing with this person admitted as a partner, because the partner has got the equal right and is not supposed to obey the instructions of his business colleague.

(2) Difficulty in removing the partner: A person admitted in the firm cannot be easily asked to leave the firm, if at all it happens, he asks for the goodwill and other benefits of assets and capital.

Conclusion

Thus, it is apparent that sole proprietorship firm is independent in its working irrespective of many business shortcomings, however, if a trader wishes to continue the business operations at small level to the extent of his capacity of financing and managing, it is considered to be the best form of business organization. But if he thinks in terms of expansion then the question of admitting a partner or employing a person as an employee is raised before him. If he takes suitable decision in this regard, it may be favourable approach, but it is still found a subject of dispute.

7

Partnership Form of Business

Sole traders found themselves incapable of running comparatively of large business. For this purpose, it is necessary that some persons should unite with their capital, ability, experience and efficiency. All the qualities necessary for the success of a business, cannot be found in one person. In this world some people have money while others have experience. For the success in the business persons with different qualities should unite, with increase in the size of business the sole trader form of business becomes insufficient; similarly in Joint Hindu Family business, also the number of the members of the family may be more but the operating member is only one, *i.e.* 'Karta'. The duties and liabilities of a sole trader increase to such an extent that he wants to encourage his faithful and best servants by making them as business partners. He might desire that a wealthy person or an efficient person might become his business partner and thus increase his business. Thus when persons with different qualities unite, it assumes the form of a partnership.

Definition of Partnership

To analyse the concept of partnership, we will study some of the definitions of a partnership:

(a) Section 4 of the Indian Partnership Act, 1932 has defined a partnership as "Partnership is the relation between persons who have agreed to share the profits of a business carried on by all or any of them acting for all."

(b) Dr. John A. Shubin: "Two or more individuals may form a partnership by making a written or oral agreement that will jointly assume full responsibility for the conduct of the business."

(c) William R. Spriegel: "Partnership has two or more members. Each of whom is responsible for the partnership. Each of the partner may bind others for debts of the partnership."

(d) Kimball & Kimball: " A partnership or firm as it is often called, is then a group of men who have joined capital or services for the prosecuting of some enterprise."

(e) Charles W. Gerstenburg: "The general partnership is a form of business organization in which two or more individuals carry on a business as co-owners for profit."

Thus, two or more persons who perform business activities are called partners and jointly they are called firm and the name in which the business is started or is carried on is called firm's name. For example, Harish Kumer, Rajinder Kumer and Anil Kumer started their business in the name of M/s. Harish & Bros. Individually Harish Kumer, Rajinder Kumer and Anil Kumer are partners of the firm, and collectively they will be called as firm and M/s Harish & Bros. is the name of the firm.

Essentials of a Partnership

The analysis of the different definitions enables us to know some of the important features of a partnership, which are as follows:

(1) Partnership agreement: To form a partnership, there must be a contract between and among the partners, it may be either in the form of 'partnership deed' or even oral: however, without agreement/contract there may not be a partnership.

(2) More than one person: There should be at least two persons to make a partnership. In ordinary business, the maximum limit of persons is 20 and in banking business the limit is 10. If the number of partners exceeds the required number it becomes an illegal partnership or a joint stock company.

(3) Business: The partners should enter into an agreement to

do some legal business. Without legal business, there can be no partnership. The purpose of the business should be moral, legal and not opposed to public policy.

(4) Sharing of profits: There must be sharing of profits among partners. Without the profit sharing among partners, it may not amount to a partnership. If a person in the partnership is not entitled to receive the share of profits, he will not be called a partner of the firm, similarly a person meant to share the losses only: will also not be considered a partner.

(5) Running of the business: The legal business of the partnership firm may be run either by all the partners, or by some of them or by one of them or even by none of them. However, legally every partner of the firm is entitled to run the business of the firm.

If any of the elements discussed above is not present in the partnership, it will not be considered a partnership firm.

Characteristics of a Partnership Firm

The following are the important characteristics of a partnership business:

(1) Unlimited liability: The liability of the members of the partnership firm is often unlimited, *i.e.*, they will be liable personally for the losses caused to the business irrespective of their profit-sharing ratio. In certain cases, some persons may be admitted in the firm with limited liability, but at least one person must be having the unlimited liability otherwise it will not be deemed to be a partnership firm.

(2) Contract or agreement: There must be an agreement among the partners, if a person who is not capable of entering into contract, he will not be considered a partner, however in some cases a minor may be admitted in the partnership with limited liability to share the profits only.

(3) Mutual relations: In partnership, the partners are the owners of the property of the firm, they are entitled as agents of the firm for each other for the business activities of the firm, they can make the firm liable by their act in discharging the duties for the firm.

(4) Number of partners: The maximum number of persons in

a partnership firm may be 20. Although this is not restricted by the Partnership Act, but the Indian Companies Acts have directed that the partnership firm of more than 20 partners shall be considered a company. In banking business the maximum number of partners may be 10.

(5) Position of partnership: The legal and business position of the partnership firm is in between Sole Tradership and of the Company form of business organization, because a partnership firm enjoys more facilities than the sole tradership and comparatively less facilities than that of the joint stock company form of business organization.

(6) Retirement of the Partners: Although every partner is empowered to leave the firm, but the unanimous decision should be taken if they want to get somebody out from the partnership firm.

(7) Profit-sharing: There must be a contract of sharing profits among the partners if there is no contract of such nature, they will be entitled to share the profits equally irrespective of their contribution in share capital. Indian Partnership Act does not lay down any specific provision for sharing the losses, the partners if they so desire may have separate ratio of sharing profits and separate proportion of sharing the losses.

With these features of characteristics of a partnership firm we can test the activities of the firm with other identical forms of business practices.

Difference Between Partnership and Co-Ownership

If there are more than one owners of a property, they are called co-owners. These co-owners have a right over such property according to their share. In ordinary language there seems no difference between a co-ownership and partnership. However, in the legal sense the following important points of difference may be studied:

(1) Contract: There should be a contract in the partnership among the different partners to carry on any legal business. No such contract is required in the co-ownership, they become the owner of a joint property and enjoy or share the income out of that property.

(2) Primary object: The primary object of the partnership is to earn profits while in co-ownership the primary object is to share the income of the property, usually they do not make any effort to earn the income from the property, while in the firm they are very much involved in making every possible effort to maximise their profits.

(3) Disposal of the share: No partner can dispose of his share in the partnership firm, while a co-owner of the property can easily sell his share to any outsider or to any co-owner of the property even without the consent of any other co-owner of the property.

(4) Agent and owner: In partnership, a partner is the owner (co-owner) and the agent of the partnership firm, while in co-ownership the co-owner is the only owner of the part of the property and he is not considered to be an agent for and on behalf of other partners.

(5) Share in kind: Often a partner gets his share in terms of money or at the time of dissolution in the form of the goods, but in the case of co-ownership, the co-owner gets his share in the form of the part of the total property of the firm.

(6) Limits of the number of member: In partnership the maximum number of persons may be 20 or 10 in case of banking business, but in the co-ownership any number of persons may be co-owners and there is no such statutory limit.

Thus, we observe that although these two seem to be identical, but they are much different in their objectives and practices.

Kinds of Partnership

The partnership business has been divided into different categories on different norms, some of the important types of the partnerships are as under:

(1) Partnership at will: Section 7 of the Indian Partnership Act does not specify the period of working of the partnership, therefore, it is always at will. Even if the partnership agreement specify any period or duration of firm, the partners if so like may dissolve the working of the firm even earlier.

(2) Joint venture: It is a short-period partnership to bear the risks of certain temporary assisgnments of contracts. Two or more

persons work together to complete a contract of profitable nature, after completion of the work, they share the profits and their amount is also withdrawn. For example, Harish Kumer and Hem Chandra enter into a contract to complete a building construction contract. Each of them contributes some amount also. After the completion of the contract, they will be getting the money and share the profits and will also withdraw their balance, if any left with the Joint Venture.

(3) Partnerships of fixed period: If some persons agree to work for a fixed period only, then it is called the partnership of fixed period.

(4) General partnership: Under this category the partners do not agree for any of the provisions of the contract. They contribute some capital and start the business. Thus in the absence of any agreement, the provision of the Indian Partnership Act shall be applicable on them, therefore it is called a general partnership.

(5) Limited partnership: If persons desire to become the partners, but do not want to bear the unlimited liability of the partnership, they may become the partner of such firm. The present law of partnership does not permit the limited partnership, in such firm at least one partner must be having the unlimited liability.

(6) Illegal partnership: When the business of the partnership firm is declared or becomes illegal, violating the provisions of any law of the country, then it is called an illegal partnership. Suppose Anita and Rosy entered into a partnership agreement to snatch the purses of the ladies and share the money received. It will be an agreement of illegal partnership and it will be void. If in case Rosy refuses to give the due share, Anita cannot file a suit in the court of law to claim her share because basically their agreement of business was illegal, therefore, it was an illegal partnership.

The above study of the different types of partnerships helps us in determining the nature of the business of kind of partnership business to be selected.

Selection of a Partner

We have already studied this problem in the previous chapter on Sole Tradership, that whether with the expanded business, we should go for the selection of a partner or appoint an employee. However, a due care is required to be given in the process of the selection of a partner.

While selecting a partner it should be kept in mind that the person should be such as can fulfil the requirements of the business. Type of business requirements depend on the nature of the business. Whatever the type of business is, we should take into consideration that he should be faithful, honest and hard-working, Special attention is required to be given to the character, habit and personality of the partner. It should also be kept in mind that only that person may become a partner who is capable of entering into a contract. A partner should not be a spectator because this tendency may lead the business to disaster. He should be having the initiative and capable of taking decisions in the routine affairs of the business. If a rich person wants to keep a partner in his business he should select an able, experienced, efficient and honest partner. But the person who does not have sufficient funds, should try to seek a rich person prepared or invest funds. Thus, the success of business depends, upon the right selection of the partners. Often the combination of money and talent may bring good results and it may be a profitable partnership for both types of persons, therefore, a person should not be in a hurry in the selection of a partner.

The personal relationship, friendship, should be a factor but these may and should not be the only criterion in the selection of a partner: the business requirements should be given the top consideration.

Difference Between Partnership and Joint Hindu Family

Although there seems to be some sort of similarity in the business of Partnership and Joint Hindu Family business in the number of members and joint ownership, however, basically these two are the different and independent form of business organizations. Some of the major points of differences are as under:

(1) Contract: Partnership is created by legal contract between and among the partners to do some legal business. In Joint Hindu Family business, a person becomes a member just by virtue of his birth, and therefore, the need of contract does not arise.

(2) Liability: The liability of all the partners is often unlimited in partnership firm, and at the time of major losses, they not only loose their capital investments in the firm but their private property is also taken away. In Joint Hindu Family business the liability of the members of the family is limited to the extent of their shares in the business, however, their personal property cannot be used to discharge the liability of the firm.

(3) Credit facilities: Since the liability of the partners is unlimited in the firm, they can manage any amount of credit or loan from different sources, while Joint Hindu Family members having limited liability cannot claim to obtain sufficient funds for the business activities of the family business.

(4) Application of law: Provisions of the Indian Partnership Act, 1932, are applicable to the relationship of the partners and their business conducts, provided there is no agreement between them. In other words, in the absence of any agreement the provisions of Partnership Act are applicable. In Joint Hindu Family business, since there is no contract among the members, the outright provisions of the Hindu Law are applicable to Joint Hindu Family relations.

(5) Effect of death: Death of a partner may dissolve the partnership but if the remaining partners want they can maintain the business of the firm of the partners, *i.e.*, the structure of the partnership is disturbed due to the death or insanity of partner. In a Joint Hindu Family, the death of the member does not affect, and his share is equally enjoyed by other existing members. Similarly, the death of Karta also does not make much difference because the next senior member of the family will resume as Karta and the business can be carried on successfully.

The basic difference between these two is that the partnership is created by agreement while the Joint Hindu Family business is a family affair in which the persons become members by virtue of their birth in the family.

Who can be a Partner?

To become a partner in the partnership firm it is essential that he should be capable of entering into a contract. Thus any major person, who is not a bankrupt nor a lunatic may become a partner. Although a minor can also be admitted in the firm, but for the profits only, such a minor cannot be allowed to inspect the accounts books. A married woman can also become a partner in the firm, but her liability in the firm shall be subject to her 'Stridhana'. A citizen of an enemy country may not become a partner in the partnership business in India.

Partnership Deed

After the selection of a partner, it is essential that formally they should prepare a partnership deed either in writing or orally. A written partnership deed on the stamp paper is considered to be a valid document for any dispute brought to the court of law. In France, Italy, U.K., Germany and U.S.A. the partnership deed should be in writing for proving their dispute in the court of law. However, in U.K., U.S.A. even if it is oral it should be supported with due evidence.

Contents of Partnership Deed

The partnership deed usually contains the following clauses governing the relationship and conduct of the business of partners:

(1) *Names, addresses and other particulars:* This deed is written in the form of an agreement, therefore, the detailed particulars of all the partners in respect of the name, father's name, residential addresses, status, profession should be properly written. Any change should be properly altered in the deed from time to time. Firm's name should also be written in the partnership deed.

(2) *Capital of the partners:* A specific provision of the amount of capital invested by each partner should be written in the partnership deed.

(3) *Profit and loss sharing ratio:* Partnership agreement or deed should specifically disclose by name of each partner, the share of profits and the share of losses they will be required to suffer. If in case even by mistake the name of one partner is left in this provision, legally he will not be considered as a partner, and he shall not own the responsibility or the liability for the losses to the firm. A person who is not getting the share of profits cannot be entrusted to bear the losses only. However, it is possible that a person is admitted to share the profits only, and he may not be required to bear the liabilities of the losses.

(4) Drawings: The amount to be withdrawn by each partner for his expenses should also be written so that in future any dispute may be avoided.

(5) Interest on capital or on drawings: Partners are entitled to receive the interest on capital investment, similarly they are liable to pay the interest on drawings. In the absence of any such agreements, neither the partners will get any credit of interest nor they will be liable to pay any interest on drawings, however, if they wish such provisions can be incorporated in the partnership deed.

(6) Duration of the firm: Although everybody wants to run the business activities for unlimited period, however, if they wish they can write the period of partnership and after the expiry of this period the contract of subsequent periods can be done.

(7) Business of the firm: Although they cannot enter into a valid contract to do some illegal business, yet they should specify the areas of the business activities to avoid any dispute in future.

(8) Division of work: The partners can write in their agreement about the activities to be performed by them. Even if anything written contrary they can subsequently enter into an agreement for doing some other activities also.

(9) Salary of commission or remuneration: Partners are not expected to receiver any benefits from the firm except thriller share in profits, however, they can provide specifically about the amount of salary, or any type of remuneration to be paid to a particular partner or to all.

(10) Application of Garner vs. Murray law: Often it is desired that they should make provisions to settle the dispute of the dissolution of the partnership of the firm. If a partner becomes bankrupt and does not pay any dues of the firm, whether this loss will be shared by the existing partners in their profit-sharing ratio or in the ratio of capital. It was decided in this case that the partners should bear the loss of capital in their capital ratio on the date of the insolvency of the partner.

(11) Goodwill of the firm: Often the disputes are found among the partners about the valuation of the goodwill of the firm either at the time of their admission or retirement or death or even at the time of dissolving the firm. They should submit the formula or the basis for the computation of goodwill of the firm so that the future disputes may be avoided.

(12) Maintenance of accounts: They can mention in writing about the method and technique of maintenance of accounts.

(13) Operation of bank account: Since every partner is entitled to act as an agent of the firm, therefore, he may claim to exercise his right for the operation of bank account, however , they can specifically delegate their power to other partners for the purpose and the norms of the operation of accounts can also be framed by them.

(14) Arbitration clause: If at any time any dispute is felt by the partners, they can refer the matter to some arbitrator instead of going to the court of law, because in courts, not only the time and money is wasted but the reputation of the firm is also endangered.

Thus, the above are not the sole provisions of the partnership deed, the partners can claim or may ask to mention any number of provisions. This Partnership Deed must be signed by all the partners and as an evidence two outsiders should also be asked to sign to make it a document of free consent of entering into a contract.

Test of Partnership

Often it creates a doubt in the minds of the students, whether a group activity of the person is a partnership or not, because many identical forms of business, *viz.*, Joint Hindu Family, Company, Co-ownership, Cooperatives are some of the example of group activities, thus we will try to clarify to the students that the group activity is not only the test, of partnership but some other factors are also required to be given due consideration. Similarly the sharing of the profits is not the prima-facie proof of the partnership. In actual practice, there are many persons who get some share of profits in the firm for one service or the other. Outsiders may consider them partners but actually they are not partners in the firm. Whether a person is a partner or not it depends on the following points:

(1) Sharing of profits: Sharing of profit is a direct proof of being a partner, it is not necessary that they should have contributed any amount in the form of capital also, but it is necessary that they are getting the share of the profits. For example,

Ram Kumar has given a loan of Rs. 50,000 to Hem Chandra with a condition that Ram Kumar will be getting the interest at 9 per cent and will also be entitled to share the profits (10 per cent of profits) and can also take part in the management of the firm. It will not be a partnership, because although the creditor Ram Kumar will be sharing the profits, still the intention is to give loan or act as creditor only, and on payment of the loan the profit sharing will also be stopped, thus it will not be a partnership. The following are also not the partners:

(a) Creditors of the firm.
(b) Manager of the firm.
(c) Widow or children of a deceased partner (without agreements),
(d) Ex-owner of the business, who has sold his goodwill to the firm.

(2) Participation in the management: If a person, who is entitled to take part in taking the managerial decision in the business of the firm, can also be considered as a partner provided he satisfies the condition of sharing the profits; because every partner is entitled to take part in the activities of the business and may run the same on behalf of the firm. Every partner is the agent of the firm, therefore, agency is an essential element of the partnership, sharing of profits and contributing the losses are not sufficient criteria.

(3) Checking of accounts books: As a rignt, every partner has access to the accounts books, he can check them and if required he can obtain a copy of the books or documents of the accounts of firm. This right cannot be given to either creditors or manager however, it is an important test of the partnership. Although a minor partner may be deprived of this right to check the books of the firm.

(4) Right to work as an agent: Every partner has a right to work as an agent of the firm. If any partner does not has this right, he may not be considered as a partner of the firm. Though he can surrender this right. Minors are not expected to enjoy this right. Similarly, creditors may also be given rights to control the activities of the firm, still they do not enjoy the right to act as an agent of the firm.

To establish the authentication of the partnership; it is

essential to satisfy the above conditions so that the partnership firm may be considered as a legal body to be governed by the provisions of Indian Partnership Act, 1932.

Essentials of an Ideal Partnership

The success of business depends upon the quantity of capital, cleverness and labour, business relations, fame, power of thought, courage, honesty, ability, education, etc. All these qualities cannot be found in one person. Therefore, the need of admitting a partner arises. An ideal partnership should have the following essentials:

(1) *Written and stamped partnership deed:* To avoid any future disputes, the partnership agreement should be written on a stamped paper duly signed and registered by all members, so that differences if any can by minimised.

(2) *Division of work according to ability:* Every person should try to work according to his best ability and capacity, therefore, interference in all the affairs may not be a successful attempt. If an engineer is trying to interfere in accounting affairs, he may not get the desired success, therefore, he should try to concentrate on purchase, production and selling activities.

(3) *Equality and fair share:* While deciding the ratio of partnership profits, it should be given due weightage to the appropriate and fair distribution of profits to the different partners on the basis of their capital invested, time and energy devoted in the business operations, often the investor trys to keep greater share in the profits of the business.

(4) *Longer duration:* The concept of short time partnership business should not be taken into consideration, because even if the firm is completing one assignment, they should continue the business and change the activities in the profitable areas.

(5) *Due weightage to partner's devotion:* In addition to the profit-sharing ratio being determined and written in the Partnership Deed, the partner should try to realise the extent of devotion of the other partner and if possible he should be suitably remunerated either in the form of additional remuneration, commission, salary, etc., so that due motivation can be maintained.

(6) *Honesty:* Honesty is considered to be the best policy in the business, however, it is a two-way affair and each one of them

should try to be honest, often it is suspected that one partner did some dishonest activities, therefore, other partner also did as a reciprocal activity of dishonesty. Every partner is an agent of the firm, therefore, as far as possible they should try to encourage the other partners also so that the atmosphere of honest dealings can be maintained to the maximum.

(7) Faith: All the partners should have due faith in each other, and without this the business activities cannot flourish.

Above guidelines are not only the sufficient criteria for the ideal partnership, however, the practical approach toward them may provide the maximum advantages to the firm.

MUTUAL RELATIONSHIP AMONG THE PARTNERS

Relations of Partners with One-another

The basic relationship arises out of the partnership deed or the oral agreement between the partners. They may incorporate as many items as they wish in the agreement. However, in practice the following two factors can only enable them to maintain cordial relationships for the better promotion of their future activities in the partnership firm.

(1) Utmost good faith: It is the primary duty of each partner to be devoted and trustworthy towards the other partners. Sense of duty and practical wisdom can give the maximum benefits to the firm. If a partner comes to know anything irregular about the other partner, he should try to influence the other partner by his efforts, instead of creating quarrelsome atmosphere. But this is possible only provided he himself is also working and influencing the other in good faith.

(2) Indemnify the losses to others for this misconduct: Nobody can call himself to be most efficient in all respects, thus everybody is subject to commitment or certain mistakes, therefore, if due to his negligence or misconduct any losses are caused to other partners, it is his humble duty to make good the losses caused to the firm or others, so as to maintain harmonious relationship. Every other person will appreciate and will neglect the losses, if there are caused in the normal course of business and without the

negligence of the concerned partners. However, even the law enforces the moral duty on the`partners to indemnify the losses caused to the firm due to the irregular activities of a partner.

The above are the suitable and harmonious criteria to be practised by the partners, so that the mutual understanding and cordial relationship can be maintained.

Rights and Duties in the Conduct of Business

The form of partnership deed is such a basic document which guides the activities and relationship of the partners in the firm, however, Indian Partnership Act, 1932 has laid down certain provisions, which can be applied if there is no specific provision in the partnership deed. The students should clearly understand that the following provisions are applicable provided there is no specific contract on the point in the partnership deed, otherwise, if there is any clause already given in the Partnership Deed than that particular clause will be applicable and the provisions given below shall not be applied. A summarised form of the different provisions is given below in respect of the rights and duties of the partners in conducting the business activities of the firm in the absence of any partnership deed:

(1) Take part in the conduct of business: Every partner entitled to take part in the business activities of the firm, and should be empowered tq manage the affairs of routine business in respect of purchases, sales, receipts and payments of funds, employ of germinate the employees for and on behalf of the firm.

(2) Attend and discharge his duties diligently: Section 12 (B) of the Partnership Act has suggested that every partner should try to discharge his duties with full devotion and diligence as if he was doing his own work.

(3) Right to express his opinion: Every partner is empowered to express his opinion and can give his advice, but it should not mean that the others are bound to accept or obey his advice. Although every effort should be made so that the decision should be taken by consensus or unanimously but often the majority decisions are also taken, therefore, the partner giving advice should take it otherwise, but the majority decision should be honoured.

(4) Access to the accounts book: Section 12 (D) of the Partnership

Act empowers every partner to have his access to the accounts books, he can check them and if required he can obtain a copy of the same. Minor partners are deprived of this right.

(5) Interest on capital: A partner is not empowered to charge any interest on his capital investment, but he can claim the interest at the rate of 6 per cent for the additional capital subscribed by him in the firm.

(6) To work without remuneration: Every partner is expected to work in the firm without charging or expecting any remuneration for the services rendered by him in the activities of the firm.

(7) Account for the private profits: No partner has a right to make any private profits out of and during the course of the business activities of the partnership firm. If a partner does so he should disclose such profits. Ordinarily he is not expected to run even the competitive business, if at all he does so, he may be subject to surrender those profits to the firm being earned by him from the competitive business.

(8) Interest on additional capital: In the absence of any specific contract, every partner is entitled to receive interest on additional capital introduced by him in the firm. The maximum rate of interest may be 6 per cent per annum.

(9) Right to be compensated: Since a partner is expected to compensate or make good the losses caused to others due to his negligence, therefore every partner in turn is also entitled to get compensation for the losses caused by other persons. Moreover, during the course of business if he sustains losses he can claim the damages from the firm.

(10) Act within the authority: Every partner should work within his authority, and he should not go beyond his rights, if at all he does and any losses are caused to the firm or to other partners, he should compensate.

(11) Indemnify the losses for negligence: He should make good or indemnify the losses caused to the firm due to his negligence and deliberate carelessness. Although nothing of the sort is provided in the Act, however, it will be decided on the basis of the circumstances of the situation.

(12) Not to assign his right to outsiders: The authority or power vested in a partner by virtue of being a partner, should not be assigned or delegated to any outsider without the specific consent

of all other partners.

(13) Right in emergency: Every partner has a right to act in an appropriate manner in certain emergent circumstances, he should act or take steps as he could do the same thing in his own and personal affairs.

(14) Rights to leave the firm: Every partner has a right to leave the firm even before the stipulated period of the partnership, but the permission and sanction of other partners shall be essential. Here permission does not mean that if he is refused he will not quit, but without the consent of other partners, he should not leave the firm.

(15) Admission of a new partner: A partner cannot admit a new person as a partner in the firm without the consent of all other partners.

(16) Right to not be expelled from the firm: A partner has a right to not be expelled from the partnership firm. Instead of being expelled he can claim the dissolution of the firm and may get his share in the net assets of the firm. In other words, if some other partners decide to expel one partner, then they cannot get success in doing so.

(17) Use of the property of the firm: A partner has to act as a trustee of others, he can use the property of the firm for the business activities of the firm in the interest of the firm, but as far as possible he should avoid using it for his private purpose, if he does so, he may be held liable to compensate for the use of the property.

(18) Ownership of the property of the firm: Every partner is the co-owner of the property of the firm to the extent of his share in the profits or in the capital investment. However, without his consent no other partner can dispose of the property of the firm. But he cannot sell in his own, which is collective and not specific.

As we have seen in the provisions of Arbitration Clause of the partnership deed, that at the time of any dispute the partners can seek help of the arbitrator for reconciliation of their cases, therefore, if need arises the arbitrator can also determine their rights and duties in certain specific circumstances.

Relation of Partners to Third Person

A partner is both owner and agent of the partnership firm. While dealing with the outsiders he is expected to act as an agent of the firm. He is expected to deal within the purview of his authority and in the name of the firm only: An act of the partner is considered to be an act of the firm. By his act all other partners will be liable individually and jointly and severally. But if the partner has done something beyond the limits of his authority, the firm and other partners may refuse to accept this liability and all such losses (if any) shall be compensated by that partner only to the third party.

Implied Authorities of a Partner

Any right or authority, which is neither clearly specified in the partnership deed nor decided orally by the partners, but provided by the law is considered to be an implied authority. Followings are the implied authorities of a partner in the absence of any specific contract:

(1) To purchase goods for the firm.
(2) To sell goods for the firm.
(3) To make payments on behalf of the firm.
(4) To receive or accept payments on behalf of the firm.
(5) To appoint employees for the jobs in the firm.
(6) To borrow funds or loan for the firm.
(7) To file a suit or defend the court cases on behalf of the firm.

A point of caution should be kept in mind by the partner that if he wants to bind the firm by his activities, he should take care of the following points:

(1) All the transactions should be done in the name of the firm,
(2) The method of transaction should be such as the purpose of binding the firm becomes clear.
(3) As far as possible firm's letter-pad should be used in all the circumstances to clarify the outsiders that the deal is in the name of the firm and on behalf of the firm.
(4) The partner should act within his authority or power.

Thus, we can say that the firm is liable for the act of the partners provided he has acted as an agent of the firm. For example, M/s. Mahavir Book Depot is a partnership firm having partners Ram Kumar, Harish Kumer and Hem Chandra. Suppose one of the partners say Hem Chandra places an order for the purchase of printing paper on the letter head of the firm, and forget to write his designation as partner or agent, this will be an act for and on behalf of the firm, but if he might have written the same letter on the letterpad of his personal name, then for this contract the firm will not be held liable and he may have to bear the losses personally.

Important: A partner cannot open an account in the bank for and on behalf of the firm, but if authorised by others, he can open and operate a bank account for and on behalf of the firm.

Implied authority does not include any of the following activities of a partner:

(1) No partner can delegate his powers to any other person.
(2) A partner cannot appoint an agent to do any work for the firm.
(3) No partner can decide or withdraw a case or settle the dispute at a loss lying in the court of law.
(4) He cannot transfer the fixed assets of the firm.
(5) He cannot decrease any claims or receipts of the firm being or due to be received by him.
(6) He cannot purchase any fixed asset for and on behalf of the firm.
(7) He cannot become a partner in any other firm as an agent of the partnership firm.
(8) Court matters cannot be referred to the Arbitrators.
(9) No partner can open a bank account in the name of the firm being an agent of the firm.
(10) No partner can accept any liability in the suit on a firm being instituted by a third party.

All these points are subject to the consent of other partners, *i.e.*, if a partner has been empowered by all other partners, he can do anything being prohibited in the above points.

Joint Liability of a Partner

Since the partners are both owners and agents of the firm, therefore, for any act performed by them for and on behalf of the firm, they can bind the firm and they are liable also. This liability is individual and in their joint capacity also. If any partner does not want to own any liability he should give due notice for the purpose to the general public before such contracts. But after entering into contract, the partner cannot escape from the liabilities of the contracts.

Wrongful Act of the Partners (Liability of the Firm)

Section 26 of Indian Partnership Act, 1932 provides that if a partner causes some loss to a third party while discharging his routine duties towards the firm or while doing something with the prior consent of all other partners of the firm, he is equally liable and others will also be liable for the act of this partner. For example, if Hem Chandra of M/s Mahavir Book Depot bribes for some favour or to obtain some secrets of some other firm. When a suit is filed by the other firm against Mahavir Book Depot, his firm had to bear a loss of Rs. 10,000 this loss cannot be recovered from Mr. Hem Chandra only, because he did this act in the interest of the firm. Similarly the firm will be held liable for any negligence of misuse of the funds by its partners. For example, Hem Chandra obtained Rs. 5,000 with an advance order for the supply of books on behalf of M/s. Mahavir Book Depot. The firm could not supply the books of Commerce for XII class within time, because he did not disclose about the receipt of the money in the books of the firm, still the firm will be held liable for the compensation to be paid to the their party.

REGISTRATION OF THE PARTNERSHIP FIRM

Getting a firm registered with the Registrar of Partnership Firms is called the registration of the firm. Although a firm is not legally bound to get itself registered, but in practice there are a few important advantages of registration, which a firm enjoys and almost every partnership firm feels it essential to get the firm registered.

Procedure for Registration

For getting a firm registered, the partners of the firm are required to submit an application along with the prescribed fees to the Registrar of Partnership firms of the concerned area. The important points of information are required to be submitted in the following form:

(1) Name of the firm.
(2) Name, Father's name, Address, Age, Profession of each partner.
(3) Name of other places, where the firm has its business.
(4) Date of admission of each partner.
(5) Duration or period of the firm's business (*i.e.,* likely to continue) the period must be mentioned even if the firm is required to continue indefinitely.

This form is required to be signed by every partner, in exceptional circumstances, the authorised agent can also sign on behalf of the partner. The name should not be kept similar or identical to the words—'King,' Queen, State, Central, Crown, Emperor, or any intention should not be expressed through the words of the name of the firm that it is patronised by the State or Central Government or any such authority.

If in case the Registrar of Partnership Firms is satisfied with the particulars submitted, he will register the firm. Often the partnership deed is obtained by the Registrar so as to regulate the activities of the partners. If they have not prepared it, the Registrar can ask them to prepare and submit for the Registration purposes. The firm is also expected to communicate the Registrar of Firms for any changes in the items of the information already submitted by the partners at the time of registration together with any change in the Partnership Deed. Following important changes are often communicated to the Registrar of Partnership Firms:

(1) Name of the Firm and its Principal Office,
(2) Change in the names and addresses of the partners.
(3) Opening or closing of the business offices or branches.
(4) Change in the nature of the business.
(5) Attainment of majority age by a minor partner should be communicated along with the decision of the person, whether he will like to continue in the firm or not.

Registrar should make necessary alteration and changes as communicated to him from time to time by the partners.

EFFECTS OF NON-REGISTRATION OF THE FIRM

Although the registration of the firm is not compulsory, however, a firm has to face the following shortcomings if it is not registered:

(1) A partner cannot file a suit against another partner: A partner of unregistered firm cannot file a suit against another partner of the firm to claim his damages.

(2) Partner cannot file a suit against the firm: A partner of unregistered firm cannot file a suit on the firm, which is not registered. Similarly, the firm cannot file a suit against the partners or any other person for realiation of its claims.

However, the following are not affected:

(a) Any person can file a suit against the firm.

(b) An outsider can file a suit against the partners for the claims against the unregistered firm.

(c) A firm incorporated outside India and not registered is also not affected by the non registration.

(d) If a partner has been declared insolvent, the official receiver has a right to recover his property from the firm.

(e) Any person can apply for the dissolution of the firm.

Thus, it is inevitable that in normal course, every partner should insist on the registration of the partnership firm, because it does not involve any legal formality, nor any activities of the firm are affected, therefore, it can be concluded that the registration of a partnership firm is always in the interests of the partners and the firm, so as to enjoy the legal protection for the firm.

Advantages of Registration

Following are the important advantage of registration, whereas there is no disadvantage:

(1) Benefits to the firm: Without registration it becomes a handicap for the firm, that it cannot file a suit against others, but

after registration it assumes its own legal entity in the sight of law and can file suits against the outsiders as well as on the partners.

(2) Benefits to incoming partner: A registered firm is required to submit all the necessary particulars to the Registrar of Partnership firms, therefore, an incoming partner may easily obtain the desired information from the office of the Registrar and can know the necessary details about the firm so as to decide whether to enter into the business of the firm or not.

(3) Benefits to the retiring partner: A partner of the registered firm can merely give notice to the Registrar of Partnership Firms and escape from the liabilities, he may not be required to give notice to the general public and creditors.

(4) Advantages to the outsiders: In business the information is always an important criterion, to judge about the working of the firm; outsiders can obtain necessary information from the Registrar about the firm so as to decide their dealings with the firm. Even the changed information can also be obtained from time to time about the constitution and working of the firm.

Thus, we have understood that there are no minus point, except the beneficial approach for the firm, partners and the outsiders by getting the partnership firm registered.

Classes of Partners

Keeping in view the business practices, the following are the important classes of partners:

(1) General or working or active partner: Such person actively participates in the routine activities and general working of the firm. Almost full time is devoted by him in looking after the activities. Normally the activities of this partner make liable other partners.

(2) Secret partner: Although these partners take active interest, contribute capital and give specific advice for the routine working, but keep their names and other particulars secret, yet their liability remains unlimited.

(3) Nominal partner: There are some persons, who merely give their name for the goodwill of the partnership firm, neither they contribute any capital, nor take active interest in the routine working of the firm. Further, they do not claim any benefits or

the share of profits from the firm. In legal terms they are called 'Partners by Holding Out' or 'Partners by Estoppel'. The simple meaning of Holding Out is that the person himself or through others publicises about his association with the partnership firm. The meaning of estoppel is that if somebody introduces one person as the partner (while he is not the partner) and that person does not stop such publicity, therefore it amounts to a 'partner by estoppel'.

Example of partnership by holding Out: Suppose Mr. Ram Kumar is a very big businessman and considered to be a rich person in Delhi city. M/s Mahavir Book Depot (i.e., partnership firm) is a firm of his sons. For some transactions, Mr. Ram Kumar spoke to some dealers that he is also the partner in that firm. With this holding out, the dealers gave some credit to the firm, the actual partners of the firm failed to discharge that liabilities, thus Mr. Ram Kumar will be liable to pay the dues of the creditors of the firm, although he was not gaining any benefits or advantages from the firm.

Example of partnership by estoppel: Continuing the above example, Mr. Ram Kumar is not the partner of M/s. Mahavir Book depot, but one partner of the Firm Mr. Hem Chandra publicised in the presence of Mr. Ram Kumar that Ram Kumar is also the partner of the firm, on this statement Mr. Ram Kumar did not object or stop Mr. Hem Chandra, the outsiders listening to this statement assumed that Mr. Ram Kumar is also the partner of M/s. Mahavir Book Depot. In this type of estoppel although Mr. Ram Kumar has nothing to do with the affairs of the firm, however, he will be liable to the unlimited extend for the liability of the firm.

(4) Minor partner: A general partner has got unlimited liability, but in certain cases, the partners with limited liability can also be admitted in the firm.

Minor is a person who has not completed his 18 years of age (21 years in case of the persons, whose guardian was appointed by the Court). In certain cases, minors can be admitted in the partnership firm for profits only. They will be liable to the extent of their capital investment. Often the minor children of the deceased are admitted in the firm in this form. Section 30 of Partnership Act provides that a person who is not major cannot become a partner, however, if all the partners agree a minor may be admitted in the firm for profits of the business.

Rights and Duties of the Minor

A minor can enjoy the following rights and duties in the working of the partnership firm:

(1) Share in the property and profits: A minor partner is entitled to share, out of profits, at an agreed rate and at the time of dissolution of the firm, he will be getting the share out of property of the firm. Similarly at the time of leaving the firm he can claim to the extent of his amount of capital after revaluation of the assets of the firm.

(2) Limited liability to the extent of capital: The liability of a minor is limited to the extent of capital invested by him in the firm. He may not be held liable to meet the liability out of private estates, nor he may be declared insolvent.

(3) Cannot file suit against the firm: A minor partner cannot file a suit against the firm or against the partners to get his share or assets and profits, till he continues in the firm. If at all he wants to file the suit, it can be for dissociating from the firm.

(4) Access to accounts books: A minor can inspect the books showing the business profits and other routine matters, while he cannot ask for the private and secret documents important for the business operations. He can claim the copy of the trading and profit and loss accounts only.

(5) Public notice after attaining majority: After becoming major, a minor (now major) is required to give a public notice within six months from the date of attaining majority, whether he wants to continue in the firm or not. In the absence of public notification it will be assumed that he wants to remain a partner and then he will be liable for all the liability after such date to the unlimited extent.

After attaining majority this minor assumes all the rights (we have discussed earlier) as an ordinary or working partner may exercise. However, we can summarise in context of the position of minor after majority, his rights will be as under:

(1) To share the profits and losses in the old ratio.
(2) His liability will no longer remain limited.
(3) He can enjoy all the legal rights as provided in the Act,

provided there is no specific agreement among the partners to this effect.

If Minor Decides not to Continue

Although a minor is required to give a public notice within six months from the date of assuming majority if he does so and intends to leave the firm after attaining majority, his position will be as follows:

(1) His rights and duties will remain alike a minor.
(2) He can file a suit against the firm to receive his share of profits and property.
(3) After giving public notice he will not be liable in any way for the activities of additional liabilities of the firm.

Thus, the law has given a very protective position to a minor, so that due to his contractual incapacity he may not be exploited but after attaining majority, he can decide on his own whether to continue in the firm or not.

OUTGOING PARTNER

Outgoing partner is a person who has been the partner of the firm and wants to leave the firm. A person can be dissociated from the firm in any of the following ways:

(a) By retirement: A person working as the partner can leave the firm with the mutual consent of the other partners. For leaving the firm, he will be required to give the notice to the firm and partners expressing his intention of leaving the firm. After serving such a notice he will escape the future liabilities of the firm. A public notice and an intimation to the Registrar of the Firms should also be given by the outgoing partner. His accounts are settled in due course of time by other partners.

(b) By expulsion: Except the concerned person, if all the partners resolve to expel a partner in the interest of the firm, they can do so. After this decision, the firm should give due intimation to all the concerned and the liabilities of such an expelled partner shall be alike the retiring partner.

(c) By insolvency: After being declared insolvent or bankrupt

a person looses his contractual capacity, thus a person without contractual capacity, cannot remain a partner in the firm, therefore, with the immediate effect, insolvent ceases to be a partner of the firm, he will not be liable for the liabilities after the date of his insolvency. Partners should settle his account and the funds are paid to the official receiver or court.

(d) By death, or insanity: On the death or on insanity of a partner, the partnership comes to an end, but if the existing partners which they can continue the firm. The accounts are settled of the deceased and his share is paid to the legal heirs of the deceased.

Restrictions on Outgoing Partner

Section 36 of Partnership Act empowers the firm or existing partner, to impose certain restrictions on the outgoing partner:

(1) He cannot use the name of the firm for his own business purposes.
(2) For the publicity of his own business he should not use his association with the firm or firm's name.
(3) He will not try to attract customers of the old firm but if the customers at their own come to him it is not important.

Rights of an Outgoing Partner

It is expected that the accounts should be settled by the firm of the outgoing partner from the date of his notice being served to the firm. However, if within a reasonable period his accounts are not settled he can claim interest on the balance due at the rate of 6 percent per annum.

DISSOLUTION OF PARTNERSHIP FIRM

According to Section 39 of the Partnership Act, the partnership is dissolved due to change in the partners, while the firm if they wish can continue but the firm can also be dissolved by the partners if they so wish or by adopting the different legal measures, Dissolution of the firm leads to closing down of the business.

Relations of the partners also come to an end as partners. A partnership firm can be dissolved in the following circumstances:

(1) Dissolution by agreement: Since the partnership is created by agreement, it can be dissolved by the existing partners any time by entering into a contract to dissolve the firm.

(2) Compulsory dissolution due to illegal partnership: There are certain circumstances in which a firm becomes an illegal partnership and the firm automatically comes to an end, *i.e.*, dissolved. Some of such circumstances are:

- *(a)* When all partners (even except one) become insolvent.
- *(b)* When the number of partners exceeds 20.
- *(c)* When a citizen of an enemy country becomes a partner.
- *(d)* The business of the firm becomes illegal due to some provisions.
- *(e)* If the business of the firm is opposed to public policy.

Thus, every partner should be alert in his routine activities so as to avoid any of such circumstances in which the partnership becomes illegal.

(3) Happening of certain events: Under the following circumstances a partnership firm stands dissolved:

- *(a)* On the expiry of the period for which the firm was formed.
- *(b)* On the death of a partner.
- *(c)* On the completion of the object, for which the firm was formed.

(4) Dissolution by notice: When there is no fixed term of the partnership business and the partnership is at will, then any partner can get the firm dissolved by giving a notice of his intention to other partners.

(5) Dissolution by court: A partnership firm can be dissolved by the order of the Court of the State. The following are the circumstances in which a court can issue orders for the dissolution of the firm on an application filed by a partner or by an outsider:

- *(a)* When a partner becomes of unsound mind.
- *(b)* When a partner other than the partner filing a suit, has become permanently incapable of performing his duties as a partner.
- *(c)* When a partner other than a partner suing has

transferred the whole of his interests to some other third parties.

(d) When a partner other than the partner suing is guilty of misconduct which may affect the carrying on of the business jointly.

(e) When the business of the firm cannot be carried on except at loss.

(f) When the court considers any other ground to be just and equitable for the dissolution of the firm.

Settlement of Accounts on Dissolution

After the dissolution of the firm, first of all the partners are expected to dispose the assets of the firm and try to discharge their liabilities of the firm by settling the payments of the creditors. In this process often a question arises about the firm s debts and private debts. After the creditors, settlements, the loans and advances of the partners are paid and the remaining, amount is given to the respective partners as per the balances of their capital and current accounts. Normally, the following procedure is adopted in the process of the settlement of accounts:

(1) Loss including deficiency of capital shall be paid first out of profits, and then these revenue losses are shared by the partners in their profit-sharing ratio.

(2) The assets of the firm are applied in the following order:

(a) In paying the debts of the firm to third parties.

(b) In paying the debts of the partners.

(c) In paying to each partner according to the balances of their capital accounts.

(d) The remaining amount, if any shall be divided among the partners in their profit-sharing ratio.

EVALUATION OF PARTNERSHIP

A detailed study of the partnership firm has been made in respect of its theoretical, functional and legal approaches, now we can evaluate whether this form of organization is suitable or not.

Advantages of Partnership

Partnership form of business organisation is often appreciated on the following ground:

(1) *Easy formation:* Alike the sole tradership and Joint Hindu Family business, the partnership firm can also be easily established by collecting the partners for contract.

(2) *More financial resources:* In partnership form of business, more capital can be managed, because every partner has got his own manner to accumulate the funds for affairs of the firm and secondly, the financiers and traders also start trusting the joint activities of the partners.

(3) *Improved business efficiency:* Persons of different calibre associate in the firm, therefore, specialised skill can be applied in the functional activities of the firm, and the efficiency in general shall be increased.

(4) *Flexibility:* In the absence of legal restriction a partnership firm is considered to be a flexible organization, because the partners can leave or join the firm by convincing the other partners, similarly the firm can also change the business if required.

(5) *Partners as specialists:* While selecting the partners a rich person may prefer an expert in sales, production, purchasing, etc. Therefore, the combination of these specialists make the business more profitable than the combination of the two rich persons.

(6) *Minority interests:* Although the routine working of the firm is carried on by majority decision, however, the attention is bound to be given to the individuals also thus often the unanimous decisions are taken.

(7) *Profit-incentives:* Every partner devotes sincerely in an expectation that he will be getting the maximum share of profits, thus they are induced to work hard.

(8) *Less speculation chances:* Every partner keeps prompt watch over the activities of the firm and of the partners, thus the partners cannot involve themselves in the speculation due to the unlimited liability of the partners.

(9) *Entrepreneurship and risky assignments:* Since more persons combine, they endeavour to take the risky assignments, which normally enable them to enjoy more profits.

(10) *Enough consultation:* In partnership, not only the partners consult themselves, but each partner has got his own friend, circle

and trys to seek advice from different sources, thus a cream or the best of the consultant's advice is used in the business.

(11) Chance to female partners also: If so desired, the females can also be admitted in the firm with limited liability to the extent of their Stridhan.

(12) Protection for the minors: Minors can be taken up in the firm with limited liability and they share the profits only. They may opt to remain in the firm after maturity.

The above advantages present a very rosy picture of the activities of the firm, however, we should also see the other side also so as to arrive at the proper evaluation of the working of the partnership firm.

Disadvantages or Shortcomings of Partnership Business

The following are the important shortcomings or drawbacks of the Partnership Firm of business organization:

(1) Secrecy: There are two aspects of this part, the secrecy is not maintained in the firm, because each and every activity is required to be disclosed to each and every partner, secondly, from the point of the outsiders, the collusion and conspiracy among the partners may cause a point of doubt in the minds of outsiders, dealing with the company, therefore, secrecy becomes a very important and negative point in partnership.

(2) Unlimited liability: The act of person doing the business, not only makes him liable but others are also subject to unlimited liability. Thus in this form, they often not only loose their capital investment, but it may also cause loss to their private property.

(3) Restriction on the transfer: A member in the partnership firm cannot transfer his share or cannot leave the firm at his will. The consent of all other partners is a must.

(4) Delayed decisions: For taking any decision, the consent of each and every partner is required to be obtained, because for the losses, each will claim the sole negligence of one person. In business, the spontaneous decisions can only enable the firm to enjoy higher profits, which is seldom possible in partnership.

(5) Mutual differences: Misunderstanding and jealous tendencies are the common weaknesses of the human beings: in partnership friends combine together to do some legal business,

and gradually they part like enemies due to basic differences in the routine working.

(6) Spirit of personal profit of benefits: Everybody wants to play safe and try to maximise his own interests, thus either they start making personal profits or become careless assuming that they are not going to get it alone, while it will be shared, thus the carelessness is also developed.

(7) Temporary existence: The above points have already made it clear that the misunderstanding and tendency towards personal profits bring the causes of dispute in the minds of partners and thus they are bound to dissolve the firm. Moreover, due to many other causes also the constitution of the firm is changed and the firm is subject to dissolution.

The above shortcomings are merely the weaknesses of human beings, and there is nothing wrong in the concept and notion of the business of partnership.

8

Selection Process of Employees

Selection of most suitable worker is a big problem for manager of human resource department. The trend towards automation and computerisation have increased importance of this process. Due to technological developments, profits stemming from efficient operations involve expeditious application of employees through effective selection and placement policy. The terms "selection" and "placement" are two different phases. Selection of employee means rejection of others. Thus, it is a negative process. On the other hand, placement is a positive process involving filling positions with the most suitable candidates. Selection stands on personal qualities of a candidate. Therefore, selection standards are adjusted to the needs of the business and labour market situations. The applicants pass or fail on specific selection standards or "hurdles" and those surviving these standards or hurdles for specific jobs are placed in vacant positions. Thus, an effective selection programme is a non-random process because those selected have been chosen on the basis of the assumption that they are more likely to be "better" employees than those who have been rejected. Then the next problem is the assignment of jobs to the newly selected individuals. Accordingly, placement relates to the question as follows: "Given the selection of N individuals to fill N various job vacancies, which individual should be put on which job?" It may be noted that in actual practice the selection and placement processes are frequently merged into a single process.

Yoder and others stress differential placement. In differential placement, attempts are made to compare an applicant's aptitudes, abilities, interests and temperament with job requirements for different jobs to ascertain for which of these he is most suitable. While traditional placement (for a single job) is effective only in a labour market marked by an ample supply of candidates, differential placement has been found to be extremely useful in a tight labour market. Indeed, differential placement makes the most effective use of human resources. The organizations can make the best use of differential placement as it specifies several positions for which an individual is suitable and provides enhanced flexibility of the work force if records of the secondary job qualifications are adequately maintained. It decreases recruiting and selection costs, absenteeism and turnover and increases job satisfaction and productivity.

While formulating selection and placement policy, attempts should be made to take in purview organization requirements as well as technical and professional dimensions of selection procedures. Decisions regarding selection and placement are line responsibilities, although these decisions can be improved through the advice of the staff personnel. Explicitly, administration and interpretation of psychological tests necessitate professional assistance. Accordingly, the crucial consideration in selection and placement relates to whether or not a professional selection and placement programme should be undertaken.

Policies on selection and placement should be based on effective blending of professional industrial relations needs, organization planning and employee development goals. As Yoder and others point out, formulation of these policies, involves several considerations such as legal provisions, objectives of employee development, organizational goals such as stability, growth, etc., union policies, integration of individual and organizational goals, technological issues, cost factors, extent of formality, etc., Briefly, an effective policy asserts the "what" and "why" aspects of the objectives.

As Blum and Naylor observe, the purpose of the selection process is to make effective use of individual differences with a view to selecting individuals who possess the greatest degree of qualities required for effective job performance. Indeed, individual differences provide the basis for the selection and placement processes. It has been found that differences between the most efficient and the least efficient workers for certain jobs such as spoon polishing are five times. This indicates advantages of developing selection methods to reject individuals with relatively less efficiency. It may be noted, as the psychology of individual differences reveals, that personal qualities of people are normally distributed. Thus, some individuals will have high amount of a certain quality as well as some will have a low amount while most of the individuals will have a moderate amount of that quality.

Although selection procedures, change from one organization to another in terms of size, industry, location, and scalar levels of jobs being filled, the selection process depends upon effective job analysis and recruitment. As Yoder and others suggest, the selection process involves seven steps as follows: *(a)* preliminary screening of applicants, *(b)* review of application blank *(c)* checking references, *(d)* physical examination, *(e)* psychological testing, *(f)* employment interview, and *(g)* evaluation of the programme.

Preliminary Screening and Review of Application Blank

It is highly non-economical to administer the entire battery of tests for selection purposes to all the applicants. It is advantageous to sort out unsuitable applicants before using the selection battery. For this purpose, usually, preliminary interviews, application blank check lists and short tests can be used. As regards screening interviews, they should be conducted by skilled and trained interviewers instead of some lower cadre clerk in the personnel department. The rejection standards for applications should be well-defined. Further, application blank check list can also be used to sort out applicants. However, the list should be determined through research and a suitable standard for rejection should be worked out. Suppose, the minimum standard for typing is 40 words per minute, the check-list should include this information. All the applicants possessing a typing speed below 40 can be straight away rejected. Sometimes, oral trade tests or aptitude tests are also used for screening purposes. Yoder and others suggest Toops' successive-hurdles technique, all selection factors are arranged in the decreasing order of importance. For example, if the aptitude test has the highest correlation among all the selection devices with job success, it would be ranked first. Likewise, if personal history has the least correlation among all factors with job success, it would come in the last. Accordingly, aptitude test can be used to screen out the applicants. Then, the next valid test will be used. Some organizations use non-objective methods such as observational technique (i.e., facial expression, etc.) and length of experience, etc. in screening applicants. This is a highly arbitrary method having only a chance validity.

Application blanks are frequently used as selection devices. These blanks vary from small one-paged sheet to several folders consisting of hundreds of items regarding the applicant's history. The application forms usually involve items such as name, address, age, marital status and dependents, schooling, experience and reference. There may be several other items depending upon the specific requirements of organization and job. As Harrell observes, these blanks provide preliminary information as well as aid in the interview by indicating areas of interest and discussion. If the application blanks consist of the proper items, the personal history items can be effectively used. Usually, the past provides indications regarding the future. The most effective predictor of job success is his demonstrated ability to perform effectively on a similar job. However, in practice, these application forms are not as effective as they appear theoretically sound. Indeed, sometimes the applicants tend to exaggerate their abilities. In several cases, the questions contained in the blanks themselves are irrelevant. In addition, sometimes the personnel department members are not aware of proper evaluation procedure of blanks and accordingly cannot make their effective use. Notwithstanding these limitations, the application blanks have been proved highly effective in several jobs. For example, several items of personal history such as age, marital status, number of dependents, etc., are found to be effective correlates of success of life insurance agents and department store salesmen. Likewise, personal history items have been found to be associated with turnover. College scholarship and other items have been compared with salaries after five years following graduation. The results revealed that college scholarship was the most important among several items for success in business. Some researchers have shown that executives are taller and heavier than non-executives, that business leaders are college graduates and have not benefitted by "family pull" in the business and that they usually come from homes of professional people, managers and business people. It may be noted, however, that these results should be interpreted with caution. Attempts should be made to constantly determine the effectiveness of personal history data for specific jobs and specific organization.

Weighted application blanks can be prepared on the basis of information regarding personal history items associated with job success. Suppose, if being under 30 years old is an advantage as an insurance agent, it is weighted high; if a handicap, it is weighted low. Likewise, if academic achievement is the least predictor of future success in salesmanship, it is assigned a low weighted value. It is markedly associated with success in executive jobs, it is assigned a relatively high weight. Thus, it is not possible to prepare a weighted application blank for all jobs in general. Rather, attempts should be made to prepare weighted application blanks for specific jobs and specific organization.

Reference Checking and Physical Examinations

Applicants should be requested to give character as well as general references in the application blanks. The previous employers and schools can provide useful information. Attempts may be made to make personal visits and telephone calls to procure objective responses. Usually, the correspondence is used to verify work history information including dates of employment, duties performed and wages and salaries received. It is an effective practice to send a brief questionnaire involving checking answers instead of requiring a great deal of writing. The enquiries should be as specific and precise as possible. General and vague questions will elicit only general and vague answers.

Physical examinations are frequently conducted and used for differential placement purposes rather than rejection of applicants. Large organizations have their own medical clinics while the small organizations refer to private clinics. The medical examinations have assumed the utmost significance in view of increasing and welfare programmes. As Yoder and others observe, physical examinations form a positive rather than a negative selection device. This helps in effective manpower utilisation by stressing differential placement involving assessment of individual's capacities and matching them with several job possibilities in the organizational setting. Attempts should be made to conduct physical demands analysis related to physical and environmental job requirements and conditions and physical capacities analysis related to the determination of how much physical activities a person can do. The physical demands of the jobs should be matched and compared with physical capacities of applicants. It may be noted that every one is handicapped physically for some jobs. Therefore, physical examinations are of the utmost significance in selective or differential placement.

Following Hanman, physical-demands analysis can be conducted by three methods—the disability method, the rating method and the specific method. The disability method stresses upon employee disabilities rather than abilities. For example, jobs are classified in terms of their suitability for persons with various handicaps such as the blind, the one-armed or the deaf. The rating method involves rating of jobs demanding "heavy lifting", "moderate lifting", "light lifting", etc. This is a highly subjective method. The specific method stresses what the employee can do. Attempts are made to state job demands as well as employee capacities in specific, objective terms enabling matching and comparison. This method also involves development of specific physical and environmental demands of job through jobs analysis enabling the personnel manager to assess specific abilities and demands for specific applicants for several specific jobs.

PSYCHOLOGICAL TESTING

General Principles

Psychological tests are used in organizations for several purposes including selection and placement of employees, transfer and promotion of employees, determining training needs and evaluation of training programmes, and counselling. Among these purposes, psychological testing is primarily used for selection and placement. The testing programme is effective if the number of applicants are large for a job. Systematic use of tests help in rejecting applicants. Thus, the testing programme is highly useful when there is considerable unemployment and abundance of applicants. However, it does not mean that it is not useful when number of applicants is less. In this situation it is useful for placement purposes enabling the manpower manager to place the individual in a job for which he is most suitable. As Tiffin and McCormick point out, it should be recognised that psychological tests are not infallible and that sometimes they reveal results which are not a true indication of the potential job success of the candidate. The effectiveness of any method depends upon the degree of improvement and not perfection. Suppose, without the use of testing programme, the turnover rate is 30 per cent and with the use of testing programme it comes down to 25 per cent. Here, the testing programme is considered as successful although it has not eliminated the turnover.

Psychological tests can be classified in several types. There may be group or individual tests, instrumental or paper and pencil tests, aptitude or achievement tests, personality and interest test, and power or spread tests. Group tests can be administered to any number of candidates simultaneously depending upon physical facilities while the individual tests can be given to one applicant at a time usually involving the utmost attention of the tester. The examples of group tests are Purdue Vocational Achievement Tests, the Adaptability Test, Wonderlic Personnel Test, etc., while among individual tests, Purdue Pegboard Tests or Manual Desterity can be cited. The instrumental tests make use of tools and usually are individual in character. The paper and pencil tests are usually group tests involving written responses. Aptitude tests assess an individual's potentiality to learn a job through adequate training and are effective if applicants do not possess earlier job experience. Achievement tests indicate how effectively an individual can perform a job or what he knows about it. These tests are useful if the candidates have prior experience of similar jobs. It may be noted that there are certain tests which when used in a particular way are classified as achievement tests and when used in other ways, can be designated as aptitude tests. Thus, the basic classification criterion should be the purpose and not the content. Personality and interest tests indicate personality and interest traits conducive to job performance and are akin to aptitude tests. A power test refers to a test where the ability of the testee to complete the test items is more crucial than his speed while speed test refers to a test where each item can be completed by most testees, but in which speed is crucial.

The tests should be tested before they are actually used. The tests should have adequate validity. The term "validity" means a test measures what it purports to measure. There are several methods of validating the tests. The present employee method and the follow-up method are largely used. The present employee method involves testing of present employees and correlating their test scores with a suitable criterion of job performance. The follow-up method involves assessing new employees at the time of recruitment, filing the test scores and subsequently determining the relationship between the test scores and the performance of employees on the job after a period of time. Although these methods have several advantages and disadvantages, the testing programme should make use of both methods to have maximum effectiveness. Indeed, there are four types of validity related to several purposes of testing. These are content validity, predictive validity, concurrent validity and construct validity. Content validity is assessed by indicating how effectively the content of a test represents the subject matter or types of situations which the test purports to measure. Predictive validity (exemplified by the follow-up method) is assessed by indicating how effectively predictions made by the test have been confirmed subsequently. Concurrent validity (exemplified by the present-employee method) is assessed by indicating how effectively the test is related to some present criterion of performance. Construct validity is assessed by determining what psychological characteristics a test measures. This is accomplished by correlating a test with another which measures the same characteristics. Factor analysis can also be used for this purpose.

In addition to validity, as Tiffin and McCormick point out, other factors determining the functional value of psychological tests include reliability, the selection ratio and the percentage of present employees who are satisfactory on the job. The reliability refers to the degree of consistency with which a test measures what it purports to measure. There are three types of reliability including coefficient of stability, coefficient of equivalence and coefficient of internal consistency. The coefficient of stability is assessed by the test-retest method. A group of individual are administered the same test twice after a period of time and then the two sets of test scores are correlated. The coefficient of equivalence is evaluated by the alternate forms method involving administration of two separate, but equivalent, forms of the test to the testees. The coefficient of equivalence is derived by correlating the scores on the two forms. Index of internal consistency is evaluated by the split-halves method. Each test is scored on each of two halves of the items ("odd" vs "even" or "chance" halves randomly chosen) and then the two sets of scores are correlated. Usually, tests with the coefficients of reliability above 0.80 are satisfactory. It may be noted that the test might have reliability but not necessarily high validity. However, if a test has low reliability, it is not likely to have satisfactory validity.

Moreover, the functional value of the test to a manpower manager depends upon the Selection ratio—the ratio of the applicants to those tested. Suppose, we have 100 applicants and place the 75 who score the highest on the test. Thus, we reduce those placed to 75 per cent of those tested. Accordingly, the selection ratio will be 0.75. Likewise, if we test 200 applicants and place the 100 who score the highest on the test, our selection ratio will be reduced to 0.50. Again, suppose we test 500 applicants and place only the 50 who score the highest on the test, the selection ratio will be reduced to 0.10. Overall, the effectiveness of the testing programme increases with decrease in the selection ratio. Thus, as Tiffin and McCormick observe, in group testing where manpower manager is interested in average, rather than individual results, he can effectively use the test with lower validity by adequately decreasing the selection ratio. Thus, in group testing a decrease in selection ratio provides a substitute for high validity. This does not mean that it is a substitute of 'no validity'. The test must have some validity to permit the utilisation of reduction in the selection ratio.

Another factor influencing the efficiency of a psychological test relates to the percentage of present employees who have been considered satisfactory. Other things remaining the same, the lower the percentage of existing employees who have been placed satisfactorily without test, the higher the percentage of satisfactory employees placed by using tests is likely to result. Let us assume that we have a test with a validity of 0.50 and use a selection ratio of 0.50 and only 5 per cent of employees placed by the traditional method are successful. Under these conditions, the expected increase to 9 per cent represents an 80 per cent increase in the number of satisfactory employees placed by the test. Indeed, if the percentages of satisfactory employees placed without the test become larger, the percentages of increase accomplished by using the test becomes smaller. Accordingly, for 90 per cent of satisfactory employees placed by the traditional method, the increase of this percentage to 97 per cent by using the test will lead to a gain of only 8 per cent in the number of employees satisfactorily placed.

Thus, other things being equal, if more complicated it is to identify and place satisfactory employees without applying tests, the more the advantage a manpower manager can acquire through a proper psychological testing programme. The Taylor-Russell tables can be used to ascertain as to what percentage of employees recruited will be effective under several combinations of test validity, selection ratio and percentage of present employees viewed effective. However, these tables should be used with caution.

A significant issue is how to use tests for employment purposes. The selection standard (critical score) on the test should vary with the market conditions. If the market conditions are tight, the critical score should be low and if loose, the selection standard should be high. Another point is that several tests should be combined into a battery. There are two methods of combining tests is a battery. These include the multiple cut-off and the multiple correlation method. In the multiple cut-off method, tests are administered one at a time and applicants who do not perform satisfactorily are eliminated with each test. Thus, the first test will eliminate all the low-scoring candidates and the remaining candidates will be administered the second test which will further eliminate more candidates and so on. The multiple correlation method involves the computation of multiple correlation between the best combination of test scores and the relevant criterion. Thus, the performance on different tests can be combined into a composite score in order to weigh each to attain the maximum correlation between the performance on the test battery and the criterion of job success. Indeed, the value of the testing programme increases by using many tests in combination because no single test gives as high a validity coefficient as does the battery as a whole.

Yoder and others suggest the inspection or the graphic method using maximum as well as minimum cutting scores. Explicitly, we may come across the fact that individuals who scored very high on the test as well as those who scored very low on the test, had a short tenure in an enterprise. These types of relationships are called 'curvilinear' and involve separate correlational techniques. Usually, the eta coefficient is used for this purpose. A study of turnover data of a company will reveal that the short tenure employees are those who have scored either below 80 or above 120 on the intelligence test. Obviously, setting a minimum critical score at 80 and a maximum at 120 will remove short tenure risks related with either very high or very low scores. It may be noted that the selection ratio discussed above assumes linearity of relationships and accordingly cannot be used for curvilinear data.

Last but not the least, adequate training of testing of testers is of utmost significance for the full advantage of the testing programme. Testing human beings is quite different from testing materials or processes. The people may react both favourably and unfavourably to test situations. Attempts should be made that they respond favourables. The testers, therefore, should have proper training to take best out of the applicants and give a favourable impression of the company to them.

Psychological Tests used in Selection and Placement

Tiffin and McCormick describe several types of tests used for selection and placement under three categories including aptitude tests, tests of personality and interest and achievement tests. Aptitudes have been grouped into five categories including mental abilities, mechanical and related abilities, psychomotor abilities, visual skills and a class of other specific aptitudes. The term mental ability has been used interchangeably with intelligence. There are several kinds of mental abilities such as verbal comprehension, word fluency, memory, inductive. Reasoning, number facility, speed of perception and spatial visualisation. Most of these tests used for selection and placement purposes are group tests. Such tests used most frequently in industry include the Adaptability Test, Otis Self-Administering Tests of Mental Ability, Wonderlic Personnel Test. The Purdue Non-Language personnel test, etc.

These tests have been effectively used in clerical and supervisory jobs and found useful in the selection of newspaper writer, teletype operator trainees, etc. However, these tests have negative relationships with performance on routine jobs such as assembly workers.

The term "mechanical ability" refers to the ability involved in working mechanical parts and equipment. This ability has two aspects—mental and motor or physical. Mental aspect relates to mechancial comprehension and the understanding of mechancial principles while motor or physical aspect relates to skills such as muscular coordination and dexterity. Mechanical ability has been used in its restricted sense involving a complex of intellectual abilities. There may be a general mental ability as well as specific abilities such as visualisation of spatial relations. The most frequently used group tests of mechanical ability include Flanagan Aptitude Classification Tests, Bennett Test of Mechanical Comprehension, Purdue Mechanical Adaptability Test, Revised Minnesota Paper Form Board, etc. There are also some individual tests, such as Minnesota Mechanical Assembly Test, Purdue Mechanical Performance Test, etc. These tests have been found effective especially for apprentices, craftsmen, mechanics and repairmen, draftsmen and engineers.

The psychomotor tests measure dexterity, manipulative ability, motor ability, eye-hand coordination and allied sensory and suscular abilities, specifically these tests involve several factors such as control precision, multilimb coordination, response orientation, reaction time, speed of arm movement, rate control, manual dexterity, finger dexterity, wrist-finger speed and aiming. Typical psychomotor tests include O'Connor Finger Dexterity Test, O'Connor Tweezer Dexterity Test, Purdue Pegboard, Minnesota Rate of Manipulation Test, etc. These tests have been found very useful in the selection and placement of packers and minor operators.

Vision tests are of special significance for practically every industrial job. Visual skills required in industry include Keenness of vision (visual acuity) at appropriate distances, discrimination of differences in distance (depth perception or stereopsis), discrimination of difference in colour and postural characteristics of the eyes (phorias) at appropriate distances. Among the major vision tests used in industry are included Ortho-Rater, the Sight-

Screener, the Telebinocular and the Vision Tester. Research results have revealed several visual job families, *i.e.*, groups of jobs which are similar to each other vis-a-vis visual requirements. These visual job families are clerical and administrative, inspection and close work, vehicle operator, machine operator, labourer and mechanic and skilled tradesman.

In addition to the above aptitude tests, there are several tests of special aptitudes such as clerical aptitude, reading speed and comprehension, vocabulary and perceptual speed.

On the basis of extensive research, aptitude tests have been grouped into three 'clusters'—intellectual ability, spatial ability and motor ability. The intellectual ability tests are highly effective in selection and the placement of general supervisors, foremen, general clerks, salesmen, protective-service workers and complex machine operators and the least effective in those of vehicle operators. The spatial ability tests have the highest validity for structural workers and the lowest for general supervisors and general clerks. The motor ability tests are found useful in selection and placement of vehicle operators, processing workers and gross manual workers.

It has been recognised that an employee may have adequate aptitude for a given job, but he is still likely to fail if he possesses a personality which causes adjustment difficulties in work settings. This necessitates identification of desirable and undesirable personality traits among job applicants. Several attempts have been made to devise tests for measuring personality and interest traits. Among the major personality tests used in industry are included the Bernreuter Personality Inventory, the Humm-Wadsworth Temperament Scale, the Guilford Series of Personality Tests, the Minnesota Multiphasic Personality Inventory, the Gordon Personal Profile, the Rorschach Projective Test, Thematic Apperception Test, etc. As regards interest tests, Strong Vocational Interest Blank and Kuder Preference Record, etc., are largely employed in industry. The major limitation of personality and interest tests for employment purposes relates to 'Faking', that is, the possibility of responses to test items which are not descriptive of the testee. Overall, personality tests appear to be more effective for selection of clerks, salesmen, protective workers and trades and crafts than for the other occupational categories. It has been widely agreed that the non-intellectual traits of personality are most significant for failures at work as well as for the effectiveness of managers. There has been more evidence of the usefulness of personality tests than of interest tests in industry.

In industry, achievement tests are used for recruitment of individuals on jobs usually demanding experience, transfer and promotion of existing employees and training purposes. Achievement tests measure actual job proficiency of the testees. Achievement tests are classified in three groups including job sample (or performance) tests, written tests and oral tests. The job or work sample tests involve utilisation of equipment alike the one which is used on the job. An example of job sample test is a miniature punch press used effectively for selecting individuals in jobs such as packaging, inspecting and several types of machine operation. Likewise, a performance test has been devised for selecting fork-lift operators. Again, several tests have been designed to select individuals for stenographic, clerical and secretarial positions. Among these are included blackstone Stenographic Proficiency Tests, the Purdue Clerical Adaptability Test and the Thurstone Examination in Typing. Usually, written tests are 'tailor made' to meet the requirements of specific training programmes. An example of such test is the Purdue Vocational Test which has been used for several trades such as the operation of the grinder, planer, lathe and milling machine. Although the achievement tests are not largely used in industry, they appear promising for not only differentiating different job groups but also different levels of ability within a job. Overall, the achievement tests are highly useful in selecting tradesmen and apprentices.

Employment Interview

The term 'interview' refers to a conversation with a purpose. The purpose of employment interview is three fold : obtaining information, giving information and motivation. Thus, the interview seeks to obtain relevant information regarding the prospective employees such as their background, training, work history, education, interests, etc. Further, it provides information regarding the enterprise, its personnel policies and the specific jobs to the applicants. Again, it seeks to establish a positive relationship between the employer and employee and motivate the prospective employees to accept the offer of appointment with the company. Interview has been considered as a communication system involving four elements – the message, the encoding device, the transmission channel and the decoding device. Explicitly, the message refers to the subject matter of the interview. The coding involves expression of information in words. The transmission channel relates to spoken words and gestures. The decoding means the interpretation of the 'message'.

Employment interview is of significance in view of the fact that it can form a better means of assessing personality than a paper pencil test. Although efforts have been made to demonstrate that several behavioural characteristics can be effectively rated during the employment interview, the results of personality assessment through such measures are unreliable. Efficacy of interviews can be improved by training the interviewers. The skilled interviewers can infer personality traits such as responsiveness, alertness in conversation, manners, presence, poise, loyalty and responsibility during the employment interviews. Overall, the interviews can be effectively used to assess motivation, personality make-up and impact of environmental and emotional problems upon the applicants.

Notwithstanding the above advantages of employment interview over paper pencil tests, it has several limitations. It is rarely possible to assess personality traits such as honesty during the interview. Stereotyping of the individual, the unconscious impact of personal bias and halo effect form the major pitfalls of the interview. Stereotyping means that interviewer tends to visualise the interviewee on the basis of a single class or category to which he belongs. Further, frequently, the interviewer tends to have unwarranted impressions of the applicants on the basis of their similarity to some other individuals whom he liked or disliked. Likewise, the interviewer is also susceptible to the halo effect. Accordingly, he tends to evaluate the total worth of the applicants on the basis of a single quality. These errors can be removed by recognising them and training the interviewer. The interviewer should attempt to maintain an objective attitude towards the interviewee and assess only those traits which are relevant for job success. Again, there are some other factors which should be considered by the interviewers. Explicitly, some of the interviewees are more at ease than others during an employment interview and give better impressions. Even though this quality of the applicant may be relevant for some jobs involving public contact, it may appear utterly irrelevant for other jobs. Therefore, these initial impressions should not be allowed to influence the final selection decisions. Further, care should be taken to have advance planning and exercise control. Without such measures the type of information received from one interviewee may differ substantially from that received from another. This will hamper the evaluation of qualities of different applicants on the identical relative basis.

There are several methods of interview including the patterned interview, the non-directive interview, the stress interview, the group interview and the panel interview. The patterned interview has also been called structure or standardised interview. This method has been designed by McMurty to assess personality traits such as stability, industry, ability to get along with others, self-reliance, willingness to accept responsibility, freedom from emotional immaturity and motivation. The rationale of this method is that an individual's past behaviour is indicative of his future behaviour. If the applicant has been emotionally stable during the past he will remain so in the future. Frequently, a form is employed to make notes and comments and rate the interviewee on each of the several traits indicated above. This approach provides a broad framework of the interview procedure for guidance of the interviewer. The method involves no questions regarding job skills which are evaluated through such measures as school and work records, reference checks and tests. Rather, stress is laid on assessing personality, motivation and interests. This method provides effective results because it uses a standard from involving a definite interview plan and specific system of recording results. Further, training of interviewers causes agreement among judgments. The patterned interview can be used in varied employment situations.

Non-directive method involves the minimum use of direct questions. Questions eliciting 'yes' or 'no' answers are avoided. It is assumed that the more the interviewee is allowed to talk freely about himself, the more he is likely to reveal his personality in the interview situation. However, the method involves scoring difficulties.

Stress interview is used in jobs where emotional balance forms an essential quality. Attempts are made to exert pressures on the candidates by exposing them to rapid firing of questions. Obviously, the interviewers appear hostile and unfriendly. This method has been frequently used in the selection of spies and sometimes that of business executives. However, there is no evidence for the validity of this method.

The group method has been divided to assess leadership. Usually, a topic is given for discussion to a leaderless group of applicants. The observers remain in the background to assess as to who assumes leadership, how he does so and how he is accepted by other participants. It has been recongnised that this method provided opportunity to rate effectively such qualities as initiative, poise, adaptability to new situations, ability to get along with others, social awareness and speaking ability. Intensive research is needed to determine the efficacy of this method for selecting individuals for leadership positions.

The panel or board interview involves use of several interviewers collectively interviewing a candidate and making rating on several traits. The methods described above should be used only if they serve specific purpose.

There are certain interviewing techniques which can help an individual to become effective interviewer. Firstly, attempts should be made to have preparation for an interview in advance. Accordingly, the interviewers should familiarise themeselves with the job in question and information about the applicants. On the basis of this knowledge the interviewer can plan the specific kind of information to be obtained during the interview. Secondly, attempt should be made to carefully begin the interview. Thus, the interviewers should establish a rapport with the interviewee and made him at ease. Further, they should familiarise themselves with the level of understanding of the applicant so that they can adapt their conversation accordingly. Thirdly, enough care should be exerted in conducting the interview. Attempts should be made to get the applicant talk.about relevant issues. The interviewers should use non-directive questions and give a pause for a few seconds after the interviewee has finished and before putting the next question. The interviewers may initially try several subjects but subsequently should return on those issues where the interviewee 'froze'. The questions should be made as clear as possible and only one question should be put at a time. The interviewers should reveal no symptoms of critical attitude towards the interviewee. The wording of questions should be appropriately framed.

Overall, as Yoder and others suggest, the procedures which can enhance effectiveness of interviews include competent interviewers, training of interviewers, suitable place for interviews, planning of the interviews, study of job description and available information about the applicant before the interview, understanding of own prejudices on the part of interviewers, putting the interviewee at ease, taking enough time, letting the interview in a friendly manner, recording the facts obtained in the interview while they are fresh and following up. Despite these guidelines, the interviewers should be sensitive and flexible enough to adapt their techniques and procedures to the specific situations.

Evaluation of the Selection Programme

As it has rightly been asserted, a selection programme is no better than its evaluation. Attempts should be made to assess the effectiveness of selection and placement through intensive research studies. For this purpose, adequate records must be maintained. There is an urgent need to determine the criteria of evaluation in advance. Employee attitude and opinion surveys can provide effective measures for evaluation. Various statistical techniques such as correlation and variance analysis can be used to indicate the efficacy of different selection methods and techniques.

It may be noted that although at present most of the selection programmes are accepted on faith, there is a growing tendency to assess selection policy, programmes, methods and techniques. Growing interest in cost/benefit analysis has stimulated constant efforts to assess costs involved in alternative practices. Likewise, public policy has compelled management to demonstrate the effectiveness of selection practices. Further, trade union have increasingly criticised selection programmes leading to their constant evaluation.

Beach outlines the areas and issues to be covered in a systematic evaluation of the selection programme. First, attempts should be made to analyse the programme with a view to determining as to whether it is in line with sound personnel management theory and practice. Second, care should be taken to assess how effectively are the programme and its procedures communicated to all the participants. Third, attempts should be made to ascertain how adequately the programme has been implemented. Fourth, steps should be taken to obtain the feedback on the image of the programme among applicants and the employment agencies. Fifth, analysis of results of the selection programmes should be conducted. Explicitly, evaluation should be performed by individuals independent of the personnel department.

Studies on Selection in India

In India, great stress has been laid on the development of measurement techniques to be employed in selection and placement programmes. Attempts have been made to use psychological tests developed in foreign countries and to standardise them on Indian population. For example, Dwivedi attempts to validate the Minnesota Multiphasic Personality Inventory on Supervisors in a large industrial undertaking in Faridabad. Ganguli examines applications of Bhatia Battery among textile workers. Some attempts have been made to devise tests. Mental ability tests devised in India for industrial uses include the Performance Test of Intelligence by Bhatia and the Group Intelligence Test by N.R. Chatterjee and R.S. Dwivedi. The aptitude tests designed for industrial applications include the New Form of Mechancial Aptitude Test by O. Ganguly, the Mechanical Aptitude Test by C.T. Philip, the Managerial Aptitude test by R.S. Dwivedi, Managerial Aptitude Test Battery by R.S. Dwivedi and Battery of aptitude Test for Card-punch operators by R.S. Das. There are several other psychological tests reported in Mental Measurement Handbooks for India which can be effectively use for selection and placement purposes. These tests can be procured from Mansayan, Delhi, Psycho-Centre, Varanasi and Purohit and Purohit, Poona.

Chatterji and Mukerjee provide a brief outline of the objective methods of selection and the rationale behind them, discuss the nature of objective tests and cite several validity studies showing the efficacy of objective tests and selections in public and private sector-organizations in India.

Chatterjee conducted a study to assess the extent of application of psychological tests in India. Of 11 large industrial undertakings surveyed, nearly one-half of the public sector and over four-fifths of the private sector enterprises did not use psychological tests and only one-forth of the public sector and a little over two-fifths of the private sector enterprises viewed that the psychological test could be used for good advantage.

Das suggests a method for selection of higher personnel which is especially useful where number of candidates is small and standardised selection methods are not available. She recommends the selection of a sample of tasks through job analysis indicating the qualities essential for job success. The task is assigned to the candidate who gives his response in writing and accomplishes it in the presence of a board of observes. The responses are assessed by these observers. She attempts to outline six such tasks—group discussion, preparation of minutes, presentation of sales appeal, plan for a sales organization, proposal for a research and a design for keeping records— as well as indicate the procedures to be followed in each case. The method appeared to have an adequate reliability for employment purposes. Das further conducted a study on a sample of four interviewers and forty-nine interviewees to assess the reliability of interview data and errors of judgement in interviewing. The mean of reliability coefficient was found to be 0.76. Leniency errors, halo effect and interviewer-trait interaction errors were found to be statistically significant.

Dhingra, Pandey and Paliwal report the progress in action-research conducted in a textile mill. The study purported to devise psychological tests for identifying prospective weavers and to determine the relationship between test scores and criterion measures. The score on selection tests were not significantly related to criterion measures except on two elemental tests. Suggestions were made to improve selection tests and criterion measures. A significant study on the selection of executives through group selection procedure has been cited by Chowdhry. The technique assisted in acquiring the confidence of the candidates in management's fair practices. In this procedure, the candidates are aware of the performance and qualifications of others.

Prasad describes selection procedure in the public sector. As soon as the applications are screened by a selection committee, the selected candidates are invited for interview. Recommendation is made on the basis of personal interviews of these candidates along with the departmental candidates. A common merit list in order of preference is then prepared for the consideration of the authority concerned. The selection committee consists of the head of the department in which recruitment is to be made, some other officer (s) of his department and a personnel officer in a advisory role. Sometimes, outside experts are also invited to join the selection committee. Usually, while recruiting for skilled jobs, trade tests are administered by members from the technical institute of the plant to the candidates. While recruiting managerial personnel, attempts are being made to use psychological tests to assess intelligence, personality and interests of the candidates. Group discussions where senior officers of the company act as observers, are also used. Finally, the chosen candidates have to appear for an interview conducted by a senior board consisting of directors, the personnel director and some senior managers. The Selection Committee makes its recommendations on the basis of candidates, performance in personal interview, group discussions, and the tests and prepares a common merit list in order of preference for consideration of the competent authority.

General plant managers have wide powers of making appointments. With the exceptions of the costs in the initial executive cadre and those which necessitate prior permission of the Government, they are empowered to make appointment for all positions in their respective plants. The appointment in the initial cadre is made by the head office. The policy of decentralisation of appointment-making power in the hands of general managers of the plant has been highly effective in the preceding several years. Initially, appointments to the executive positions are made on a contract basis for five years. Subsequently, after the satisfactory services of five years, the contract is extended upto the age of supernnuation (*i.e.*, 58 years).

Davar describes manpower selection practices in several Indian undertakings such as IOC, TELCO, L&T, Hindustan Lever and ACC Ltd. Of these, the selection procedure of Hindustan Lever Ltd. seems highly comprehensive. The procedure consists of three stages—the completion of the application form (or the preliminary screening), the preliminary interview and the final board procedure. In the first stage, the applications are examined with utmost care to determine to what extent the candidates meet the minimum qualifications for the job. The candidates who tend to meet these standard requirements are requested to fill up a detailed application form involving factual information and attitudinal and personality data. Then, a strict standard for rejection is used and attempts are made to expose a brief preliminary interview to as many applicants as feasible. This leads us to the second stage.

The second stage involves a preliminary interview consisting of 10 to 20 minutes and purporting to discover as to whether or not the candidate is worthy of further consideration. The interview is conducted by one manager who tends to discuss during the interview the nature of the job in question, the future career opportunity for the candidate and the company's policy in this respect. Frequently, before finally determining the issue of further consideration, the candidate is exposed to a further interview by another manager. After the completion of this fact finding and rejection stage, the final board procedure is adapted.

The final board procedure starts with the group method of selection. The board consists of four members including the personnel director, the director of the division for which the candidate is being considered, a senior manager of the same division and another senior manager. The board meets under the chairmanship of the director of the division concerned. The final board procedure may extend up to a full working day and involve six to ten candidates. At the very outset, the candidates are given a copy of the case study to be discussed subsequently. The chairman tends to introduce each board member to the candidates who, in turn, are required to introduce themselves individually to the board usually with the help of a specimen introduction sheet distributed to them.

Frequently, the candidates are required to participate in two group discussions. In the first discussion, the group members are either requested to select a topic themselves or a topic given by the board itself. After the completion of this discussion, there occurs a short interval during which the board members discuss among themselves their impressions of the participants in a separate cabin. Thereafter, in the second round, the case study distributed earlier is discussed. In addition to these discussions, the participants are also requested to prepare a precis of the subject discussed during the first round. The board members further discuss their opinions about the candidates and rate each of them on the qualities as follows : style of self-expression, general knowledge and knowledge of the subject in question, clarity of thought and logic, lucidity of expression, tolerance of others' views, persuasiveness and leadership. This follows a lunch break and thereafter individual interviews are conducted. This structured in nature and attempts are made to explore various items given in the application form. After the completion of the interview the board members discuss their impressions. Each board member is then required to indicate his comments for each candidate under the heads as follows: self-expression, group discussion, individual interviews, precis and summing up. Finally, a consensus is reached and at the same evening, the candidates are communicated the final decisions of the board. The following day, the selected candidates are required to take medical examination.

It may be noted that sometimes variations in the selection procedure as described above is allowed. Whatever be the procedure, observes Davar, the selection programme forms an important event in the entire process of acquiring and developing managers. The Hindustan Lever adequately stresses a systematic yearly review of its existing manpower resources to meet growing future requirements. Accordingly, on the basis of an integrated, well-designed forecast of manpower needs, efforts are made to recruit and develop managers constantly.

Overall, as Chatterjee observes, the management in Indian industries has recently recognised the importance of psychologists in selecting the right men for the right jobs. Unfortunately, because of the paucity of standardised selection techniques and tests, the management could not use them in selecting personnel for a long time. However, the situation has improved substantially now and attempts are being made to devise standardised tests for selecting personnel for different jobs.

9

Authority and Responsibility in Business

The words authority and responsibility have different meanings in management science. One speaks of an authority on nuclear physics. The shop superintendent complains that the union is undermining his authority, the design engineer authorizes a certain design. This text is concerned with managerial authority. A standard definition adhered to by many writers in the area of management is that authority is a legal or rightful power, a right to command or to act. It is a power to command others to do or not to do certain thing which the possessor of the authority deems appropriate and necessary to realize the objectives of the enterprise. This concept of authority implies the possession of the power to impose sanctions and to coerce, for without such a power to enforce an order, the enterprise would become disorganized and chaos would result.

Authority is the key to the managerial job. Throughout this text a manager has been described as the one who performs the five managerial functions and who also possesses authority. The performance of the managerial functions along with the possession of authority are the essentials of a manager. Without authority he is not a manager. Authority makes the managerial position real, enabling the manager to order his subordinates to act as he directs them. In case the subordinate refuses, the manager's authority include his power and right to take disciplinary action, in the last instance to discharge the subordinate. This of course, is the least desirable procedure, and such drastic action should only be used in extreme cases.

Every successful manager knows that in order to induce his subordinate managers to perform the required duties it is best not to invoke authority, but to utilize other ways and means to get the job done. As a matter of fact, in practice it has come to the point where many managers are disinclined to speak of authority at any time. They would much rather talk about "responsibility" or "tasks" and "duties" which they have, instead of stating that they possess authority. Some managers consider it better human relations to state that they have the responsibility for a certain activity instead of saying that they have authority within that area. Using the words responsibility, task, and duty in a loose sense allows the manager to avoid the big stick. Using these terms in their proper sense, it should be noted that having authority delegated to the manager means that he has the power and right to command; tasks and duties are assigned to the manager; responsibility is accepted by the manager, it is exacted from him, but not delegated to him.

Authority is the rightful legal power to request a subordinate to do a certain thing or to refrain from doing so, and if he does not follow these instructions the manager is in a position, if need be, to take disciplinary action, even to discharge the subordinate. There probably are much better ways of exercising one's authority than to dismiss the subordinate, and there probably are better human relations practices which will bring about the desired results. However, there is the danger of confusing the issue as to what authority is, where it lies in the organization and how it manifests itself. Regardless of how the manager applies authority the point is that the manager must have it. Without it he is no manager, his job is not real. Without the right to command there would be no superior and no subordinate. Without authority only anarchy and chaos would result.

The Source and Nature of Authority

Much has been written and said about the source and nature of authority. The early students of management took authority for granted and had little doubt about its nature purpose, and origin. To them it was a necessary building stone in forming an organization. Henri Fayol speaks of authority as "the right to give orders and the power to exact obedience". And he goes on to say that authority is not to be conceived of apart from sanctions, reward or penalty, which goes with the exercise of power. However, since then, different views have been expressed regarding the nature and source of authority. There are primarily two schools involved. One is called the "formal authority theory," and the other is known as the "acceptance theory of authority."

Formal Authority Theory

The formal authority theory traces delegations of authority upward from any managerial position, from the various subordinate managers up to the president of the company who, in turn, receives his authority from the board of directors, who in turn receive their authority from the owners or the stockholders. Therefore, to follow the formal theory, the ultimate source of authority is principally in the institution of private property, in the legal aspects of private property as guaranteed by our legal system and the constitution of the United States. "Under our democratic form of government the right upon which managerial authority is based has its source in the constitution of the United States through the guarantee of private property. Since the constitution is the creature of the people, subject ot amendment and modification by the will of the people, it follows that society, through government, is the source from which authority flows to ownership and thence to management." The formal authority theory, then, views the concept of authority as being power-transmitted, from the basic social institutions to the individual managers.

In a business enterprise authority originates at the top of the institution (of private property) and is delegated by the owners to their representatives, the directors, president, managers, and from there further on down to the various subordinates. In social groups, where private property does not exist, the origin of authority can be traced back to the elements of an institution, the basic folkways and mores of that particular group. For instance, in political or religious organizations the authority originates from social institutions, the democratic process, the system of government, and so on.

The Acceptance Theory of Authority

There is a large group of writers in the area of management who do not agree with the formal authority theory point of view. It is common to read definitions of the concept of authority like the following: "Authority is the relationship that exists between individuals when one accepts the directive of another as authoritative, that is, when the individual receiving the directive weighs the consequences of accepting it against the consequences of rejecting it, and decides in favour of acceptance. The authoritative nature of the directive is confirmed when the person accepting the directive acts in accordance with it, within the confines of his understanding and ability."

This definition obviously is based on the familiar expressions of the behavioural school represented by Chester Barnard, Mary Parker Follett, Herbert Simon, Robert Tannenbaum and others. They state that the true source of authority of the manager is the acceptance by his subordinates. Barnard states his "approximate definition of authority" as follows:

> Authority is the character of communication (order) in a formal organization by virtue of which it is accepted by a contributor to or "member" of the organization as governing the action he contributes; that is, as governing or determining what he does or is not to do so far as the organization is concerned. According to this definition, authority involves two aspects: first the subjective, the personal, the accepting of the communication as authoritative, the aspects which I shall present in this section; and, second, the objective aspect —the character in the communication by virtue of which it is accepted....... If a directive communication is accepted by one to whom it is addressed, its authority for him confirmed or established. It is admitted as the basis of action. Disobedience of such a communication is a denial of its authority for him. Therefore, under this definition the decision as to whether an order has authority or not lies with the persons to whom it is addressed, and does not reside in "persons of authority" or those who issue these orders.

Other writers of this school state their views similarly. The key aspect of the acceptance theory is that the manager has no real authority unless and until the individual subordinate confers it upon him.

Tannenbaum, following the general thinking of Barnard, develops a rule which governs the individual's acceptance of authority and says "an individual will accept an exercise of authority if the advantages accruing to him from not accepting exceed the advantages accruing to him from not accepting plus the disadvantages accruing to him from accepting; and, conversely, he will not accept an exercise of authority if the latter factors exceed the former." Barnard states that a subordinate can and will accept a communication as authoritative only when four conditions obtain simultaneously: *(a)* He can and does understand the communication, *(b)* at the time of his decision he believes that it is not inconsistent with the purpose of the organization, *(c)* at the time of his decision he believes it to be compatible with his personal interests as a whole, and *(d)* he is able mentally and physically to comply with it.

It is self-evident that a communication which cannot be understood does not carry authority. A manager cannot expect a subordinate to carry out an order given to him in a language which the subordinate does not understand. Furthermore, a manager does not normally give orders which would not be in accordance with the objective and the purpose of the enterprise. If he does issue an order which seems to be such, it is imperative that the manager explain, to his subordinate why this order is consistent with the purpose of the organization. Finally, a manager should not give an order which the subordinate cannot physically fulfil. Barnard states that in most orders these four conditions are fulfilled.

Barnard also explains that there exists "a zone of indifference" in each individual within which orders are acceptable without consciously questioning the authority. These orders are within the range of requests and duties which were generally anticipated when the subordinate accepted employment with the organization. Similarly, Tannenbaum speaks of a "sphere of acceptance" and expresses essentially the same thought as Barnard does when the latter speaks of the "zone of indifference."

Some of the advantages that Tannenbaum lists which accrue

to the subordinate by accepting the authority are the following: Contribution to the attainment of the enterprise propose, approval of fellow workers, rewards from the superior, action in accordance with the subordinate's own moral standards, and response to qualities of leadership of the superior. If the subordinate refuse to accept authority, he loses all of these advantages, and, in addition to this, he will experience the disadvantage of social disapproval expulsion from a group, formal disciplinary action, and economic pressures.

Another writer of the behavioural school of thought, Benjamin Selekman, seems to straddle the question by stating "It is true enough that the management executive must, directly or indirectly, obtain consent to his decision from the men under him; the importance of such consent now receives ever-increasing recognition. Nonetheless, the manager still wields authority over his workers as of right—a right delegated to him by the owners of the business."

The writer feels that it is unrealistic to subscribe to the acceptance theory of authority within the area of management. Many of the thoughts expressed by the exponents of the acceptance theory are valid in the discussion of the concept of leadership, but, in the concept of authority, it is difficult to imagine that a subordinate has the choice of accepting the authority or paying the consequences for not accepting the authority. There is very little choice left if the only alternative is not to accept and be dismissed from a position. Also, it should be noted that the subordinate's power to disobey cannot possibly deprive the superior of his authority. Furthermore, a manager cannot run a business without knowing whether or not his authority has been accepted by his subordinate in each and every instance. Even Barnard emits that his definition of authority might appear to many as a platform of chaos.

The exponents of the acceptance theory look at authority without considering the sanctions. If subordinates confer authority on their superiors, they must also confer upon them the right to levy sanctions even to the point of coercion. But Barnard ignores this aspect of sanctions, and Tannenbaum mentions the disadvantage of coercion merely in the calculation the subordinate makes when he determines whether or not to obey. It is not clear whether or not this reference to coercion of Tannenbaum's means that the subordinate has conferred upon his superior the right to levy sanctions.

At this point it is interesting to note that several decades ago Henri Fayol anticipated some of the problems which seem to have influenced the writings of the behavioural school of thought. He called our attention to the fact that a "distinction must be made between a manager's official authority serving from office and personal authority, compounded of intelligence, experience, moral worth, ability to lead, past services, etc. in the makeup of a good head personal authority is the indispensable complement of official authority." Marten Mandeville suggests taking the slight liberty of substituting the word "leadership" for the term "Personal authority." By doing this the meaning of the English translation of Fayol's writing is not altered but it shows up that Faylo pointed to the difference between the leadership concept and that of authority.

In his article Mandeville concludes that the arguments and confusion concerning the nature of authority revolve around different ways of looking at organization, whether organization should be considered as a structure built to achieve some objective or "as a dynamic aggregation of social beings." All of these schools, however agree that authority is one of the foundation stones of organization and probably the key to the entire organization.

> The concepts started with authority being placed in one person who then delegated it downward to other persons who acted for him in various capacities. The influence of the military command can be seen here. The next step was the idea that authority was connected with the work to be done and appeared throughout the organization as a necessity for the accomplishment of tasks. Finally, we arrive at the notion that authority does not exist unless it is effectively executed and that it is therefore something which is granted by a subordinate to his superior or to some one else. Thus the meaning of the word has come full circle. While all of these concepts are valuable to our understanding of the subject of administration or management, they have certainly stretched the meaning of one word to its limits.

The writer shares with Mandeville the opinion that when the behaviourist school discusses authority they really do not mean authority; probably something else, perhaps the concept of leadership. "The nature of authority seems to be the right to see that tasks are accomplished. There is something more fundamental in the concept of 'authority' than the inclination of someone to work or not toward for an organization."

Without discounting the importance of formal authority, it is well to remember that, since it is the manager's job to get things done through people, he will do all he can to avoid relying on the sheer power of his formal authority. He will refrain from speaking of authority he possesses and will prefer to talk about "responsibility" or "tasks" and "duties" assigned to him. He will bring into play aspects of leadership and motivation so that his subordinates will voluntarily and effectively carry out their assigned tasks. Then it will not be necessary for the manager to fall back on the formal authority which in the final analysis makes his managerial job real.

Additional Sources of Authority

In addition to the above-mentioned theories, other writers in the area have enumerated other sources of authority.

Mention should be made of authority by law. In this instance the rightful power is granted by law. It gives the office holder the necessary power so that the legal requirements will be met. Also, authority often comes from personal qualities or technical competence. In this instance, the authority adheres to the individual. It cannot be delegated or assigned and reassigned. A person who is a recognized expert in one particular field is often referred to as an authority on certain problems. In this instance the person has authority because of what he knows. His decision is accepted not because of any position he holds in the organization but because of his authority of knowledge. If someone is known as being an authority in a certain school of painting, this authority adheres to this individual only and cannot be delegated by him to anyone. Nor is it something that a manager can assign to someone else.

Naturally, it is desirable to fill managerial positions with an executive who, besides being cloaked with administrative authority by his superior, also possesses technical authority because he is an expert in the problems involved with his position.

This is not always possible, and in some instances it is advisable that such an executive receive further training to help him achieve this personal technical authority.

Limits of Authority

There are definite limitations to the concept of authority, either explicit or implied. Some stem from internal and others from external sources. Authority is limited, like all social institutions, by such restrictions as our codes, mores and folkways and laws. Over the period of time many legal, political, ethical, social, and economic considerations have put limitations on the concept of authority. The articles of incorporation set limits to the authority of the officers. The by-laws may place further restrictions on the manager's authority. The executive's authority is restricted by the enterprise's objectives, policies, procedures, and programmes. There are many laws which clearly limit the authority of a manager; for instance, laws referring to collective bargaining and the establishment of labour unions. This, in turn, leads to further limitations imposed by contractual obligations; to mention one, the manager's limitations in handling workers' complaints and grievances.

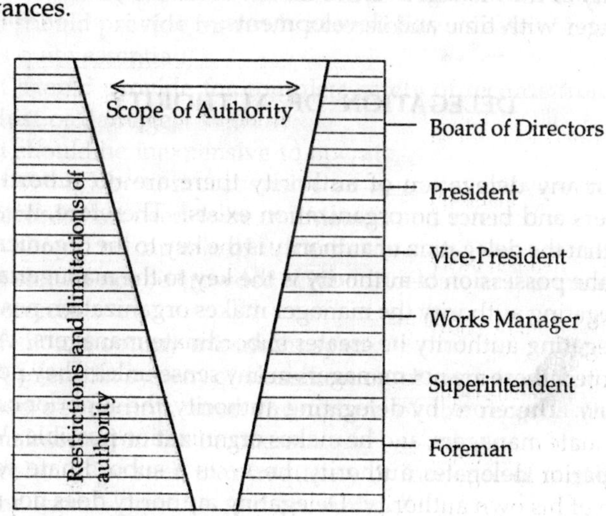

Figure 9.1

Furthermore, it is common that each manager in a particular position is subject to specific authority limitations spelled out in the assignment of duties and delegation of authority. It is conceivable that a branch manager of a manufacturing plant has the authority to make capital expenditures up to five thousand dollars, whereas for a local warehouse manager this authority is limited to possibly one hundred dollars. It can be generally stated that there are more limitations on the scope of authority as one descends the managerial hierarchy. This is why one speaks of the tapering concept of authority. The lower down in the managerial hierarchy, the more restrictions of the authority; the higher up in the managerial hierarchy, the less limitations and the broader the scope of authority, as shown in Figure 9.1.

In addition to these various limitations on authority there are a number of other "constraints" which seriously limit authority. There are biological constraints which limit authority just because the human being does not have the capacity to do certain things. No subordinate can be expected to do the impossible. In addition to biological constraints there are physical constraints, technological constraints, and even economic limitations on the authority of the manager. These limits of authority will be subject to changes with time and developments.

DELEGATION OF AUTHORITY

Without any delegation of authority there are no subordinate managers and hence no organization exists. Therefore, it can be stated that the delegation of authority is the key to the organization, just as the possession of authority is the key to the managerial job. By delegating authority the manager makes organization possible. By delegating authority he creates subordinate managers. As we have noted, these are not managers in any sense unless they possess authority. Therefore, by delegating authority, the superior creates subordinate managers, and he makes organization possible. When the superior delegates authority, he vests a subordinate with a portion of his own authority. Delegating authority does not mean that the superior manager surrenders his authority or gives his authority away. The delegating manager always retains his overall authority which was assigned to him to perform his functions.

Delegation of authority merely means the granting of authority to subordinates to operate within prescribed limits. Because of this process of delegation, the subordinate receives authority from his superior, but the superior still retains all of his original authority and does not surrender any. A good comparison can be made between delegating authority and imparting knowledge. The teacher in school shares knowledge with his students who then possess the knowledge, but the teacher still retains the knowledge too.

The Scalar Principle

Through the process of delegation, authority is distributed throughout the organization. It flows downward from the source of all authority at the top, usually from the chief executive. Although in a corporation the president is subject to the higher authority of the board of directors and its chairman, for all practical purposes he is the single source from which authority flows to the rest of the organization. The broad authority necessary to run the enterprise is delegated to him by the board of directors, and he in turn must delegate authority to others and these in turn will delegate further down the line. There must be a chain of direct authority relationships from superior to subordinate throughout the entire organization and this is commonly known as the scalar principle.

There must be a clear line from the ultimate source of authority to the lowest ranks in the organization. "The scalar chain is the chain of superiors ranging from the ultimate authority to the lowest ranks. The line of authority is the route followed—via every link in the chain—by all communications which start from or go to the ultimate authority. This path is dictated both by the need for some transmission and by the principle of unity of command, but it is not always the swiftest". This chain of command must be clearly understood by every subordinate and must be closely adhered to or else the risk exists of undermining authority which ultimately would mean undermining the managerial position. The term "flow of authority" might give the erroneous impression of a continuous stream, whereas in reality such a delegation is discrete and often more of a trickle.

The Process of Delegation

Newman succinctly points out that there are three chief aspects to the process of delegation of authority: (1) the assignment of duties by an executive to his immediate subordinates; (2) the granting of permission (authority) to make commitments, use resources, and take all actions which are necessary to perform the duties; and (3) the creation of an obligation (responsibility) on the part of each subordinate to the delegating exclusive to perform the duties satisfactorily. These three aspects of delegation are inseparably interrelated, and change in one will require adjustment of the other two.

Assignment of Duties

In the assignment of duties the manager decides how the work is to be divided among his subordinates. He will consider the best allocation of these duties in order to achieve a happy balance between an effective span of management and a reasonable number of managerial levels. In checking his functions and duties the chief executive will examine them to see which he can delegate to others and which he cannot assign to a subordinate. There are some duties which are so routine that there is no doubt that the manager would do best to assign them to one of his subordinates. There are other functions which he can delegate to subordinates who possess the necessary skill to perform them effectively. And then again there are those functions which he cannot delegate and must do himself. A number of managerial duties are borderline cases and could fall into either one of these groups. Decisions as to whether or not the manager can allocate a specific duty to subordinate will often depend on the executive's general attitude and the subordinates he has available.

The Granting of Authority

The second aspect in the process of delegation is the granting of authority to make commitments, use resources, and to take the actions which are necessary to perform the allocated duties. To be specific, duties are assigned and authority is delegated not to people but to positions within the enterprise. But unless these positions within the organization are manned by people, the assignments and the delegation of authority are meaningless. That is why one commonly speaks of the delegation of authority to subordinates instead of delegation of authority to subordinate positions.

In this stage the superior confers upon the subordinate the right to act and to decide within a limited area. It is necessary for the superior to determine the scope of authority which is to be delegated to the subordinate. This scope of necessity depends on the area of authority which the superior manager himself possesses. The scope of authority is intrinsically related to the duties assigned to the subordinate, and any change in those will necessitate a change in the scope of authority. Generally speaking, the wise manager will see to it that the scope of authority which is delegated to a subordinate is adequate for the successful performance of the assigned duties. But the scope should not be larger than necessary.

It is obvious that clarity of the scope of authority of each subordinate manager is necessary for an organization in order to have clear and not fuzzy lines of authority. It is not enough that the clarity of the scope exists merely in the mind of the delegating executive. The scope must be just as clear to the subordinate manager and to the minds of the other managers. Fuzziness can only lead to confusion, conflicts, and duplications of efforts.

Specific or General Delegation

Delegation of authority can be specific or general, and it is obviously more desirable that it be specific. It often happens that a superior delegates authority in a broad sense to his subordinates. He merely tells them to take charge and to do whatever they deem necessary. This manner of delegation cannot be considered a satisfactory way to delegate authority. It is much better to be precise and clear instead of letting the subordinate guess how far his authority may go. If the limits of his authority are clearly defined there will be no need for him to wonder how far it goes and to experiment by hit and miss. Therefore, it is advisable to be clear and specific as to the extent of the delegation of authority.

It is preferable, if appropriate, that the scope of authority be set down in writing for this will provide the subordinate with a clear guide at all times. Charts, manuals, and job descriptions will be of considerable aid in the manager's endeavour to clarify the scope of authority. Although the delegating manager has clearly written down the scope of authority, he has the obligation of checking from time to time to see whether or not the subordinate is keeping within the delegated limits. He also should bear in mind that as conditions and circumstance change additional clarification and interpretations of the scope of authority might become necessary. This is primarily so if there should be a change in the assignment of duties.

On the other hand, there are times when the scope of authority cannot be made too specific. This is particularly true in a new enterprise or in some new venture within an existing organization. It can happen that the superior himself does not fully realize how much is involved in a new activity, and he threrefore cannot be specific as to the amount of authority he should be delegating to his subordinates. Because the extent of the new activity is not known, it is understandable that in such a case the delegation of authority cannot be specific. But once the new task has begun to take shape, the subordinate would be wise to clarify his area of authority by discussing it with the superior or vice versa. By that time both know what is involved in the new activity.

Shared and Splintered Authority

The superior may at sometime delegate authority to two or three subordinate togather, for he may want the authority over a given situation to be hard by them. This is known as "shared authority". For example, the president of a corporation might want the vice-president in charge of production, the sales manager, and the chief engineer to share the authority of deciding which products will be carried in the product line for the coming year. In this instance, the three executives share the authority to make this decision. All three together have the authority.

In addition to the concept of shared authority, there is the concept of splintered authority which is frequently found in organizations. Splintered authority "exists wherever a problem cannot be solved or a decision made without pooling the authority delegations of two or more managers." In this instance, the individual manager possesses all the authority he needs to make the decision within his own department. However, the problem under consideration concerns a question which bridges more than one department. In order to solve this particular problem, the several managers pool their authority to make the decision. If it is necessary, however, for managers to pool their authority frequently, it is wise to re-examine the delegation of authority, checking to see whether or not some managers have been delegated too much or too little authority.

In checking into the varies applications of splintered authority, the superior manager would do well to find out whether or not such a pooling of splintered authority was applied to problems which, though not specifically included in the area of authority, still could be reasonably expected to fall within their level of the managerial hierarchy. It is conceivable that several subordinate managers had pooled their authority in order to decide problems which the top manager wished to retain under his own authority and therefore had purposely not delegated. The author has had occasion to observe instances where the pooling of authority has led subordinate managers to make decisions on problems which the superior manager wanted clearly and specifically reserved for himself. Following the exception principle (discussed below), the problem should have been handled by referring it to the executive who is their common superior.

The Exception Principle

The proper assignment of duties and the necessary scope of delegated authority will tell the subordinate manager the area within which he specifically alone is to make the decision. Should a problem come up which is beyond this scope, the subordinate manager must refer it upward in the organization. He is to decide all those matters within his authority limitation, but he does not have authority over those which do not fall within this area. These exceptional problems must be referred upward; this is what is commonly known as the exception principle. Koontz calls it the authority-level principle.

There is great temptation to ignore this exception principle, but ignoring it will mean the weakening of the delegation of authority. There is a temptation for the incompetent and insecure subordinate to refer too many appeals and tool many "exceptions" to the superior. In such an instance, the superior manager should make it clearly understood that the problem is within the area of the subordinate's decision-making power. On the other hand, there is the temptation for the superior manager to make a decision concerning an activity where he once made the decision himself, but since he had delegated this authority and assigned the duties to a subordinate manager, he must refrain from deciding unless the problem brought to him is clearly an exception.

Revoking of Delegated Authority

Delegated authority can be recovered by the grantor. Whenever the manager delegates authority he does not divorce himself of this authority. He has the authority to revoke whatever he has delegated to his subordinate. As time changes, and activities change, there is often the need to revoke authority which has been delegated and to realign various authority relationships. Managers often speak of reorganizing and realigning. What they mean by this is the revoking of authority and its reassignment to someone else. After the manager has revoked authority from his subordinate managers, he can exercise this authority himself, or he can re-delegate it to some other subordinate. He may even delegate more authority than the previous subordinate manager had, or he may redelegate less authority, depending on the circumstances. Naturally, a wise manager will see to it that such realignments and reshuffling of authority do not take place too often. Every subordinate manager can understand the necessity for reassigning authority from time to time, but if this happens too often the morale of the subordinate managers is greatly impaired.

Extent of Delegation

Whether or not a manager delegates authority is not the problem. What is important is the extent to which he delegates authority—how much or how little. An organization with the tendency to delegate authority freely is spoken of as an organization with decentralized authority, and one where little authority is delegated to subordinate managers is called an organization with centralized authority. Delegation of authority, therefore, is a tendency and not an absolute. A manager who is not willing to delegate authority freely automatically limits the number of executives and the size of the enterprise. He himself is limited in what he can accomplish in a day's work and limited in the number of subordinates he can effectively manage. Hence, the growth of the enterprise is stiffed. In order for the undertaking to grow, therefore, the manager is obligated to delegate increasingly more authority to his subordinates.

Learning to delegate authority effectively is an art which for many executives takes years to acquire. It is advisable to stress the importance of delegation of authority in the early stages of a management development programme, and it remains a constant task and continuous problem for top management to see to it that it is done. Much, of course, depends on the basic philosophy, the outlook, and the manager's personal attitude toward the extent of delegation of authority. He must be willing to give subordinates a chance. He must be willing to let go. The author has observed managers who felt that they were best able to perform the managerial functions themselves, and instead of delegating authority for making certain decisions to their subordinates, they preferred to hold on to this authority and to make the decisions themselves. In so doing they were unable to spend much of their time in thinking, in making more important decisions, and performing duties which probably could have contributed more to the objectives of the corporation. This kind of fallacious behaviour is often found with executives who have been promoted from one position to a higher position. They still want a claim to the authority which they had in the lower position instead of willingly delegating that authority to someone else.

It is often the desire of such executives to maintain tight control over the duties assigned to them. Such one-man domination has serious drawbacks, however, which will sooner or later reveal themselves. The dominant manager is so overburdened with work that he cannot possibly carry out all his duties at the time when they should be performed. Furthermore, he too can make a number of mistakes just as his subordinates could. In addition to this, the subordinate is stiffed, and the chances for keeping well-qualified sub-ordinates in this unit are remote. There will not be a potential replacement for this domineering executive, and in case of a sudden emergency the future of this unit is endangered.

Inasmuch as delegation of authority is a special kind of relationship between the executive and his subordinate, there are certain personal attitudes which play an important role in this art of delegation . The willingness to let go, of course, includes the willingness to let others make mistakes. It is difficult for a manager to watch his subordinates make mistakes which will ultimately cost the corporation money, but unless the subordinate makes some mistakes, he will never learn. A wise manager is willing to let his subordinates make a mistake, provided the magnitude of this mistake is not such that it would seriously harm the corporation. Serious and constant mistakes, of course, will be avoided by the supervisor's counselling and guiding of his subordinate. The writer does not advocate that the manager sit idly by watching his subordinate makes mistakes merely for the sake of delegation of authority, but at times the price of the mistake is well worth the experience for the subordinate manager. The cost of this mistake must be considered as an expense in the subordinated's training and as an investment in the future life of the organization.

The manager must show a willingness to trust his subordinates, without which trust he will not be able to delegate any authority. Very often he camouflages this lack of trust by stating that the subordinates are not quite ready. Often they are ready, but it is the manager who is not ready to delegate authority, and it is he who is the stumbling block. It is conceivable that the quality of performance may suffer, but it would suffer also when the superior tries to perform too many duties himself. If the superior feels that his subordinate is not well enough "seasoned", then it is upto him to train and coach him so that he becomes capable of doing the work.

Often the problem is not so much the lack of trust and confidence in the subordinate as it is the superior's fear of the subordinate's potential growth. The executive might feel that by delegating authority to the subordinate the latter would excel himself in such a way that he would lose the valuable services of his subordinate. There exists, furthermore, a different kind of fear of the subordinate's potential growth which keeps the superior from delegating authority to him. The author has had occasion to observe this kind of fearful thinking on the superior's part in many organizations when the delegating executive has about reached the limits of his own advancement. Men in this situation have usually been willing to delegate authority freely as long as they could see a possibility of their own advancement. But once there was no further advancement possible for them, they began to guard their own positions more cautiously, and may believed that one way to do this was to delegate less and less authority.

All in all, the manager should not be too severely criticized for being reluctant in delegating authority. It is advisable to move cautiously and judiciously in delegating. After all, it is not possible for him to delegate his responsibility to the subordinate manager, and he still remains responsible for whatever his subordinate will do. Therefore, the manager must set up and exercise board controls to assure himself that the authority which he has delegated will be properly used. He must have a way of knowing that the authority which he has delegated will be used to support the company objectives. Often his inability to establish and exercise the proper controls are the real reasons for ineffective and sparse delegation. How to set up controls and how to control will be discussed in the chapters dealing with the managerial function of controlling.

Delegation by Results Expected

Whenever a manager delegates authority he must bear in mind the duties and functions which he has assigned to his subordinate. He must also bear in mind the results which he expects his subordinate to obtain. In delegating by the results expected, the delegator must state exactly what he expects, when he expects it done, and by whom. It is also the delegator's responsibility to make certain that the delegate knows what is expected of him. Edward Schleh points out the significant advantages which delegations by results will produce. Delegation by results will, first of all, lead to real accomplishment on the subordinate manager's part instead of merely "spinning his wheels" with a great furry of activity and without producing much of value to the company. If the superior manager delegates by results expected he will be able to set up standards for the job which will lend themselves as standards of performance. Right there and then the delegating executive sets up a system of realistic controls. Lastly, delegation by results expected will help to minimize politics in the enterprise. If the expected results have been clearly laid out and thus standards and controls to measure them have been defined, it becomes difficult for a man to achieve success based on anything else except his record.

As pointed out above, the granting of authority is intrinsically and directly related to the duties assigned to and results expected from the subordinate. The delegator must make sure that he has delegated enough authority so that the subordinate is able to obtain these results. There is no need to delegate more authority than necessary, but the subordinate must have enough in order to perform the functions. The subordinate, on the other hand, can only be expected to accept responsibility for those functions for which he had enough authority. He does not expect more authority than he need for this would be loose management.

Unity of Command

The delegation of authority must flow from one superior manager to one subordinate manager. The only exceptions are the instances of shared authority discussed earlier in this chapter and the applications of functional authority which will be discussed in Chapter eight. Except for these, the delegation of authority flows from a single superior to a single subordinate, and each subordinate reports to only one superior. This is what is known as the principle of unity of command, and it is one of the most widely recognized principles of management.

Situations occur, however, when two or more superiors delegate authority to one subordinate. Both have assigned duties to him and have delegated authority, but the subordinate's difficulties of serving two or more masters are obvious. Ever since biblical times it has been pointed out that it is difficult, if not impossible, to serve two masters. It is bound to lead to unsatisfactory performance by the subordinate, and it results in a confusion of authority. The subordinate does not know which of the two superior has the authority which will contribute more toward his success and progress within the enterprise. Having only one superior to whom to report eliminates conflicts of this sort. The principle of unity of command will be discussed on several occasions within this text and primarily in the discussion of the various line authority relationships. Within our present framework of the discussion of delegation of authority, however, the principle of unity of command means that the delegation of authority for a particular activity flows from a single superior to a single subordinate. The author has often observed instances where this basic principle of unity of command was disregarded and violated in practice. Eventually such situations always resulted in conflicts and organizational difficulties.

The Permeating Effect of Delegation

A manager cannot expect to have a good organization unless the principles of delegation of authority are carried out properly and promptly. An organization cannot function efficiently unless the guides for the delegation of authority have been adhered to. The chief executive sets the keynote for delegation of authority within his organization. If he is the type of executive who sincerely believes in delegating the necessary amount of authority to his various subordinates, this attitude and philosophy of delegation will perneate throughout the entire organization. There will be an atmosphere which removes the element of fear and frustration and which will reward the executives for good delegation instead of penalizing them. If the chief executive, however, is the opposite type, and very reluctant and sparing in delegating authority, he is in reality creating a "one-man organization". Then it can only be expected that all the subordinate managers will have the same reluctant attitude towards the delegation of authority.

Frequently, the writer has seen in practice many instances of faulty and weak delegation of authority. Often it was a case of psecudodelegations; often the weaknesses were caused by fuzzy delegations; and then again such weaknesses were caused by subordinates who did not want to accept responsibility, who were not well enough trained, or who continued to go to their superiors for their decisions. In reality, however, all of these shortcomings were caused by top management. It is upto top management to furnish the proper environment, to see to it that the proper principles of delegation are pursued and that the subordinates are properly trained and coached.

Myles L. Mace has devised an amusing list of "business birds" and grouped them according to their willingness to delegate authority. Some of the species are: the White-Shirted Hover—a bird who gives a subordinate job to do and then perches on his shoulder, or the Pin-striped whoopster—a bird who, like the hover, watches closely over his subordinates and becomes very raucous when subordinates deviate from the way he thinks the job should be done, etc., etc. To this rather pointed list Koontz and O'Donnell add additional well-known types of "birds" such as the Duck-Billed Coubletalker—a bird who really never made clear what authority he meant to delegate, and the Black and White Organization Creeper—a bird who delegates authority and then creeps around the structures to lower-level subordinates and thereby nullifies the delegation. Many of these are exceedingly well-known to practitioners in management.

RESPONSIBILITY

The third major aspect of delegating authority is the creation of an obligation on the part of the subordinate to the superior executive for the satisfactory performance of the assigned duties. The acceptance of this obligation by the subordinate manager creates responsibility. This is the third and final aspect of the process of delegation and without it the delegation is not completed. Therefore, the concepts of responsibility and authority are closely related to each other. The term "responsibility", along with the term "authority", is often misused, however, and misunderstood in the area of management. It is common practice to use expressions such as keeping subordinates responsible, delegating responsibility, or carrying out a responsibility. Actually, what is meant is duty, task, activity, or authority. Responsibility is the obligation of a subordinate to perform the duty as required by his superior. Thus the essence of responsibility is obligation.

By accepting his employment, by excepting the obligation to perform the assigned duties, the subordinate implies the acceptance of his responsibility. It results from a contractual agreement in which the subordinate agrees to perform such duties in return for rewards. It stems from the superior-subordinate relationship in which the superior manager has the authority to require the performance of specific duties from a subordinate. The authority to perform and accomplish the specific job flows from the superior to the subordinate, and responsibility is the obligation which is exacted from the subordinate to accomplish these duties. This concept of responsibility gains in magnitude as we ascend the managerial hierarchy.

Responsibility may be continuing or it may be terminated by the accomplishment of a single action and never happen again. The relations between the president of a corporation and the works manager is an example of a continuing obligation. If, on the other hand, the president arranges for someone on the outside to spend sometime at the corporation to evaluate the salary structure of the company, this responsibility is discharged with the accomplishment of the study and recommendations.

"Delegation" of Responsibility

Often managers speak of delegating responsibility to their subordinates. In spite of this very common remark, it must be stated that responsibility cannot be delegated or shifted to the subordinate. The manager can delegate to a subordinate the authority to perform and accomplish a specific job. But he does not delegate responsibility in the sense that once duties are assigned, the delegator is relieved of the responsibility for them. This delegation of tasks does not relieve the executive from his own responsibilities for these duties as he must continue to supervise, direct, and control the subordinate to whom he has delegated authority. A manager can delegate authority to a subordinate, but a superior cannot delegate any of his responsibility.

Although a president of a company may and of necessity has to delegate to a works manager authority to perform his tasks and services, and while the works manager in turn may delegate and of necessity has to delegate a portion of the authority received, neither of them delegates any responsibility. As defined above, responsibility is the obligation of a subordinate to perform the tasks assigned. It is an obligation which is owed to one's superior, and this obligation cannot be shifted or reduced by assigning duties to another.

When the president is called upon by the board of directors to explain performance in the area of production, for example, he cannot plead as defense that he has "delegated the responsibility" for such activity to the works manager. The president must answer to the board of directors. He has remained responsible. Although the president had delegated authority to the works manager the responsibility still always remained with him. A manager cannot shift responsibility to his subordinates. In the earlier discussion in this chapter of delegating authority, it was pointed put that although the manager has delegated varying amounts of authority to subordinates he has not divested himself of any authority, and that he has retained as much authority as he had prior to delegating. The same pertains to responsibility. Regardless of the extent to which the manager create on obligation on the part of the subordinate to perform satisfactorily the assigned duties, he still retains the ultimate responsibility along with his authority. The delegator does not absolve himself from his own responsibility for effective performance of his subordinate.

Newman calls attention to the fact that the same kind of reasoning holds true in other kinds of responsibility and he cites the example of Mr. A borrowing money from the bank and then reloaning it to his son. This transaction with his son in no way reduces Mr. A's obligation and responsibility to repay the money to the bank.

It is important to note that although the responsibility has not been removed or shifted by delegation some recognition must be given to the operating situation. Delegations and redelegations are necessary in order to achieve the large tasks which the president and the works manager have. Although he will exercise and employ the best managerial practices, the works manager cannot be sure that each and every one of his subordinates will use the best judgment. But allowances must be made for errors, and in appraising the achievement of the president some attention should be paid to the degree to which the president must depend on subordinates to get the job done. This is more a matter of standards than a question of responsibility.

Accountability

In addition to the concept of responsibility, some writers have developed the concept of accountability. This latter term is largely used by military organizations, and in this connection to be accountable means to keep accurate and adequate records and to safeguard public property. Aside from government and military circles, there are a few writers in the area of management who distinguish between accountability and responsibility. Peterson and Plowman hold that "to be accountable is to be answerable for one's conduct in respect to obligations fulfilled or unfulfilled". Accountability is a reckoning that is required by a superior of a subordinate as a result of a "liability for the proper discharge of duties." Following our concept of responsibility which defines responsibility as the obligation of a subordinate to perform the duty as required by his superior, the concept of accountability is included and embraced. Hence, only the term responsibility will be used in this text although "being accountable" will at times be referred to in the discussion of controls where the term has more meaning.

Authority should Equal Responsibility

One of the most widely recognized principles of management is the requirement that authority and responsibility should be coextensive. This means that the subordinate must have been delegated enough authority to undertake all the duties which have been assigned to him and for which he has accepted responsibility. A subordinate manager cannot be expected to accept responsibility for activities for which no authority has been delegated. In other words, "to keep someone responsible" that "someone" must have authority to perform his duties. The superior manager cannot exact any responsibility from a subordinate for any activity for which the subordinate does not have the authority. On the other hand, it is poor management to delegate to a subordinate more authority than he needs to perform the duties which he undertook to perform.

The subordinate needs all the authority he should have, but he should not have more than that. Inequality between delegated authority and responsibility produces undesirable results. If authority exceeds responsibility a misuse of authority can easily result. On the other hand, the one who accepts responsibility without adequate authority to take the necessary actions to perform his duties is likely to find himself in a most embarrassing and frustrating position. There are, however, some situations where the strict application of this principle would not be advisable. For instance, in emergency situations executives often exceed the bounds of their authority without any criticism.

It sometimes happens that managers are delegated authority for a task for which they actually cannot accept the responsibility. For instance, consider the case of a sales manager to whom enough authority has been delegated to enable him to fulfil his assigned duty of selling the entire output of the factory. The sales manager, in turn, has accepted the responsibility for sale of the factory's output and for obtaining the planned sales volume. On the other hand, he has accepted responsibility for something for which he really cannot "be held responsible". He cannot compel customers to buy. Similarly, unforeseen economic conditions and unexpected maneuvers by competitors will greatly affect sales. In reality the sales manager has accepted responsibility to use all material and human resources available to him to obtain sales. He can be "held responsible" only for using his best efforts, but not for more.

This principle of coextensiveness of authority and responsibility is a generally recognized and accepted one. However, from time to time it has been questioned. Urwick, although generally advocating the basic concept, seems to agree with Barnard in his challenge of the principle of parity in authority and responsibility on the ground that at times individuals are placed in a position where they have responsibility but cannot have authority. At times executives often which for subordinates who are "more willing to assume more responsibility". McFarland feels that in so doing the superior manager is actually inviting his subordinate managers to bid for authority which he has not as yet seen fit to grant them and to accept responsibility ahead of time. Newman speaks in a similar vein when he discusses what he calls the "sense of responsibility". He states that we often expect a man to have a feeling of responsibility that exceeds his scope of authority. "The concept of civic responsibility, or being 'my brother's keeper', places a heavy responsibility on an individual without giving him permission to run the local government or direct the actions of his brother." Newman feels that his sense of responsibility involves a moral concern. A similar thought is expressed by General Clay in the following statement : "...... I would never be satisfied with the individual who is not continually seeking to add to his responsibilities, to increase his authority, and who in case of doubt never hesitates to make decisions which are not being made by others perhaps more directly responsible."

The author agrees with the thinking that such an extended concept of responsibility is at times very real and very potent, and he has seen it in operation on many occasions. It is primarily only the vary good executive who has this sense of responsibility. This does not man that he is to exceed his limits of authority and to step into some other manager's area of authority. This also is not to be construed as condoning the "empire-builder". Barnard goes even further in stating that a good executive can get action for which he cannot be given authority of command. He points out that in most organizations, many members high and low in the managerial hierarchy, who have little or no authority to command, "are properly held accountable and responsible."

Although this idea of an extended sense of responsibility ought not to be overlooked, it does not alter the basic principle of coextensiveness of responsibility and authority. The concepts of authority and responsibility so closely related to each other that for all practical purposes the entire process of delegation can become ineffective unless they are coequal.

10

Control and Communication in Business

The main purpose of control is to maintain production, selling administration and finance functions at the highest level of efficiency. With this inview plans are made and all segments of the business are coordinated. This also involves predetermination of performance at costs at the level of efficiency explained in the preceding chapter. Actual performances and cost compared with predetermined performances and costs and variances are analysed—divided into their component parts and reasons found for their existence so that management can take corrective action, thereby bring about the desired objective.

It was also explained in the last chapter that budgeting control and standard costing employ these techniques. The former achieves the necessary coordination of plans and control through department and functional budgets.

Standard costing provides a much more detailed control and it, therefore, particularly important for controlling production costs. In most of the enterprises the two techniques are generally combined so that there is a system of standard costing which employs coordinated budgets.

The main purpose of computing variances, is to inform management and employees of all the vital facts which affect the efficient running of the business. Communication thus establishes the critical link for control and coordination. Accounting and budget reports comprise a large proportion of the reports needed by the various levels of management. Reports concerning the financial situation are essential to most, if not all, managerial policy decision.

Communication is a two way traffic. Basically communication function means to inform management of the activities of the business; it also means to inform the employees of the intentions of management; and again serve as a feed-back to management regarding the result of their decisions.

Management thus requires information for decision-making and control and for their purpose information system is organized to provide the necessary intelligence on a timely basis to help management plan, execute and control.

It was also explained in introduction that the business policies in general and finance functions in particular are affected by the decisions of:

(a) Shareholders—(Government in case of public enterprises).
(b) Board of Directors
(c) General Managers
(d) Functional Manager including the Finance Manager.

The information system is devised with a view to help the above interests to play their role in taking decisions and exercising control. A large number of reports are drawn for this purpose, they can be broadly classified as routine and special reports. Routine reports have fixed periodicity—such as daily, weekly, monthly, quarterly, annual, or other suitable duration. The following is the general classification of reports under this head:

(1) Annual Published Accounts for Shareholders and Public
(2) General Management Reports
(3) Production Reports
(4) Sales Reports
(5) Distribution Reports
(6) Administration Reports
(7) Research and Development Reports.

In addition, there is unusual or special information which is necessary to overcome a particular problem: a special report is prepared to cover this type of situation.

Information System in a Private Sector Unit

The method of information and communication is different in private sector units. No uniform procedure is followed. The features of communication for various levels of an organization for private sector undertaking are mentioned:

(i) Information sent to the shareholders: Management transmits information to the shareholders through its annual reports as well as through special reports. The special reports cover any change in major objectives and policies contemplated by the board to directors and management which requires approval by shareholders, such as proposed merger or a change in the number of authorised shares of capital. This is very rare and the particular corporation never has their occasion in 31 years of its establishment.

There is however a uniformity in respect of the information sent via the annual accounts which furnishes information according to Companies Act. Besides the detailed account of financial progress during the past several years, the chairman's speech (reports) gives a description regarding: *(a)* firms products, *(b)* firms market, *(c)* plans for research and development, *(d)* expansion plans, *(e)* description of employees relations, and *(f)* firms dividend policy. The chairman's speech also reviews the past performance, present position and future prospects.

(ii) Information prepared for the board of directors' meeting: To fulfil their responsibility for both the shareholders and management, the board of directors require certain information necessary to the formation of corporate plans as well as performance reports depicting the progress of corporate affairs. Data required by the board is for: *(a)* formulation of objectives and policies, and *(b)* checking overall performance of the business organization.

In most of the private concerns the Board of Directors are not operational executives. Therefore, reports are designed to serve as a basis for future planning and informational purposes rather than as a basis for controlling activities. For example in framing dividend policy the directors are furnished with the following information: *(a)* the composition of share capital, *(b)* the characteristics of stockholder ownership, *(c)* the capitalisation of the firm, *(d)* fixed capital requirements, *(e)* the status of the firm's credit standing, *(f)* characteristic of past earnings, and *(g)* the forecast of the economy.

Reports prepared for planning and informational purposes are generally brief. Instead of including the analysis of deviation, the report generally explains any variation which exists. There financial data are usually presented in charts, graphs and tables. Visual presentation through charts, graphs and tables enables them to ascertain quickly and accurately the activities of the firm in relation to: *(a)* planned operations, *(b)* previous operations, and *(c)* operations of similar business enterprises. The following are the most usual type of information prepared for the Board's meeting

(i) statement of financial conditions,
(ii) statement of total income and expenses,
(iii) statement of income and expenses by products or division,
(iv) financial and operational ratios depicting overall efficiency, profit position, liquidity position, and capital structure position.
(v) comparison of actual operations with predetermined standards for the period under consideration.
(vi) comparison of actual operations with past experience and similar business within the same industry. Classification and general indices of business conditions, and
(vii) summary of sales data (total sales by area, orders received, and back orders).

In addition to the above routine information the board requires specific financial data from time to time in order to solve special planning problems such as *(i)* a change in level of production, *(ii)* replacement of equipment, *(iii)* expansion of capital equipment, *(iv)* sources of new short-term and long-term funds, *(v)* inventory policies, *(vi)* investment policies for short-term funds, and *(vii)* credit policy.

To help the board in taking right decision, the top

management dissects the special reports into three categories: *(a)* a definition of the problem to be resolved, *(b)* managements analysis of the problem, and *(c)* the alternative solution which management recommends.

(iii) Information content for general manager: The General Manager occupies the third scale level and is primarily responsible for the efficient operation of the firm's activities. His duties are largely coordinative and executives. Generally, the General Manager coordinates finance, and operates, executives assist him in the performance of his managerial duties. The financial information which is submitted to the General Manager and top level committees are more detailed than that submitted to board of directors. The following reports are submitted periodically to the General Managers:

(1) The financial budget—This is a summary of the operating budget and the capital expenditure budget.
(2) Funds Reports.
(3) Balance sheets and profit and loss statements—monthly, quarterly and annual.
(4) Statement of income and expenses by product lines or divisions. It also gives a detailed analysis of variation for the financial budget.
(5) Financial comparisons with regards total operating efficiency, and efficiency of working capital, flow of funds, changes in fixed capital, and relative earnings position.
(6) Forecasts and future financial requirement.

Apart from these routine reports, special financial information is also furnished whenever any change in the operational process is contemplated for example in expansion of physical plan and equipment, product mix, sales prices, volume of inventory to maintain, sales policies, quality of product, working capital and research.

A popular method of furnishing daily information to General Manager is to display the figures regarding daily output, (compared with daily target), expenses operating and fixed, daily profit or loss figures on the board fixed at his room. Visual picture of performance trends and comparison are also displayed which gives overall picture at a glance.

(iv) Financial information to colleagues managers: In addition to supplying financial data upward, the financial executive also supplies data to his colleagues who are equal in managerial status. In other words, financial data are supplied horizontally as well as vertically in the organization.

The Finance Manager makes available to the Sales Manager who is on the same scale level, information regarding effects on profits when actual sales deviate from budgeted sales valumes. The data is processed according to product and separately for each geographical area.

The Finance Manger is also responsible for the transmission of performance information to the Production Manager which reveals budgeted costs, actual costs, percentage of deviations, and the effect upon profits of the deviation between actual and budgeted costs.

(v) Communication below the line: Transmission of financial information to the lower level is absolutely necessary for coordination and organizational purposes. This is achieved by issuing Manual which law down the code of conduct and established methods by which financial data are to be reported to Finance Manager. Changes and revisions in the regulations and procedures are notified by office memorandums.

The use of office memorandum as a means of communication below the line is the special feature of Public Enterprises to the concerns. Some are general circulars; affecting the behaviour of all the public enterprises; others are meant for the concern for which they are issued. The copies of these memorandum are circulated to all the divisional heads, sectional officers, superintendent and others in the line organization.

However, in both public sector and private sector units, the use of Financial Manual is encouraged mainly for two reasons. First, written objectives and policies are the best means of assuring consistent action by all members of the financial organization. Second in order for objectives and policies to be carried out, they must be supported by procedure. The only way to assure this is to put all financial policies in writing. It is not enough to include in the policy manual the exact details of all company policies; each should be carefully explained in order to avoid misinterpretation by members of the various financial subfunctions.

Public sector units have to prepare about hundred more

reports which they periodically sent to government agencies, including their controlling ministries. These reports, covering areas such as General Management, Financial, Personnel and Establishment, Operation/Construction etc., are generally in the form of progress of routine reports. The major reports include monthly and quarterly progress reports, monthly cost statements, quarterly financial reviews, reports relating to use of powers delegated to the top management production and construction reports and return prescribed under various statutes. All the reports required except those specific under Companies Act etc. statutes or by the controlling ministry are not adopted by each public sector organization.

Government thus receives information in several capacity. In some public sector undertakings it holds majority shares along with the private individual shareholders and therefore receives the copy of the audited annual report and accounts, with directors's report and chairman's speech as representative of the owner of the shares of the undertakings. It also enjoys a specific position as supplier of long-term loans and guarantor of funds; as such its capacity is that of an investor or creditors, in which position, it expects certain information. As the agency accountable to the parliament and the public in general for the invested public funds it needs some other facts. Certain information it seeks as the agency for the overall development of the industry in the particular sector. But the information sought by the government under various statutes and regulation is for macro planning and social control which is beyond the scope of management information system.

A management reporting system subserves three basic objects: *(a)* strategic planning, *(b)* management control, and *(c)* operational control.

These three distinct aspects can be identified with the following levels of management. Strategic planning of public sector is the responsibility of: *(i)* Planning commission, *(ii)* Finance ministry, and *(iii)* Administrative ministry.

This is done within the framework of the policy objectives laid down by the Parliament. The board of directors is also associated.

The management control is exercised by the administrative ministry board of directors and the General Manager. Operational control is exercised by functional directors and departmental heads. Thus, over study on Management Information System with regards public sector enterprises will cover only the information flowing to those three levels of management.

In processing and compilation of data for purpose of planning and controlling there is little difference between the public and private sector units. Most of units still follow the traditional practice. The information in the form of Daily or Sectional Reports are received in the Statistics of Management Account department which prepares various types of statements. Most common type of Reports which are used upto Board level (and also passed on the administrative ministry in case of public enterprises) are the following:

(1) Comparative statement of management ratios,
(2) General operating statement,
(3) Divisional operating statement,
(4) Sales operating statement,
(5) Variance analysis statement,
(6) Labour efficiency report, and
(7) Departmental operating statement.

The Anatomy of Management Information System

The concept of 'Management Information System' which is being used here is somewhat different, than the 'information' as present' collected', 'assembled' and 'processed' in most of the private and public concerned. The various activities of the firm which involve collecting, processing, storing and reporting of information can usefully be considered as a system. In actual practice, these activities take place in separate parts of an organizations as sub-system, to the extent that information function has common goals, resources and resource management, it can be viewed as one system. Basically, the information system comprise: *(i)* data collection and its recording, *(ii)* Processing, and *(iii)* Processed date generates meaningful reports.

The reports could be periodical reviews, analytical reports and control or action statements. The characteristics of a good information system are that its records are as detailed and accurate as possible and the flow of information into and out of the system takes place automatically within appropriate time spans. The system should be able to process the information and provide meaningful reports for decision making at different levels of the division to the degree of detail required by such level. A well designed information system is able to perform these functions automatically, besides it also automatically monitors the transaction and activities by comparing results with established criteria.

An examination of collection assembling and dissemination of data in some of the public and private sector units shows that there is not much 'systematic approach'. The data does not flow on continuing basis and the reports prepared with the help of inadequate data are difficult to analysis. No care is taken to draw reports to suit the special managerial needs for different levels of management. The later point is specially important to explain.

It was pointed out earlier that the reports are required of different levels of management for different purposes. Operational control has almost a day-to-day emphasis while planning needs are best met by choosing a time span long enough to throw up trends. It is also a characteristic of the control process that the shift from operational control to planning simultaneously involves shift in terms of management reporting from internal (organizational) data to external (environmental) data and from financial to non-financial information. An examination of the contents of the reports of the public sector units how that no such distinction is made. The same set of information which if furnished to the ministry is also presented to the board and is circulated among all the divisional heads. Repetition of the same information in different forms of reports is generally made. There are two very important features of these reports. Firstly, they are too many and secondly, they are too bulky. Generally they contain a large number of details in comparison to minor nature and often the most significant and critical figure is lost in those voluminous details. The long narrative reports as they are at present, prepared result in shifting the focus from significant to minor details. To a certain extent the ministries themselves are responsible; they often call information for ad hoc purposes, which does not fall in the area of the functions defined above. In this connection it is necessary that the authority seeking information must be clear about its role and prepare a system of information that should be based on a proper and realistic examination of the information requirement of the users and must be related to their management objectives.

Time factor is the most important consideration of these reports. There are instances where the reports are sent after too much lags and by the time the information is received, the report becomes out of date and quite irrelevant to a particular situation.

The study team on public undertakings set up by the administrative Reforms Commission pointed out, among others the following defects in the present reporting system in public enterprises insofar as these relate to the government:

(i) a rational and up-to-date system of reporting is yet to be designed for providing the government with timely information about the true picture of the enterprises;

(ii) in many cases, an unduly large number of reports and returns are being obtained from the public enterprises and at too frequent intervals;

(iii) the form and contents of the reports need to be modified to cut out non-essential information and concentrate on important items of information that the government requires for exercising control at key points; and

(iv) adequate experts cells do not exist in the controlling ministries or at a central point in the government for processing the reports and returns and for taking follow up action on them.

The Committee on Public Undertakings in their first report on the National Building Construction Corporation had also pointed out that "despite the submission of reports and returns neither the administrative ministry nor the Ministry of Finance were aware of the difficult financial position of the corporation in time." In the 5th Report on the Oil and Natural Gas Commission, the Committee remarks that the commission submitted about 55 periodical reports and returns without the ministry getting a clear picture of the problems and progress of the commission.

This violates the fundamental principle of reporting. Communication implies that a person receiving the information understands the nature and significance of material contained in the report he receives. When communication is generally effective, management's action and decisions are likely to be based on relevant facts which they receive rather than on untested impressions and guesses. However, there are reasons to believe that accounting reports to management have not always achieved their intended purpose because the reports were not understood, recipients lacked the time required to grasp the meaning, or the content of reports were not relevant to problems facing the persons who received them.

A great deal of managerial effort and time is required to develop Management Information System for an enterprise. This effort is justified primarily on the grounds that the activities of all sub-units of the enterprise must be focussed on common and agreed upon enterprise objectives: each component of an enterprise must contribute in attaining the enterprise goals. To ensure *conformance*, reports become an integral aspect of effective management. It is fundamental that *performance* reports must encompass all the activities and tailored to the characteristics of each particular environment. The development of an effective information system depends upon and presupposes a detailed documentation of the functions and activities of the division concerned; a clear formulation of inter-relationships between different activities and the rules and procedures according to which decisions are made and further action is generated. It means that an information system can be successful only when it is connected with other important finance functions—planning, controlling such an integrated approach is made in the following chapter.

STOCK EXCHANGES

The investors want liquidity for their investments. The securities which they hold should easily be sold when they need cash. Similarly there are others who want to invest in new securities. There should be a place where the securities may be purchased and sold. Stock exchanges provide such a place where securities of different companies can be purchased and sold. Stock exchange is a body of persons, whether incorporated or not, formed with a view to helping, regulation and controlling the business of buying and selling securities.

Stock exchanges are organized and regulated markets for various securities issued by corporate sector and other institutions. The stock exchanges enable free purchase and sale of securities as commodity exchanges allow trading in commodities. The following definitions explain the meaning and scope of stock exchanges:

Definitions

Pyle: "Security exchanges are market places where securities that have been listed thereon may be bought and sold for either investment or speculation." Stock exchanges allow trading in securities both to the genuine investors and speculators.

Securities Contract (Regulation) Act, 1956: "Stock exchange means anybody of individuals, whether incorporated or not, constituted for the purpose of assisting, regulating or controlling the business of buying, selling or dealing in securities".

According to this definition, the stock exchange allows trading in securities under certain rules and regulations.

Hartley Withers: "A Stock Exchange is something like a vast warehouse where securities are taken away from the shelves and sold across the countries at a fixed price in a catalogue which is called the official list."

Hartley calls stock exchange a warehouse where all securities are kept and traded on specified prices. It may not always be that every type of security is purchased for sale, there may be investors who do not bring their securities to the market but keep them only as investments.

Husband and Dockeray: "Securities or stock exchanges are privately organized markets which are used to facilitate trading in securities." As per this definition the stock exchanges are the organized places where securities are purchased and sold.

Characteristics of Stock Exchanges

From the definitions given earlier, the following characteristics or salient features of stock exchange come out:

(1) It is a place where securities are purchased and sold.
(2) A stock exchange is an association of persons whether incorporated or not.
(3) The trading in an exchange is strictly regulated and rules and regulations prescribed for various transactions.

(4) Both genuine investors and speculators buy and sell shares.

(5) The securities of corporations, trusts, governments, municipal corporations, etc., are allowed to be dealt at stock exchanges.

Functions of Stock Exchanges

The stock exchanges play an important role in the economic development of a country. The importance of stock exchanges will be clear from the functions they perform and discussed as follows:

(1) *Ensures liquidity of capital:* The stock exchanges provide a place where shares and stock are converted into cash. The exchanges provide a ready market where buyers and sellers are always available and those who are in need of hard cash can sell their holdings. Had this not been possible then many persons would have feared for blocking their savings in securities. It is because of exchanges that many persons invest in securities and they can again convert them into cash.

(2) *Continuous market for securities:* The stock exchanges provide a ready market for securities. The securities once listed continue to be traded at the exchanges irrespective of the fact that their owners go on changing. The exchanges provide a regular market for trading in securities.

(3) *Evaluation of securities:* The investors can evaluate the worth of their holdings from the prices quoted at different exchanges for those securities. The securities are quoted under the free atmosphere of demand and supply and the prices are set on the basis of free market. Stock exchanges are helpful in evaluating any type of security listed there.

(4) *Mobilising surplus savings:* The stock exchanges provide a ready market for various securities. The investors do not have any difficulty in investing their savings by purchasing shares, bonds etc. from the exchanges. If this facility is not there then many persons who want to invest their savings will not find avenues to do so. In this way stock exchanges play an important role in mopping up surplus funds of investors.

(5) *Helpful in raising new capital:* The new and existing

concerns need capital for their activities. The new concerns raise capital for the first time and existing units increase their capital for expansion and diversification purposes. The shares of new concerns are registered at stock exchanges and existing companies also sell their shares through brokers etc. at exchanges. The exchanges are helpful in raising capital both by new and old concerns. The intending buyers also remain in touch with the exchanges for investing money in securities.

(6) Safety in dealings: The dealings at stock exchanges are governed by well-defined rules and regulations of Securities Contract (Regulation) Act, 1956. There is no scope for manipulating transactions. Every contract is done according to the procedure laid down and there is no fear in the minds of contracting parties. The safety in dealings brings confidence in the minds of all concerned parties and helps in increasing various dealings.

(7) Listing of securities: Only listed securities can be purchased and sold at stock exchanges. Every company desirous of listings its securities will apply to the exchange authorities. The listings is allowed only after a critical examination of capital structure, management and prospects of the company. The listing of securities gives privilege to the company. The investors can form their own views about the securities because listing a security does not guarantee the financial stability of the company.

(8) Platform for public debt: The increasing government's role in economic development has necessitated the raising of huge amounts for this purpose. The stock exchanges provide a platform for raising public debts. The stock exchanges are also organized markets for government securities. However, there is no provision for a separate counter for government securities but these are traded through brokers dealing in these securities.

(9) Clearing house of business information: The companies listing securities with exchanges have to provide financial statements, annual reports and other reports to ensure maximum publicity of corporation operations and working. The economic and other informations provided at stock exchanges help companies to decide their policies.

Listing of Securities

Listing of securities means permission to quote shares and debentures officially on the trading floor of the stock exchange. Every security issued by companies cannot be traded at a stock exchange. The stock exchanges fix certain standards which the company must fulfil before getting the securities listed.

Requirements for Listing

Any company intending to get its securities listed at an exchange have to fulfil certain conditions. The following informations must be filed with the exchange for getting a security listed:

(i) Memorandum and articles of association.
(ii) Copies of all prospectuses or statements in lieu of prospectuses.
(iii) Copies of Balance Sheets, audited accounts, agreements with promoters, underwriters, brokers, etc.
(iv) Letters of Consent from Controllers of Capital Issues.
(v) Details of shares and debentures issued and shares forfeited.
(vi) History of the company in brief.
(vii) Details of issues of bonuses and dividends declared.
(viii) Agreement with managing director, etc.
(ix) An Undertaking regarding companies with the provisions of the Companies Act, 1956 and Securities Contracts (Regulation) Act, 1956 as well as rules made therein.
(x) A list of the highest ten holders of each class or kind of securities of the company.

The stock exchanges are empowered to withdraw or suspend the admission granted for trading following any breach of conditions.

The securities are classified into: *(a)* cleared securities, and *(b)* non-cleared securities. Cleared securities enjoy forward trading facilities while non-cleared securities have only cash trading and are on the cash list. If the shares are fully paid and have listing privilege for three years the exchange may grant the status of cleared securities. The securities must be widely distributed and have public interest only then they can become cleared securities.

Procedure for Dealings at Stock Exchanges

The buying and selling at stock exchanges is not allowed to outsiders. They have to approach brokers who are members of the exchange and the dealings can only be through them. The following procedure is followed for dealings at exchanges:

(1) Selection of a broker: The first thing to be done is to select a broker through whom the purchase or sale is to be made. The intending investor or seller may approach his bank for this purchase. The banks have appointed their own brokers at exchanges and they contact for dealings on behalf of their customers. On a recommendation from the bank the client's account is opened by the broker. The bank assures about the financial condition of the client.

(2) Placing an order: After selecting the broker the client places an order for purchase of sale of securities. The broker also guides the client about the type of securities to be purchased and the proper time for it. If a client is to sell the securities then the broker tells him about the favourable time for sale. The broker is told to purchase shares, their, number and price to be paid. Sometimes a definite price is given on which the purchase is to be made, sometimes the tentative price is told, sometimes the minimum price to be paid is told, etc. The broker will try to make purchases as far as possible to the nearest price offered by the client. The broker is given some choice for bargaining. The same type of choice is given to the broker for selling the securities.

(3) Making the contract: The trading floor of the stock exchange is divided into different parts known as trading posts. Different posts deal in different types of securities. The authorised clerk of the broker goes to the concerned post and expresses his intention to buy and sell the securities. A deal is struct when the other party also agrees. The bargain struck by an outcry mentioning the price and number of securities contracted by both the clerks. The bargains is noted by both the parties in their note books. The slip giving brief details of the bargains is put in a box for making announcement in the official price list for publicity.

(4) Contract note: The buying and selling brokers prepare

notes after their mutual contract next day. The seller is sent to selling note and the buyer is sent a buying note. The details of securities traded are given mentioning their number, price, etc.

(5) Settlement: The spot dealings are settled there is full. The selling broker hands over the transfer form and share certificates to the buying broker after receiving the price. The settlement for ready delivery and forward contracts is done with a different procedure.

Settlement of ready delivery contracts: The settlement in different stock exchanges is done between three and seven days of the transaction. If the settlement is done by giving actual delivery of securities on receiving the price it is called liquidation in full. In another method the dealings are squared by adjusting price differences only.

Settlement of forward delivery contracts: The forward delivery contracts are done for speculative purposes. Only the active and broad market securities are traded in forward contracts. The settlement of forward contracts can be done in any of the three ways:

(a) *Liquidation in full:* The securities are delivered and payment is received or vice-versa after crossing all intermediate purchases and sales.

(b) *Liquidation by payment of differences:* The purchase and sale are offset at the ruling price by paying or receiving the difference amount. The securities are not delivered but only the difference of prices contracted and current prices are received or paid as the case may be.

(c) *Carry over to the next settlement:* When the buyer does not want to settle the contract but wants to carry it to a future date then it is called carry over. The buyer will have to pay certain amount to the seller for this concession and the amount paid is known as Badla or Catango charge.

11

Coordination in Business

Henri Fayol considers coordinating to be one of the functions of the manager. According to him, to coordinate is to harmonize all the activities of a concern in order to facilitate its working and its success. "It is to bear in mind in any activity whatsoever, technical, commercial, financial or other, the obligations and consequences such action involves for all the functions of the business." He states that in a well-coordinated enterprise the following facts are to be observed: Firstly, each department should work in harmony with the rest; secondly, each department, division, and subdivision should be precisely informed as to the share they must take in the communal task; and thirdly, the working schedule of the various departments and subdivisions should be constantly attuned to circumstances. He concedes, however, that there three requirements are not always fulfilled, and the lack of coordination is apparent in three ways: First, each department knows and wants to know nothing of the others; secondly, water-tight compartments exist between the divisions and offices of the same department as they do also between different departments; and thirdly, no one thinks of the general interest. "This attitude on the part of the personnel, so disastrous for a concern, is not the result of preconstructed intention but the culmination of non-existent or inadequate coordination."

To remedy this situation Fayol suggests a weekly conference

of departmental heads. These conferences are to be held not for the purpose of drawing up the plan of action but to facilitate the carrying out of the plan in the light of current events. If such weekly meetings of departmental heads for purpose of coordination cannot be held, or if the meetings must be held at longer intervals, Fayol suggests the use of liaison officers in the interim. These liaison officers could generally be staffed employments who would perform these functions during the time when meetings could not be held.

It is noteworthy to cite the different views of coordination taken by some of the writers in the area of administration and management. For example, Ralph C. Davis looks on coordination primarily as vital phase of control. L.A. Allen cites coordinating as one of the managerial functions alongside planning, organizing, motivating, and controlling. However, he goes on to state that most of this coordination will be accomplished automatically. If sound objectives, policies, procedures, and organization are established. Mooney defines coordination as "the orderly arrangement of group effort, to provide unity of action in the pursuit of common purpose." He calls coordination the first principle of organization, and by this he means that coordination expresses all the principles of organization in toto—nothing less than that. Ordway Tead, although admitting that he will not find universal acknowledgement of his views, finds it valuable to identify the coordinative functions as a separate function. According to him "coordination, in short, is administration at its most creative."

Defining Coordination

Coordination might best be considered not as a separate function, but as a process by which the manager achieves orderly group effort and unity of action in the pursuit of common purpose. He brings about this process as he performs the five basic managerial functions of planning, organizing, staffing, directing, and controlling. Coordination is the orderly synchronization of efforts of the subordinates to provide the proper amount, timing, and quality of execution, so that their unified efforts lead to the stated objective, namely, the common purpose of the enterprise.

To quote Tead, "coordination is the effort to assure a smooth interplay of the functions and forces of all the different component parts of an organization to the end that its purposes will be realized with a minimum of friction and a maximum of collaborative effectiveness". Coordination pertains to the synchronization and unity of the actions of a group of people within an organization, and one of the important goals of every manager is to achieve this coordination. Chester I Barnard even went so far as to say that under most circumstances "the quality of coordination is the crucial factor in the survival of organization."

Coordination is not a separate and distinct activity of the manager; it is a part of all the managerial functions of palling, organizing, staffing, directing and controlling. It transverses the entire process.

Coordination and Cooperation

The term coordination should not be confused with cooperation for there is considerable difference between cooperation and coordination. Cooperation indicates merely the willingness of individuals to help each other. It is the result of a voluntary attitude of a group of people. Coordination is much more inclusive, requiring more than the desire and willingness of the participants. For instance, consider a group of men attempting to move a heavy object. They are sufficient in number, willing and eager to cooperate with each other, and trying to do their best to move the object. They are fully aware of their common purpose. However, in all likelihood their efforts will be of little avail until one of them, the manager, gives the proper orders to apply the right amount of effort at the right place, at the right time, and then they can move the object. It is conceivable that by coincidence mere cooperation could have brought about the desired result in an instance such as the above. But no management can effort to rely upon such a coincidental occurrence. Thus, although cooperation is always helpful and its absence could prevent all possibility of coordination, its mere presence will not a sure coordination. Coordination is superior in order of importance to cooperation.

Self-Coordination

Although it is the manager's job to effect coordination, this does not mean that the subordinate should be exempt from doing all he can to aid in this effort. In this connection Alvin Brown speaks of "self-coordination." He defines self-coordination as "the effort of independent responsibilities to achieve the harmonious or reciprocal performance of their own responsibilities." In other words, according to him, each person in a group takes cognizance of the effects of his own performance upon others and thereby coordinates his activities with those of others. Herbert Simon speaks in this connection of the concept of self-adjustment. Needless to state, the wise manager will do all in his power to promote voluntary coordination. However, neither the principle of self-coördination nor the concept of self-adjustment is a substitute for coordination. It takes the efforts of the leader or the manager to bring about coordination, and the goal of the enterprise cannot be successfully obtained without it.

Although a capable manager can do much to instill into his subordinates a concern for the common good, it will not be possible to convince the subordinate that, in the final analysis, he will not be judged by the way he has performed his individual responsibilities. It is unrealistic to expect subordinates to consider their responsibilities second to the welfare of the entire enterprise.

Attaining Coordination

Coordination is not easily attained. Each functional interest in the enterprise stresses its own coveted opinion of how the purposes should be accomplished, and each tends to stress one or another different policy or method of emphasis depending upon the experience of the department. The same problem of the different viewpoint applies as between the several levels in the managerial hierarchy. It takes real thoughtfulness listening power, and goodwill to see properly a problem of work relationships of the group above or below. In spite of the cooperative attitude, self-coordination or self-adjustment of each member of a group, there will be duplication of actions and efforts, and even possibly conflicts of efforts unless the manager synchronizes all these efforts. Through coordination he brings about a total accomplishment far in excess of the sum of the individual parts. Each part is of significant importance, but the result which is achieved is greater than the mathematical sum of the individual achievements. This is because of the manager's successful coordination of efforts.

The task of securing harmonious action belongs solely to the manager, and it cannot be delegated to a specialist or to a single department. The manager, from his vantage point, is in a better position than any special "coordinating department" to view the various functions and to determine whether or not they are coordinated in a way that will bring about the desired results. It is absurd to think that the task of securing coordination could be shifted and assigned to a department created for this purpose.

Although the need for coordination is obvious in all kinds of enterprises, it is not easily achieved, and the task of coordination is becoming increasingly complex. These increasing difficulties arise for various reasons, of which growth of the enterprise is one. With growth the task of synchronizing daily activities becomes more complicated. With the increase in the number of position the need for coordination and the necessity for synchronization to secure the unified results increases. A more complex organization structure involving more subordinates brings about added problems of communication. All of this makes coordination more difficult.

Specialization is another source from which problems of coordinations stem. Modern business has become increasingly complex due to the fact that it is necessary and desirable that the various functions be performed by specialists. Specialization in turn brings about the need for more coordination as it arises from the diversity of tasks to be undertaken and of persons to carry them out. It emerges as soon as the operations begin to be multiple or complex, by reason of the fact that more than one person is concerned with them. Marshall Dimock goes so far as to say that administration is the coordination of the work of specialists. It must furthermore be kept in mind that, due to our age of specialization, the tendency of dividing each activity into smaller specialized parts brings with it an attitude in those specialists performing the parts that their activity is the most essential. It is understandable that they attach under importance to their own activity.

Human nature itself presents problems of coordination. Each executive is preoccupied with the work in his own unit and hesitates to become involved in other areas without considering that his activities might have significant bearing also on them. It is also at times understandable that each manager tends to think primarily of the welfare of his own department without the necessary consideration of the enterprise as a whole. This will particularly be true if his total compensation is determined in relation to the financial performance of his departmental activities.

Vertical and Horizontal Coordination

Within the concept of coordination one must distinguish between vertical and horizontal coordination. By the term "vertical coordination" we mean the coordination between the various links of the different levels of the organizational unit. For instance, consider the coordination between the vice-president in charge of manufacturing and the works manager, between the works manager and the superintendent, between the superintendent and the formen, and so on down the line. Looking at this situation vertically, levels of authority are super-imposed upon each other, and it is necessary that the activities assigned to the several levels of the enterprise be coordinated. This vertical coordination is secured by delegated authority, together with the means and manner of directing, supervising, and controlling. Although a manager will be very reluctant to rely on this power of authority—and in most cases he will not—it is well to remember that in the event that one subordinate within the vertical line is a hindrance in achieving coordination, he ultimately may have to be removed from that particular position. Although the power of delegated authority will carry great weight, vertical coordination cannot be achieved by the sheer weight of authority itself. This vertical coordination should come about as a by-product of the superior's efficient and expert performance of his managerial functions. This will be discussed shortly.

By the term "horizontal coordination" we are referring to coordination between horizontal departments on the same level in the managerial hierarchy. In this direction, as well as in the vertical direction, coordination cannot be ordered; it must be achieved in the nature of a by-product. Coordination in the horizontal sense refers to working arrangements which are necessary between, for example, the vice-president in charge of production, the vice-president in charge of sales, and the vice-president in charge of finance in their planning and implementation of a new promotional programme. Coordination is needed between them so that, at the time the sales department is ready to sell the new item, the production department will be in a position to fill the orders, and the financial arrangements have been made so that the necessary funds are available to have the raw materials, parts, and so on, and to be able to carry the necessary amount of outstanding credit. Each and every one of the executives involved in this coordination is a manager of his own departmental function, and between them horizontally there cannot be an edict, a fiat, to coordinate. These men do not have authority over each other. In order to achieve the pre-determined goals of the enterprise, it is expected that these men will coordinate their activities. If the need arises, however, organization structure will make it possible to carry a question on up in the managerial hierarchy to a senior executive who directs the activities of all the groups involved. Here, too the senior executive cannot rely on the sheer weight of authority to achieve coordination. It must be brought about in a different fashion.

Coordination of the various functions between independent managers of the different departments is facilitated in a small enterprise due to proximity of working arrangements, close contacts, and short lines of communication. However, when a large company is involved, the problems become more complicated, and it is the fine art of the superior manager to achieve coordination in this horizontal sense. The ideal solution, of course, would be if the various executives would voluntarily recognize that their jobs and goals are in harmony with the goals of the other departments and of the total enterprise. If all would view their activities in this light, coordination would automatically be achieved without the special efforts of the manager.

The Principles of Mary Parker Follett

Mary Parker Follett, in her discussion on coordination, has presented several fundamental "principles of organization." In the first principle she states that coordination can be achieved by direct contact among the responsible people concerned. Miss Follett believes that coordination can be obtained more easily by direct interpersonal horizontal relationships and direct personal communications, which bring about agreement on methods, actions, and ultimate achievement. Second, she calls to our attention the fact that coordination can be achieved more readily in the early stages of planning and policy making. Direct contact must begin in the very early stages of the process. If the executive of one department meets with the executives of the other departments and confronts them with a finished policy and he in turn is confronted by them with an already finished policy, coordination of course will be found difficult. But "if the head of the production department, while he is forming his policy, meets and discuss with the other heads the question involved, a successful coordination is far more likely to be reached. That is, you cannot, with the greatest degree of success for your undertaking, make policy-forming and policy-adjusting two separate processes." Achieving coordination in the early stages of planning and policy making is essential.

As the third principle of coordination, Miss Follett states that all factors in a situation are reciprocally related. As a matter of fact, this third principle shows us exactly what the process of coordination actually is. When A works with B and he in turn works with C and D, each of the four finds himself influenced by the others, influenced by all the persons in the total situation. "This sort of reciprocal relating, this interpenetration of every part by every other part, and again by every other part as it has been permeated by all, should be the goal of all attempts at co-ordination." As the fourth principle of coordination, Mary Parker Follet states that coordination is a continuing process, something which must go on all the time. This, of course, is self-explanatory. Coordination cannot be left to chance, and the manager must constantly work at it so that he will not be suddenly confronted by unforeseen developments.

Coordination, a By-Product

Obiviously, coordination is something which cannot be ordered. It is something which is to be brought about by the efforts of the manager as he performs his managerial functions. If he performs his five managerial functions efficiently and expertly, then coordination will be forthcoming. There will be no need for special coordination as such.

As the manager performs his first function, namely, that of

planning, he must strive for coordination immediately. This is precisely what Mary Parker Follett is referring to in her second principle. The planning stage is the ideal time to bring about coordination, and the manager must see to it that the various plans are properly interrelated. He should discuss the various plans and alternatives with the managers of all departments so that at an early time they will have the opportunity to express any doubts and objections. If they have been engaged and involved in planning at the initial stages together with the executive, then the changes for coordination are good. For instance, the thoughtful manager will plan an advertising campaign in conjunction with the production manager, the sales manager, the vice-president in charge of finance, the publicity manager, and so on. At that early time, as he performs his managerial function of planning, he is attempting to achieve coordination by synchronizing the efforts of all the men involved. One of the overriding factors in efficient planning is the constant thought pertaining to coordination.

The concern for coordination should also be prevalent when the manager organizes. As mentioned before, Mooney considers coordination as the very essence of organization. The reason for organization is to obtain coordination. Whenever, the manager groups and assigns the various activities to subordinates, and when he creates departments, the thought of coordination should be the one which is uppermost in his mind. In the process of organizing, the manager also defines relationships between departments. He should define them in such a manner and set them up in such a way that coordination will result. By placing related activities which must be closely synchronized in the same administrative unit, coordination will be facilitated. Coordination is an essential part of organizing, and unless the manager bears in mind how these groups are to function together, the organization will not be a successful one.

At this occasion of organizing the manager should keep in mind that clear-cut organization and procedures with which all persons concerned are familiar will greatly contribute to coordination. Often poor coordination is caused by a lack of understanding of who is to perform what or due to the fact that the manager did not clearly delegate authority and exact responsibility. Such fuzziness can easily lead to the duplication of efforts instead of to their synchronization. It is conceivable that, due to this void in organization, two executives both feel that they are responsible for the same activity. The purchasing department and the maintenance division, for example, might both consider it their function to buy repair and spare parts, and this may lead to difficulties with the suppliers.

In order to obtain coordination while organizing, the manager must look at it both vertically and horizontally. Vertical coordination is secured due to the fact that levels of authority are superimposed upon one another. In order to assume that the organization will also produce the proper coordination horizontally, the manager must make certain that the total efforts of the various functional, territorial, and divisional units are directed to wards a common effort and that the heads of these various activities are under the over-all direction of an executive who will make sure that the various activities are in harmony and bring about the desired results. The organization must be so set up that, in the event that the various managers of the sales, production, finance, and promotion departments do not coordinate their efforts, there will be a common superior to all of them who will bring the various activities into line and coordinate them. It is, of course, much more desirable that the various functions coordinate their efforts voluntarily.

Many managers, in order to insure voluntary coordination among the various functions, introduce committees into the organizational set-up. Some writers strongly recommend the creation of such committees in order to accomplish the objectives of the enterprise as a whole, as these committees' will give the various unit heads occasion to hold formal and informal meetings. Often the manager creates the committee for the particular purpose of bringing together the men whose activities need to be coordinate, and by so doing the manager provides a setting which will bring about voluntary coordination horizontally. All of these activities are performed by the manager as he fulfils his function of organizing. Again we state that in fulfilling this function a constant over riding thought in the manager's mind must be the need to achieve coordination.

When the manager performs this function of staffing he should bear coordination in mind. He should make certain that he will have the right number of executives in the various positions to assure the proper performance of their functions. He should see to it that those executives are of such quality as to willingly cooperate and coordinate their efforts.

When the manager directs he is also involved with coordination. The very essence of giving orders, instructions, coaching, and teaching subordinates means to coordinate their various activities in such manner that the overall enterprise objective will be reached in the most efficient way. In assessing the aid which good directing and supervision can give to coordination. Alvin Brown goes even so far as to define coordination as "that phase of supervision which is devoted to obtaining the harmonious and reciprocal performance of responsibilities of two or more deputies." The supervisor can never completely relieve himself of the duty of watching the progress of the various activities under his direction to be sure that they are proceeding harmoniously. The manager's expertness in effectively directing his subordinates will bring about coordination. The latter will be well informal and will understand how their activities affect those of the other executives and subordinates. Every directive which is given should take into account the effect this particular action will have on the other departments and other executives.

In our discussion in Part V regarding the various techniques of direction it will be pointed out that, among others, the manager will use free and open discussion and group decision-making techniques with his subordinates in order to achieve the necessary coordination. At that time it will be shown that in order to obtain coordination it is vital that the various subordinates have an opportunity for free and open discussion and for an interchange of ideas so that the various problems of a particular directive are properly understood. In sum, as the manager performs his directing function he will invariable coordinate.

Last, but not least, controlling has a direct bearing on coordination. As cited previously, R.C. Davis considers coordination as a vital phase of control and nothing else. As will be discussed in Part VI on the controlling function, the manager must, by checking and observing, learn whether or not the current activities are in conformance with the desired activities, for this is necessary in order to bring about the desired coordination. Frequent evaluation of operations helps to synchronize the efforts of the subordinates. If while controlling the manager finds that the performance is not as planned or as directed, he should immediately take remedial action so that whatever deviations have occurred can be remedied. By doing this he assures coordination at least from then on. As he controls he will discover if and where there has been a lack of coordination. The very nature of the controlling process is one that brings about coordination, the synchronized effort which in the final analysis will lead the organization to the desired and started company objectives and goals.

Good communications will be of immeasurable help in the coordination of the various activities. There must be continuous and full flow of communication which will give the various subordinates all the necessary information needed for coordination. Personal contact is probably the most effective means of communication to achieve coordination. However, there are many other additional devices which can be used, such as written communications, reports, procedures bulletins, and numerous modern mechanical devices which will insure a speedy dissemination of the necessary full and accurate information to the various subordinates who must of necessity have this information to insure proper coordination. Newman rightfully points out that "since coordination is concerned with the interrelationships of separate activities, it can be no better than the transfer of information about those activities to some common point or points, where the devetailing takes place." The recent developments in automatic data processing can be of considerable help in this direction.

Liaison Men and Coordination

Coordination should result from the effective execution of all managerial functions. Although coordination will always remain the line manager's responsibility, sometimes special employees have been charged with the task of coordination. It is conceivable that in special situations where the direct personal contact of executives of the various functions is not frequent enough to provide all the informal information that is desirable liaison men may be utilized. Such a liaison man is thoroughly familiar with operating conditions in his division, explains these to other divisions with which he is in close contact, and at the same time reports their conditions back to his own unit. In large business concerns with widely scattered headquarters, offices, plants and branches, a liaison man's usefulness and appropriateness can at times be justified.

These liaison men do not have authority to commit their operating divisions, and their use should never be considered a substitute for more direct means of securing coordination. This device was extensively used during World War II when the position of coordinator or expediter or liaison officer was created to assure coordination between various departments, suppliers, resources, subcontractors, and so on. No doubt, this was appropriate and filled a need in times of war or emergency, and such measures could also be advisable as a temporary relief in any management situation. However, if there is a constant need for expediters in an organization under normal conditions, then it becomes necessary to check into the organizational set-up and into the manner in which managerial functions are performed. The chances are that something remains to be desired in reference to management and/or the organization. There should not be any need for expediters or specialists who do nothing but coordinate.

External Coordination

In addition to the need for internal coordination there also exists the need for outside coordination, coordination, with factors external to the enterprise. There are a number of external factors, such as changes in the competitive situation, governmental activities, technological advances, and the interest of the general public, the owners, and the employees, which add to the difficult task of coordination. There must be coordination between the enterprise and other enterprises such as shippers, suppliers and carriers. And coordination should exist between the enterprise and the world economy at large.

It should be pointed out that the manager's knowledge of how to obtain coordination is becoming broader, not only due to the emergence of new tools and devices, but also due to his better and more thorough understanding of effectively performing the five managerial functions. The manager's ever-increasing problems of coordination can only be offset by an ever-increasing knowledge of how to perform his managerial skills.

12

Office Management

Office is to a business what the main spring is to a watch. Prof Donald Cousins says that "the office of successful business organization must be the brain of the whole concern." Stephenson describes the office "as that of a business enterprise which is devoted to the direction and co-ordination of its various activities." Thus a office is the nucleus of the varied activities of the enterprise. It is the office that plans for business are chalked out, the business policies are executed and the records of the business transactions are kept. "It is the seat" says Stephenson, "not only of the administrative activities which determine the policy of whole business, but also of the principal executive activities whereby that policy is carried into effect." Hence office is the centre of administration and execution of business policies.

Importance of office for modern business, trade and industries is summarised as follows:

(a) Office is the Concrete Proof of the Existence of an Enterprise. Office and its branches are identified with the business they transact. In case of banking and insurance enterprises office is "the only visible embodiment of the business which is carried on."

(b) It is a Place where Plans for the Business are prepared and Policies are framed. A trading concern has to plan ahead its

purchases, sales, campaigns, financial resources, etc., keeping in mind the trends and tendencies in the markets. Specialised personnel are appointed to work out the plans. They prepare appropriate plans for the guidance of executive authorities in the office. On the basis of the plans, the policies are framed by the administrative heads of the office. In the words of Stephenson, "on the selling side, plans are made for advertising campaigns, for opening up new territories by salesmen and for undertaking market research. On the side of financial administration, measures must be taken to control the capital resources of the concern to utilise them in the most productive manner. These activities of the office are fundamental to the prosperity of the business."

(c) It is through office that the Administrative Policies of the Business are executed. Different departments are set up to put into effect the policies decided earlier. Office is constituted by the operative group of executive personnel whose function is to implement the business plans and policies laid down by the higher administrative authorities. It can, therefore, be called the medium of management. Progress and prosperity of a business enterprise is preconditioned by effective managerial control. This managerial control is exercised through office organization.

(d) Correspondence which is a Constructive Force in Modern Business is one of the Main Functions of a Commercial Office. Incoming letters are handled through the medium of office. Incoming letters are forwarded to the concerned departments for prompt and suitable replies. Outgoing letters in a business concern are described as the "Couriers of Commerce" and the "alpha and omega" of business. Hence, there should be efficient arrangement for conducting correspondence with customers. In the words of Stephenson, "letters which are sent out are the silent ambassadors of the business." Commercial office acts like the clearing house of correspondence. Correspondence department in the office ensures prompt attention to the incoming letters and timely despatch of appropriate letters to outsiders.

(e) Office is a storehouse of Records. Incoming letters are filed for future reference. Similarly copies of outgoing letters are filed for the purpose of records. Trading Returns, Financial Records, Reports and other statistical materials are also filed for ready reference. Commercial office thus preserves these records intact and makes them available as and when required.

Thus, a modern office is the fountain-head of planning, control, coordination, communication and records.

Office Organization

The location, the premises, the layout and the equipment of the office determine and display the grace underlying the whole organization.

Essentials of an Efficient Office Organization

(1) Location: The central parts of a city or a town are ideal sites for locating the offices. The site must be so located that it is easily accessible to the customers and others. Proximity to banks, post offices, railway stations, bus terminus, government offices, etc. should be taken into account while locating an office on a particular site. The area in which it is located should be such as would be frequently visited by the buyers. It is rather false economy to established the office on some cheap site in an out-of-the-way locality.

(2) Premises of the office: Office should be housed in spacious premises with cheerful surroundings. The office building must be large enough to meet the requirements of the business and there should be also sufficient scope for possible extensions as and when necessary.

The office building must be well-ventilated. Light, ventilation and sanitation are important matters to be attended to in office organization. Adequate natural light and air should be streaming into the building through windows and ventilators. Wherever and whenever necessary, there should be provision for artificial lighting. Electric lights are in most common use in modern offices. Big commercial undertakings have air conditioned offices which are most pleasant to the staff working there.

Poorly-ventilated and unclear office building and premises are repulsive to the staff as well as visitors. Prof. Donald Cousins points out that proper ventilation and sanitation in offices have an important bearing on efficient organization and rapid transaction of work.

(3) Lay-out: Various departments in the office should be systematically arranged in order to ensure quick work and more

effective supervision and control. Scientific layout of the office departments facilities most economical working. Well-designed and elegantly arranged departments create lasting impression on the visitors and boost the morale of workers in the office. As Prof. Cousins says, "a well-arranged, well-kept office is a great asset on account of the favourable impression it produces."

General layout of the office premises should be highly attractive. Inner layout also should be such that it has good effect on the customers and other visitors. Layout has an advertising value.

The various departments of the office should be arranged in proper contiguity. The purchases and sales, warehousing, despatching and advertising departments should be adjoining one another. The Cash and Accounts department should be adjacent to each other. But the Cash Department should have separate room well marked out from other departments. The cashier's room should be well fortified to prevent any mishaps. Correspondence and Filling departments should be arranged in close contiguity. The chambers (rooms) of Managing Director, General Manager and Secretary should be also within reasonable proximity. In addition to these departmental rooms the modern offices should have separate provision for Waiting and Reception Rooms, Telephone Cabin, Lavatory and Dressing Rooms, Canteen and Recreation Halls.

Office rooms of Managing Director and the General Manager in particular should be tastefully and artistically decorated.

Convenience, utility, and principles of taste and art are the criteria of scientific layout of office.

(4) Furniture: All the office rooms should be well-furnished. Adequate tables, chairs, cupboards, racks, etc., should be provided in each department according to its requirements. Suitable furniture has much to do with the efficiency of the office staff. Furniture of appropriate size and good workmanship should be supplied to the staff so that they can work with ease and comfort. The clerical tables should not be arranged face to face, so that gossip among the clerks while on duty can be avoided. Furniture of superior quality should be placed in the rooms of top officers like Managing Director, General Manager, etc. The furniture in the Reception Hall also should be elegant and of superior quality.

(5) Stationery and equipment: Stationery used in the office

should be of standard quality. The hightone stationery produces favourable impression. Catalogues, Price Lists, Invoice, Letter-heads, Envelopes, etc., should be of suitable size and the paper used in preparing them should be of superior quality. Papers of different colours are also used for distinguishing different categories of correspondence. Ink, type-ribbons, files, folders, diaries, paper-weights, etc., should also be of good variety. "The quality of stationery", says Thomas Evelyn, "is of much ,more consequence than is generally recognised, for, if it is unduly cheap and poor in appearance, a bad impression is given to customers." Every commercial office now-a-days has modern equipment depending upon the nature and scale of business. Typewriters, telephone, filing cabinets, are mostly used in many offices. In addition, labour saving devices like comptometres, copying machines, dictaphones, cheque and address writing machines, etc. are employed in offices of large undertakings in order to enhance their working efficiency.

(6) *Office staff:* Appointment of office personnel is the most significant aspect of office organization. Various departments on the office should be adequately staffed to ensure smooth business, operations. Office staff should be well-qualified and experienced. There should be provision for giving training to fresh recruits so that they will be able to handle their respective jobs with confidence and competence. Pay and other conditions for the staff should be fair and reasonable. There should be recognition for efficient workers. Contented staff is usually and surely a sound asset of the firm. Staff should be provided with amenities for their recreation, viz., sports, entertainments etc.

(7) *Functional division of work:* The main principles in allocation of office work are specialization, correlation, and business connection. Functions are allocated to different persons according to their suitability. Different activities concerned with the administration of the business are grouped together under a department. Efforts are also made to coordinate the work of several departments. The work of control and coordination is vested in the top authorities like Board of directors, General Manager, Secretary, etc.

Functional division of work ensures the benefits of specialization. It would also be possible to define and fix responsibilities on individuals with reference to a particular work.

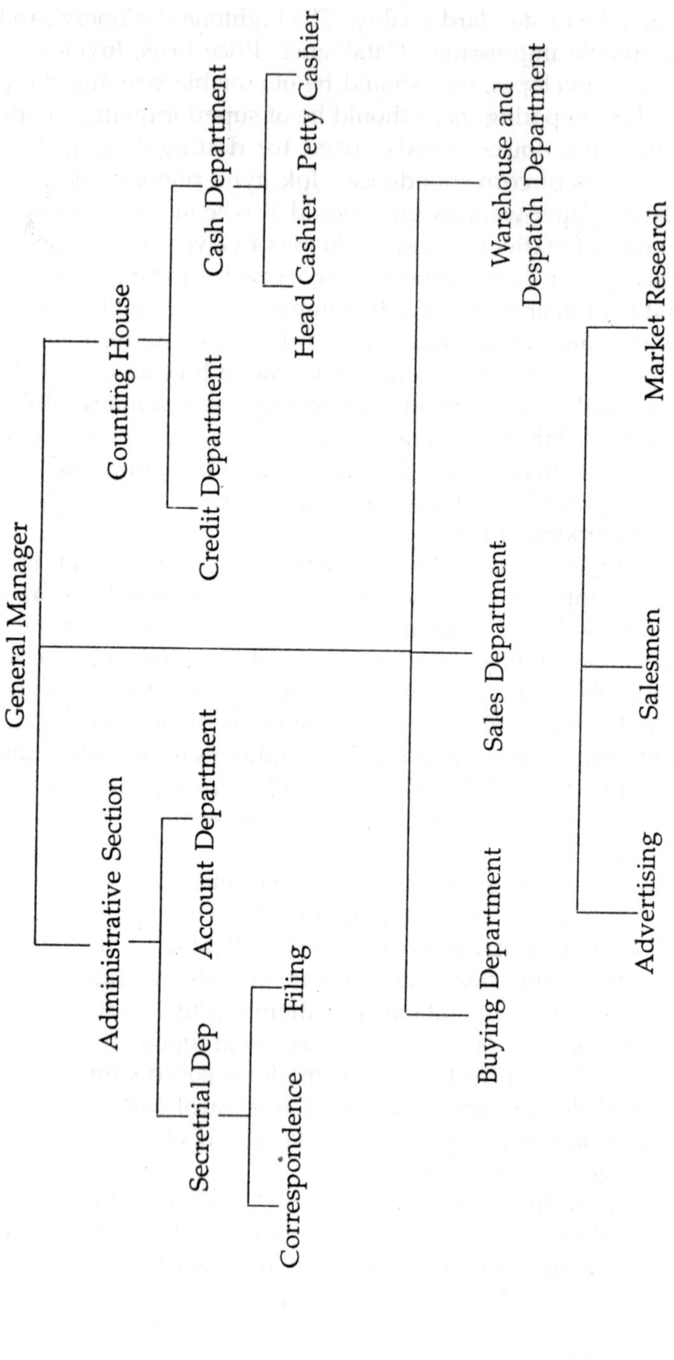
General Manager
Administrative Section
Counting House
Sales Department
Account Department
Secretrial Dep
Filing
Correspondence
Credit Department
Cash Department
Head Cashier
Petty Cashier
Buying Department
Warehouse and Despatch Department
Advertising
Salesmen
Market Research

Such clear cut division of duties among different individuals would lead to greater diligence in their work. They may show independence, initiative and push in their work.

Organization of the office of a trading concern based on functional division is illustrated by the following chart:

Note: Sometimes Credit and Warehousing Departments are organized as sub-department of the sales organization. The work of some of these departments are briefly discussed here.

Departments of Commercial Office

Following are the main departments in a commercial office of a typical trading concern:

- *(a)* Purchases Department.
- *(b)* Sales Department.
- *(c)* Cash Department.
- *(d)* Accounts Department.
- *(e)* Correspondence Department.
- *(f)* Filling Department.

Purchases Department

Successful selling depends upon careful purchasing. Buying of goods is a delicate task. Therefore, expert buyers are appointed to make judicious selection of goods required for the business. Buying department calls for requisitions from other departments. Orders for the goods requisitioned by different departments are placed with established suppliers after full inquiries. Manager of the Sales Department informs the Purchases Manager to procure such type of goods as are likely to command more demand in the market. Accordingly the Purchases Manager calls for quotations or tenders from different suppliers and places orders with those who offer most favourable terms.

Functions of Purchases Department

(a) Buying right type of goods. The Purchases Department has to see that the goods bought are to standard qualities laid

down in the Sales Manager's requisition. In a trading concern goods are bought for sale. Hence, purchases should be made keeping in mind the saleability of the goods within a short time. Size, variety, colour, brand and other properties of goods should be taken into account while making an order for purchases.

(b) Buying required goods in adequate quantities at the right time. Purchases department should be always in touch with the markets and must study the relative prices, quality and availability of different types of goods. Quotations and samples of different grades of goods should be obtained so as to be able to place orders at the required time. It should endeavours to keep a steady flow of supply.

(c) Buying accurate type of goods in favourable markets. The Purchases Department should buy goods on most economical terms. Quality, however, must be sacrifices in the name of economy.

(d) Keeping the records of all the purchases made from time to time. The requisition notes, the purchase orders, invoices—all should be kept on record so that goods received as per order may be compared with them. Full particulars should be entered in Stock sheet and then passed on to the Warehousing Department.

Sales Department

Importance: Sales Department is the most important department in a commercial organization. The efficiency of a business firm is primarily measured by the volume of sales turned out during a given period. Sales or turnover of goods is the barometer of business profits and reputation. Goods are produced or purchased in anticipation of demand. Hence, the Sales Department has to create demand for goods in order to clear the stock within a short time. It is the job of the Sales Department to promote the 'sales and maintain and further increase the turnover. It is the embodiment of all the varied activities and efforts undertaken to boost the sale of goods in question.

Functions of the Sales Department

The main functions of the Sales Department are as given below:

- *(a)* to inquire into the needs, tastes and buying habits of different classes of consumers in the market;
- *(b)* to measure the strength of the competitors in a particular line of business;
- *(c)* to look out for new and profitable markets;
- *(d)* to organize advertisement campaigns and other sales promotion activities in order to create, maintain—and extend the demand for goods;
- *(e)* to collect orders from customers directly or through salesmen or agents;
- *(f)* to execute orders by timely despatch of well-packed goods;
- *(g)* to determine the most appropriate and economical method of selling goods;
- *(h)* to frame policies relating to price, credit and discount; and
- *(i)* to arrange for after sale service and render other services to customers for gaining there goodwill.

Sub-Departments of Sales Department

To perform the above-mentioned functions more effectively, sales department is divided into following sub-departments:

- *(i)* Sales Personnel—consisting of counter salesmen and travelling salesmen.
- *(ii)* Market Research.
- *(iii)* Advertisement.
- *(iv)* Sales promotion and after-sale service.
- *(v)* Warehousing, Packing and Despatching.
- *(vi)* Credit and Collection.

Note : Credit and Collection and Warehousing are sometimes organized as separate departments.

The Sales Manager Communicates his requirements of goods to the Purchases Department. Findings of the 'Market Research' conducted by his department forms the basis of his requisition. Requisitioned goods after they are received, are stored in the warehouse at one central place or in warehouses at different convenient centres to facilitate quick handling of orders. He appoints salesmen and allocates sales-territories to them to canvas business in their respective territories. Simultaneously, advertisements are made through different media to win over customers. Quotations in the form of price-lists, catalogues, brochures, etc., are sent to the prospective buyers in expectation orders from them.

Sales Manager, thus, collect orders directly or through salesmen. These orders are executed in time. Applications for credit accommodation, if any, from the customers are considered and may be sanctioned on the advice of the Credit Manager. Goods are then packed and forwarded to the customers. The amount due from customers is collected as per agreement by the Credit and Collection Manager or by the Counting House.

Management of Business Correspondence

Correspondence is essential for an effective system of filing. Whatever be the method of filing, all the materials to be filed are first to be divided into suitable categories to facilitate ready and accurate reference. Invoices, vouchers, receipts, letters, legal documents, etc., are to be analytically classified so that they are readily accessible whenever required for reference in future. The papers and documents so classified are to be filed separately. "No filing system", says Thomas Evelyn, "can possibly be of much use unless it is accompanied by effective method of classification."

Methods of Classification

Following are the main methods of classification:

(1) Alphabetical Method;
(2) Numerical Method;
(3) Alphabetical-Numerical Method;
(4) Geographical Method,
(5) Subject Method.

Alphabetical Method: In this method letters and records are classified and arranged in alphabetical order. It is the most suitable system of filing inward and outward letters. In case of inward letters, surnames of the senders and in case of outward letters, surnames of addresses are taken into consideration. There is a separate file for the contents beginning with each alphabet. For example, letters received from individuals or firms whose name begin with alphabet 'A' are filed in the folders, boxes, binders marked with 'A'. Suppose letters from following business firms are received:

(i) Automatic Electric Private Limited; *(ii)* Bharat Industrial Cooperatives; *(iii)* Ideal Book Service; and *(iv)* Kakade M.G. and Bros.

Letters sent by these firms are filed underseparate files marked with A, B, I and K respectively. If two or more names begin with the same alphabet, the second alphabets in the names are taken into consideration for classification. For example, if there are two letters—one from Ideal Book Service and another from International Book Depot, then the letter from the former is put first and that from the letter is placed next (I-d; I-n). If the surnames of individuals are the same, the alphabets of their proper names will be the basis of classifications.

When the numbers of correspondents is large, a plan of forty guide cards is followed according to "forty division system" —A, BA, BE, etc. Letters are classified according to this order and put into separate folders bearing on their tops the characters BA, BE, etc. In case of letters received from casual and occasional correspondents, a miscellaneous folder is kept at the back of the drawer and its contents are arranged alphabetically. If letters are being regularly received from a customer, a separate folder may be provided for all such letters and the folder is put into the drawer in the correct position according to the names of the customers.

This system is very simple. Moreover, there is no need to compile separate index since the guide cards or the labels themselves serve the purpose.

Numerical method: Under the numerical method each correspondent is given a number and that number is shown on all his correspondence. The correspondence pertaining to him is filed in a separate folder which bears that particular number on its tab. Folders with their guide cards tabbed with numbers are arranged in numerical order in the drawers.

This system is particularly useful in filing invoices. Entries of purchases and sales in their respective journals bear reference to the numbers of invoices relating to each transaction. These invoices are later filed even on a horizontal file in their numerical order. This system is also used in classifying numerous letters received by a firm having a large number of customers.

However, this system is of any use only if a comprehensive index is separately prepared, because it is not possible for any filing clerk to remember correctly the number of every invoice or customer. An index showing the particulars relating to a number has to be compiled. This is absolutely essential both for correct filing and quick reference. Small index cards containing useful information about a customer are prepared and stored in separate drawers to facilitate reference to their files. The index card bears prominently the number allotted to each file.

This system is simple and flexible and avoids the possible confusion that may be caused when many correspondents have the same name. The index card system furnishes some useful statistical information about the number of customers, the number of letters written to them or received from them, the limit of credit, if any , granted to them, etc. It serves the purposes of reference and information.

"This system", says Stephenson, "ensures the greatest accuracy and is virtual necessity where the subject matter requires much cross reference. "The only possible objection to this system is that much labour has to be put in to prepare the card index without which reference to the file is not practicable. The number must first be ascertained from the card and then the reference to the main file can be made. Both filing and finding the file take much time and involves much labour. But as Professor Donald Cousins points out, the card index may be used to record such information (relating to a firm or a subject) as may be worth more than the labour spent in compiling it.

Alphabetical-numerical method: Under this system, papers are classified broadly into alphabetical sections and then numbers are allotted to different documents for the purpose of their sub-classification. Suppose a letter is written to Mysore Sandal Soap Factory. It is first classified into M.Y. category and then given a number, say 15. It follows, therefore, that the letter can be found in the 15th folder of "M-y" section. This method is thus a combination or synthesis of the first two methods. This is widely used for filing and finding specimen signatures of the clients and depositors of a bank. Even in libraries books are first categorised into alphabetical sections and then each of them in that section is given serial number. The cupboard bears the label of alphabet and serial number of foods stored in it. This facilitates very quick reference. This system does not require a separate card index arrangement. It avoids the confusion of names of the same alphabet common in alphabetical classification. At the same time it does not necessitate preparation of a separate index. In special advantage is that it has the exactness of the numerical system.

Geographical method: Under this method all correspondence relating to a particular area is clubbed together. Papers belonging to any geographical territory are grouped first and then are re-arranged according to numerical or alphabetical order. A separate file is maintained to contain letters and other records pertaining to each geographical division. The method is, therefore, just a modification of the system discussed earlier. Initial classification, however, is geographically oriented. A trading concern which has a net-work of branches at different places would file its correspondence with the branches on the basis of geographical division. This geographical classification may refer to a state, district or a city. Suppose a Bombay firm has branches at Poona, Hubli, Banglore, Kolhapur and Sholapur. Papers pertaining to Hubli and Bangalore branches are filed separately since these cities are in the state of Mysore, while papers relating to Poona, Kolhapur and Sholapur are classified under the head 'Maharashtra'. A firm having branches in other countries may similarly classify its correspondence and other records country-wise.

The system is particularly helpful for exploring the commercial possibilities in different areas and facilities areawise comparison. Efforts of salesmen working in different territories can be evaluated easily by means of this classification. This system is particularly used in multiple-shop or chain store system and mostly in all concerns having business outside its head office. This is meant for a business where "territorial grouping is of leading importance."

The subject method: Under this method papers are classified into separate categories on the basis of the subject to which they refer. A firm may have an Order File or an Invoice File, or a Salary File. Papers dealing with a particular subject are put together and then re-arranged alphabetically or numerically. Instead of the names of the correspondents, subjects are mentioned on the guide cards or the file labels in alphabetical order. Numerical method also may be used to provide for sub-divisions of the subject or for individual correspondence coming under the subject. This method is useful "where the subject is of more importance than the name of the correspondent." This method is most commonly used in libraries. Books are classified into subjects like Accountancy, Economics, Law, Geography, History, Essay, Commercial Correspondence etc. Then they are placed under the respective subjects in alphabetical or numerical order.

When negotiations are proceeding over a particular matter, this system is most suitable. The entire correspondence relating to that matter (subject) is found in one file and hence its classification is useful for reference. A perusal of the whole file maintained on the basis of the subject gives the whole idea of the matter which would be great help in properly pursuing that matter.

Indexing

When various files are maintained for different purposes, indexing is essential to find out the particular file needed for reference. In a large firm with wide assortment of records relating to numerous transactions, use of index is inevitable to trace any file containing the specific information which is required for reference. One of the main aims of filing is "accessibility" to records. Indexing helps in enhancing the utility of the filing system from the standpoint of easy and ready accessibility.

An index is a ready guide to locate the required file. It is compiled in order to single out any information from files, books or ledgers. For example, an index is attached to a ledger. Accounts in the names of different customers are opened on different pages of the ledger. Index shows in alphabetical order on what folio of the ledger a customer's accounts appears. Indexes of different types are likewise prepared to find out the letters or records relating to a particular customer or subjects.

Types of Indexing

Indexes are mainly of the following types:

(i) Book Index *(ii)* Vowel Index, and *(iii)* Card Index.

(i) *Book index:* Generally index is in the form of a book. This is also known as Ordinary Index. Each page of the books is supermarket with a letter of the alphabet. Names beginning with that initial letter are listed on the corresponding page. Names beginning with initial letter—A would be written on the page or pages marked A, those with B on pages headed by B and so on. The folio of the ledger, the number and category of file or the number of folder relating to that name would be shown horizontally against the name. In fact, the index book is divided into alphabetical sections. Each section has the leaves cut away at the side so that initial letters of all the sections are visible at a galance.

(ii) *Vowel index:* This is an improvement upon the ordinary index system. In a big firm list of customers would be very long. It would, therefore, take considerable time to find out the name under reference. In order to facilitate quick reference book index is modified by vowel classification. The books is as usual, divided into sections based on the initial letter. Each initial-lettered section is further classified into six-sub-sections according to the five vowels A, E, I, O, U and Y. The page where an entry is to be made is determined first by the initial letter and then by the vowel or Y, occurring after the initial letter. For example, the name "Canara Bank" would be entered under the initial sections of C and in the vowel sub-section A, the name "Central Bank" would appear under the vowel sub-section E in the initial section C. This is usually used in big firms which have to record many names.

(iii) *Card index:* The Card Index is a modern innovation which has been found to be most convenient and useful for the ready tracing of documents.

Under this method, references are not entered into books.

They are shown on cards. Cards are made of uniform size and are often coloured differently to distinguish the purpose in view. The usual size of the card is above 5" x 3". These cards contain the names and other particulars to be indexed. They also bear number of file where those names and particulars can be found. These names or subject cards are placed in drawers or boxes of suitable dimensions. These drawers or boxes are divided into alphabetical sections by means of smaller guide cards. Index cards are placed between these guide cards in dictionary order (strictly alphabetical sequence). Suppose it become necessary to refer to some correspondence from a firm called "West Coast Papers Mills Ltd". We have to first pick up the card in the index drawers under the letters. "W-e" in the section indicated by the guide card "W". The name index card contains the reference to the file number of the "West Coast Paper Mills Ltd". That file is later found out from the filing cabinets.

Index cards can be used for various purposes. They are commonly used in libraries to enable prompt issue of books from different sections. They are also used to show the name, address, credit terms, order placed, etc., of each customer. Index cards for indicating the stock position of different goods are also prepared. Particulars of each employee are also shown through the card system.

Advantages of Card Index System:

(i) The card index system ensures quick and accurate reference to files. The card index gives the file or the folder number where the required material is placed. Hence reference to such file would be easier.

(ii) New cards may be inserted whenever any fresh matter is required to be indexed. Thus, this is "flexible and adoptable" method.

(iii) The arrangement of cards can be easily altered in any manner whenever felt desirable. Alteration does not cause dislocation of the system.

(iv) Old and out-of-date material may be removed by removing the relevant cards.

(v) Card index is capable of expansion. "It never gets full", because new names may be added without disturbing the dictionary order.

(vi) As explained earlier, card index can be used for different purposes, viz,. recording particulars of customers, employees, stock quotations and other documents. Specimen signatures of depositors in a bank are also indexed on card system.

13

Management of Accounts Department

The Accounts Department is like a guide to other departments. Transactions relating to purchases, sales and cash are recorded in the different sets of account books. Purchases are noted in purchases Journal, and Sales Journal is used to record the sales. Cash receipts and payments are entered in the Cash Book. Entries in these books are then posted to the Ledger under different account heads. Maintenance of accounts help in ascertaining the financial position of the business enterprise.

Accounts disclose the profit or losses, indicate the amount payable to others as well as the amount due from others and reveal the state of assets and liabilities of the enterprise.

The Accounts Department is headed by a Chief Accountant. Under his guidance and control, entries of different transactions relating to the business are made in the relevant books of accounts. As Prof. Donald Cousins says, "the Accountant utmost importance and upon the accuracy and lucidity of the work of his department much depends." It is the paramount duty of the accounts department to see that all the accounts are kept up-to-date, so that the most recent information on all details of the business is at hand for the manager's information.

The accounts department maintains following main types

of books of account:

(a) Journal
(b) Subsidiary Journals
(c) Ledger
(d) Cash Book
(e) Petty Cash Book

Books of accounts are periodically balanced and a Trial Balance is prepared to verify the arithmetical accuracy of the accounts kept. Towards the end of the year final accounts are compiled. These include Trading Account showing the Gross Profit, the Profit and Loss Account showing the Net Profit, and the Balance Sheet showing the state of Liabilities and the Assets as at the end of the year.

Cash Department

Cash Department in a commercial office is invested with great responsibility. It is concerned with the receipts and payments of cash. It functions under the charge of an officer known as Cashier or Treasurer who regulates the cash transactions. In a big concern this department is headed by Chief Cashier assisted by subordinate officers and clerks in separate charge of receipts and payments. For handling minor payments a Petty Cash Clerk is also appointed on the staff of this department.

Functions of the Cash Department

Important functions of the Cash Department are as follows:

(a) Acknowledgement of remittances in cash or through cheques from customers. Official receipts are issued for the amount received.
(b) Amount received in cash or through cheque is paid into the bank from day to day.
(c) Cash receipts are entered into the Cash Book.
(d) Payments are also made through this department either in cash or by cheques under proper authority. All payments are backed by corresponding vouchers approved by the sanctioning authorities.
(e) Payments are recorded in the Cash Book on the basis of

related vouchers.

(*f*) Vouchers and counterfoils of receipts are separately filed to facilitate verification.

(*g*) Cash Balance on hand and at Bank are verified from time to time. A Bank Reconciliation Statement is prepared at least in a month.

Cashiers are not usually permitted to record entries or make postings in any book of accounts other than the Cash Book. Fidelity bonds are also taken from Cashiers handling large sums of money. This is as a precaution against possibilities of fraud and misappropriation.

Correspondence Department

Importance. Correspondence holds the key to business expansion. Correspondence is communication with outsiders by letters with a view to building up business. Reputation of business undertraining depends in no small measure both upon the quality of the letters which are sent out and upon the way in which correspondence is dealt with. Efficient organization of the Correspondence Department is, therefore, essential to successful business.

Correspondence work is entrusted to the charge of a competent officer who is generally known as the Secretary. The department is divided into branches – one for handling inward correspondence and other for expediting the drafting and despatch of letters addressed to outsiders. Every office follows a particular line of routine to deal with the matters of business correspondence. A brief description of the routine usually followed in a modern office is discussed here.

Inward Correspondence

The starting point of the correspondence work is the incoming letters. Incoming letters may pertain to orders, remittance, complaints from customers or may be relating to offers, quotations, invoices etc., form the suppliers. Prompt handling of such letters is essential from the standpoint of business goodwill. In the words of Thomas Evelyn, "the organization of inward correspondence is very important, for on this depends the prompt despatch of orders, the safe handling of remittances, adequate attention of complaints, and in general, smooth running of the business as a whole."

Correspondence Department of the office, therefore, has to observe the following routine:

(i) *Receipt of letters:* A small businessman receives his letters from the postman on his usual delivery rounds. A large business undertaking has a numbered Post Box at the post office. Letters addressed to the firm are all put into the numbered box from which they are collected once or twice a day by the mail staff of the office. Members of the staff who are expected to open the letters are usually required to be present in the office earlier in the morning than the other staff so that the day's work in other departments may not be delayed.

(ii) *Opening the mail:* The concerned clerks open the letters and sort them in the presence of responsible official. Envelopes are carefully opened and their contents are safely taken out. Enclosures are particularly verified with the details specified at the foot of the letters. Any discrepancy has to be reported to the authorities for cheques, bills of exchange, etc., are specially checked with the amount indicated in the letters.

(iii) *Stamping or marking the letters:* As soon as letters are opened, they are stamped or otherwise marked with the date and time of their receipt. Below is a specimen of a rubber stamp affixed on incoming letters:

Ashoka Traders Ltd.
No.....................512 S
Recd..................10.9.1977, 10.30 a.m.
Ackd..................
Ansd..................

The stamp indicates the serial number of the letter, the date and the time at which the letter is received. Sometimes a specific alphabet may be used to identify the letters with any particular department. For example, the character "S" may be used to denote sales. The stamp also contains the space lines to be filled up when the receipt of letter is acknowledged and when reply to it is sent. This stamping or marking on the letter is intended to fix "responsibility for any delay which may occur in replying to it."

(iv) *Record of letters received:* Brief particulars of each incoming letter are then entered into an Inward Letter Book (or Letters Received Book). This book shows the date of receipt, serial number, name of the sender, a brief note of the subject matter, the department to whom the letter is forwarded and the date and nature of reply. We give below a specimen of the Letters Received Book.

Letters received Book

SARITA TRADERS LIMITED

Date	*Reference No.*	*Name of the sender*	*Nature of Communi- cation*	*To whom referred*	*Date of reply*

This register is periodically checked by the Secretary.

Distribution of Letters

Incoming letters have to be promptly forwarded to the concerned departments for timely replies. As soon as letters are stamped and their record is made in the Letters Received Book, they are sorted departmentwise and sent to the concerned departments.

Outward Correspondence

The organization of outward correspondence is of vital significance. Importance of outgoing letters cannot be minimised. Letters should be drafted in impressive language and couched in courteous style. The object of correspondence is expansion of business and creation of goodwill. Both these depend upon the favourable impact caused by letters written to the customers. Therefore, replies to customers' letters and any other communications to the outsiders have to be drafted by qualified clerks under the supervision of competent officials. Clerks prepare rough draft to letters to be written and place them before the departmental authorities for their approval. The approved copies of all the letters are then sent to typists. Typed copies alongwith the enclosures, if any, are again brought before the departmental executives for their signature. Important letters are sometimes dictated by the higher officers themselves. Stenographers take these letters in shorthand and the full text is later sent to the typist.

Types of Outgoing Letters

Usually outgoing business letters are of following types:

(a) Sales letters describing the selling points of the goods and inducing the prospective buyers to purchase them.

(b) Circular letters containing some information useful to customers, viz., reduction or increase in prices, change of business address, appointment or removal of agents, etc.

(c) Letters of quotations enclosing price lists and catalogues in reply to customers' inquiries.

(d) Letters advising execution of customers' orders.

(e) Adjustment letters in replay to letters of complaint for customers.

(f) Letters requesting customers to pay their dues.

Stereotyped Letters

Letters sending quotations, statement of accounts, etc., are usually stereotyped. Standard froms are used for these purposes. They are usually printed or cyclostyled before hand and they are sent to the concerned customers after "matching in" their names and addresses. The use of form paragraphs' is also made in sending routine replies. Set paragraphs are drafted to cover regular matters of routine and each incoming letter is dealt with by making number of paragraphs to be sent in reply to the customers' inquiries.

Correspondence in Suspense

Correspondence in any matter which remains incomplete is to be kept separately in a 'Suspense File'. Reminders or any other communications relating to that subject are also to be kept in the

Suspense File only.

If a particular case needs reference to more than one department, correspondence relating to that case is circulated to all the concerned departments each of which attaches to it its own Reply Slip. All the reply slips so collected are compiled in the form of a single letter.

Suspense file facilitates "Follow up" in case of incomplete correspondence.

Completed correspondence. Completed correspondence with all the copies of replies is sent to the Filing Department for filing and record.

Despatch of Correspondence

After letters are typed and signed by the concerned authorities, they are sent to the Despatch Clerks for forwarding them to the respective address. The Despatch Clerks have to perform the following functions:

(i) Folding of letters neatly and inserting them in the envelopes.

(ii) If the letter has any enclosures like cheques, invoice, catalogue, etc., they have to be checked and numbered by adhesive labels. Despatch clerks have to see that all these enclosures are also inserted alongwith the letters in the envelopes.

(iii) Envelopes are then to be closed and sealed, gumming and sealing machines are used for the purpose in big modern offices.

(iv) After envelopes are sealed, they are addressed clearly. The despatch clerk sees the inside address typed on the letter and writes the same on the envelope. The name of the firm, the street name and number, post box number, if any, name of the town and the State constitute correct address. Complete address should be put on the envelope to ensure quick delivery and prevent wrong delivery.

Window envelopes are now in common use. Most of the letters already contain the address of the firms or persons to whom they are being sent. These letters are so folded that the addresses of the recipients typed on the letters are visible through the transparent window envelopes. This saves time taken in writing the addresses on the envelopes. Confidential letters are, however, usually sent in closed envelopes with complete addresses typed thereon.

(v) Then postal stamps are affixed on the envelopes. Envelopes alongwith their contents are weighed in order to calculate the total amount of stamps required for sending them through post. Letters which are to be sent by registered post or by express kept separately from ordinary mail and necessary additional stamps are affixed on such envelopes as per postal regulations. In big concerns instead of affixing adhesive stamps on the letter covers, franking machines are used to make a red printed impression on the envelopes. Franking is subject to the control of the local post office.

(vi) *Record of outgoing letters.* Before sending letters to the post office, particulars of each letter are entered in the Post Book or the Outward Register. This post book shows the value of stamps supplied to the Despatch Clerk, the date and the number of letters posted, the names and places of addresses, the value of postal stamps affixed to each letter and the signature of the person despatching the letters.

We give below a specimen of the Post Book (Outward Register):

Stamp in hand		*Date*	*No.*	*Name & Place of addresses*	*Postage affixed*		*Signature of Despatch Clerk*
Rs.	*P.*				*Rs.*	*P.*	

Post Book serves following objects:

(a) It acts as a check on the despatch clerk in respect of the stamps used. The despatch clerk is required by the Cash Department to produce this book everyday for verification of the purchase and use of postal stamps. This prevents possible misuse of postal stamps by the despatch clerks.

(b) It acts as a record of letters written to different individuals and firms in the course of business. "As a record of letters posted, the Post Book is referred to when doubt arises as to whether a particular letter was sent or not."

(vii) After the entry is the Post Book, letters to be sent to outside places are put into post bag.

(viii) Letters meant for local delivery are noted in the Peon Delivery Book. The peon delivers the letters to the local addresses and gets their signatures as a proof of having received the letters in the relevant columns of the Peon Book.

Specimen of a Peon Book

Date	*Name & Locality*	*Nature of Communication*	*Peon's Name*	*Recipient's Signature*

Filing Department

Letters received and also the copies of replies thereto and the copy of every letter sent out are then sent to the Filing Department to be preserved in files.

METHODS OF FILING

Meaning and Aims of Filing

Filing means the systematic classification of records and their safe preservation. It is the storing of letters, papers and documents so that they can be readily found when required.

It aims is "to provide a mechanism whereby business record may be stored so as to be readily available when required." Thus "by filing we mean *(a)* the putting away of letters and other documents to preserve them from dirt and damage, and *(b)* the arranging of them according to some plan so that any letter or document can afterwards be laid hold of quickly should it be wanted."

Aims of filing include: *(i)* preservation of records in safe position, *(ii)* storing the records, and *(iii)* systematic arrangement of records to facilitate reference.

Importance of Filing

As indicated in the preceding chapter, one of the important functions of a modern commercial office is preservation of records. Records are to be preserved to enable their use for reference in the course of business administration. The nature, the range and the pattern of modern business have been such the memory alone cannot help in the successful management of any business firm. A sale transaction for example, passes through different phases before it culminates into a bargain, viz., enquiries, quotations, order, settlement of terms, etc. Accurate, records of all these stages have to be kept to follow-up the transaction sometime it becomes necessary to resort to past records to argue a case or settle a dispute. Business is a continuous process and hence the business policies have to be shaped out not only according to current trends but also on the basis of past experience. In that case reference to previous records becomes essential. Moreover, numerous letters are written to customers in reply to their letters. Records of incoming and out-going correspondence have to be kept for ready reference. Thus, it is necessary to preserve records of enquiries, quotations, orders, invoices, statements of accounts, vouchers, receipts, contractual documents and legal deeds etc., in a well-arrange form. Preservation of the different types of records would be possible if there is an efficient system of filing.

Organization of Filing Department

Filing Department should be organised with efficient staff and necessary equipment. It is headed by the Chief Record and Filing Officer who should be an expert and experienced in the technique of filing. Other personnel in the department should also be capable of classifying the records correctly and filing them in perfect order. The department should be supplied with standard equipment and materials cabinets, drawers, folders, index cards, etc.

Filing Department may be organized in two ways:

(a) Under Centralised System

(b) Under Departmentalised System.

Under centralised system, files relating to all correspondence of the office are preserved and accommodated at one central place which may be called Filing Room or Record Room. It is entrusted to the charge of a senior officer.

Under Departmental system, files pertaining to a particular department are maintained in that very department. A separate filing clerk may be appointed in each department to maintain the records and file them. The departmental head is responsible for the files relating to his department.

The centralised system is advantageous in many respects: *(i)* it is effective; *(ii)* it may result in economies of time, money and space; *(iii)* the departmental head is saved from the botheration of maintaining records and he can devote himself to the main tasks in his department.

But the efficiency, reliability and alertness of the personnel would be necessary to work the system effectively.

Essentials of Good Filing System

In addition to the above considerations the organizations of filing system should meet the following requirement:

(i) It should be simple and easily workable.

(ii) It should be suited to the nature and size of the business.

(iii) It should provide for ready accessibility, as ease of reference is quite essential.

(iv) It should provide for complete safety of records from dirt, dust or damage.

(v) It should be inexpensive to operate.

(vi) It should be comprehensive so as to cover every type of records that need to be maintained and referred to.

(vii) It should be capable of further extension.

(viii) It should not be crowded with out-of-date and unnecessary records.

(ix) It should occupy minimum space.

(x) A scientific system of classification of records should be in use depending upon the nature of the records usually maintained in the business.

(xi) It should be such that frequency or inudence of mistakes is the least.

(xii) Files containing important documents and confidential correspondence should be kept under lock and key under the charge of responsible executive officials.

Methods of Filing

Different methods of filing are employed by different commercial concerns depending upon the nature, the size and the scale of their business operations. We can classify the methods of filing under two heads: *(i)* Old methods of filing, and *(ii)* New Methods of filing.

Old Methods of Filing

Old methods of filing include:

(1) Spike File.
(2) Docketing.
(3) Box-File.

(1) Spike file: This is the simplest method of preserving business letters and other records. It is perhaps the most traditional type of filing.

In this device, there is a metal or wooden plate on which a spike is firly fitted. The spike is a thick steel wire resembling a long nail with a sharp projecting point. It stands vertically fixed on a small wooden or steel base. Letters which are intended to be filed are punched through the sharp point of spike. They pile up one above the other on the base plate. Letters are passed through the spike wire as and when they are received and can be said to have been filed otherwise.

This method is usually used by retail traders and other petty shopkeepers and firms receiving very few letters in a week or a month. In other commercial offices also it is used for filing papers which are not so important and which are to be preserved for relatively shorter period.

This type of filing is simple and inexpensive and does not require any elaborate organization. Spike file is just hung on a wall. This system, however, is highly unsuitable for filing the vast and varied correspondence of modern commercial enterprises. It does not ensure safety of records from dirt of damage since there is no protective cover. It does not also facilitate prompt reference to past records. In order to pick out any previous letters required for reference, the whole bunch of subsequent letters has to be taken out and later has to be reinserted. In this process records are likely to be spoiled and mutilated. Hence it is most inconvenient.

(2) *Docketing or pigeon-hole system:* Docketing is also one of the orthodox methods of filing although it is being used in a few commercial offices even today. Its use is most common in Post Offices and Insurance Companies.

This method of filing consists of two steps:

(i) Docketing of letters, and other documents,

(ii) Insertion of docketed papers in the particular pigeon-holes.

(i) A docket is a brief note indicating the contents of the letter invoice or any other document. Letters and other papers to be filed are folded to a uniform size and on the outside of each a brief description of its contents is given. Docket of letters should indicate the name of the parties, their addresses, the date of receipt, the subject referred to, and the date on which reply is sent. The docket for invoice should show the name of the parties, their addresses, the date and the amount of the invoice. The docket thus gives readily a rough idea about the nature of the correspondence and the contents. We give below two specimens of dockets:

DOCKET ON LETTERS	DOCKET ON INVOICES
Name	Name............................
Brief Address...........	Address........................
Date............................	Date................................
Subject........................	Amount
Replied on	

(ii) *Filing the docketed letters:* This method of filing is also called Pigeon-hole method. In this system "a set of pigeon-holes is provided." There is a wooden or steel case consisting of square holes. The case or the shelf is open from one side. Each pigeon-hole bears usually an alphabetical label. But the label may refer to any geographical area, political region or the name of a place.

After the docketing of documents is complete for the day, they are put into their respective pigeon-holes. For example, a letter written by Popular Book Depot is inserted to the pigeon-holes bearing the label 'P'. The pigeon-holes may be cleared at periodical intervals, say a month or a quarter. The documents in each hole are carefully sorted and neatly bundled. Each bundle bears the relevant label. The labelled bundles are then put in boxes on which also labels are affixed.

This system is useful in small commercial offices with limited number of correspondence. But in almost all post offices which have to handle large number of letters, this method is commonly used. Letters are sorted place-wise and put into the pigeon-holes bearing the related place-label. After the sorting of all the letters is over, holes are cleared and letters are put into the mail bags meant for particular places. Even in the office of Insurance Companies, docket system has been found to be convenient. Each policy holder is given a code number and the contract documents and correspondence relating to him may be put into the hole bearing the code label.

But in modern offices which are to expendite large number of correspondence this method becomes cumbersome. It may be a convenient device for sorting letters and other papers, but if is unsuitable for ensuring the safety of records. The whole set of pigeon-hole occupies a fairly large space and it requires much effort and time to docket the documents and then file in the correct holes. The system is also inflexible. In the words of Thomas Evelyn, "this system may be extremely cumbersome in any office dealing with much correspondence."

(3) The box file: In this system, letters and other documents are sorted out alphabetically and arranged in serial order. These are found together in the form of a book according to chronological sequence. This system consists of loose manila sheets which are used to classify the documents according to alphabetical order. An index is provided by marking the alphabets on the sheets. This facilitates quick reference. This system is an improvement over the pigeon-hole system of filing.

New Methods of Filing

Due to the limitations of the old methods, modern commercial offices have adopted improved methods. These are:

(1) Horizontal System. (2) Vertical System.

(1) Horizontal or flat system: Under this system, papers are filed one above the other data-wise. Papers are punched with holders at the side or the top and are placed flat through the mental spikes fitted to the filing receptacle. The filing receptacle may be in the form of a book, box or drawer. Usually these are cardboard covers provided with two metal hinges to hold together the punched papers. In many modern offices drawers with specially designed cabinet are used for filing.

This method is simple and flexible. It facilitates easy reference to the current documents since they are filed in chronological sequence. Main effect of the system is that reference to previous records would be inconvenient, because to get hold of any previous letter, other letters which are filed above it have to be taken out. Or, the whole file has to be carried even when one single letter or papers to be referred to. In this process the contents of the file are likely to get torn or otherwise worn out. Moreover, insertion and detachment of papers take much time.

There are two types of horizontal or flat filing system:

(i) Loose-sheet system *(ii)* The lever-arch system.

(i) Loose-sheet system: Under this system there is a box like arrangement with a lid and hinged side. Loose tough paper sheets are arranged inside the box. These sheets bear either an alphabetical or numerical marking which could serve as an index to the filed documents. Letters and other documents which need to be filed are first to be classified into alphabetical or numerical order. Then they are interposed between the index sheets below the figure or the alphabet to which they belong as per their classification. These files may be arranged in the form of drawers. Now springs of sheet prongs are being used to hold the papers in good grip.

This method is usually used to file current catalogues, price-lists, bills of lading and other papers which need very frequent reference. As soon as current documents become dormant they are transferred to the store room to facilitate future reference.

(ii) *The Lever-arch system:* Under this system there is provision for a double spring arch over which papers are placed and a cover on which a spring presses to preserve the documents from dirt or dust. Contents of the file lie flat. Distinguishing feature of this system is its fastening device. It consists of double arch of thin metal tube or thick wire which can be adjusted through a spring contrivance for opening and closing. Papers are specially punched or perforated for opining and closing. Papers are specially punched or perforated with two holes and are put through the two projecting spikes. At the back of the spikes and fitting tightly over their points, are two arches which turn sideways to enable insertion of any additional papers. In order to insert any document in the middle of previous papers or to remove any of them, the papers above the point required are turned upwards and backwards over the arch. The arch then can be opened and the concerned papers may be inserted or taken out. The arch is later closed and the top contents in the file are restored to their normal position.

Two points should be kept in mind to make this system effectively useful. Firstly, punch holes should not come too near the edge of the paper or documents, and secondly, contents should be kept neat and straight.

These files can be made up of thick cardboard or may be designed in the form of special cabinets. Alphabetical or numerical index may be provided for each of the cabinet.

Advantages of the Lever-arch System:

(a) Letters and papers are not misplaced since they are firmly fastened on the arch.

(b) Insertion of papers in the middle of the file is possible without any dislocation.

(c) Reference to previous records is made convenient. There is no need to take out other papers while referring to any past correspondence or document. Main defeat of this system is that insertion and removal of papers takes a long time when the correspondence is very bulky. In that case more than one file can be used to facilitate convenient handling of different records.

(2) Vertical method of filing: In this system papers are placed side by side in vertical position. "The contents stand upright usually on their left-hand edges and face foremost." Documents which are to be filed are first put into folders and these folders stand upright in alphabetical or numerical order and are accommodated in drawers of suitable size and design.

The drawers are generally about 24 inches long, 12 inches wide and 10 inches deep. At the bottom of each drawer, there is a rod of thin metal which runs from fronts to back. This rod is meant to hold the folders together. For maintaining a large number of vertical files, a cabinet containing several drawers is used. The cabinets may be of wood or steel and are usually supplied in tires of four or five drawers.

Inside the drawers, folders are placed in alphabetical or numerical order. A folder is a strong and stiff paper or linen-jacket in which letters and other papers are put. The folder serves as protective cover each folder bears the name of the customer or other correspondents and the reference numbers. The letters pertaining to a party are put into the folder which can be picket out whenever required for reference.

A series of guide cards made of heavy manila paper is provided in each drawer. These guide cards divide the folders into defferent sections usually in alphabetical order. The guide cards have projecting tabs which indicate different sections of folders. This provides a key for ready reference.

It should be remembered that the papers in a vertical file are not tied or fastened together in any way. Only the guide cards are strung. Papers to be filed are merely slipped into the proper folders and whenever any letter is required for reference its folder is just lifted out. It can be reinserted with ease after reference has been made. If any folder is required for reference at leisure, it can be taken out and a card with a memorandum about its whereabouts may be inserted in its place. Such cards are called Absent Cards or Outcards.

Advantages of Vertical System of Filing:

(i) Since letters and other papers stand upright any of them can be easily picked out for reference without disturbing other records.

(ii) No time is lost in insertion or removal of papers, because

they are not tied together. It is, therefore, simple and flexible.

(iii) The capacity of drawers and cabinets is larger than that of a flat filing receptable. The range of reference is therefore wider.

(iv) In the course of reference to any document, it is not necessary to turn over or touch other documents. Hence, there is least likelihood of other papers being worn out.

(v) The documents are placed in thick folders and hence greater safety of the records is ensured.

(vi) Index cards facilitate quick and accurate reference. Each index card is projected above the other. Therefore, indications on each are immediately visible and distinguishable for reference.

The main defect of this system is that the papers taken out for reference may not be carefully reinserted. Immediately after the reference is over. Hence, officials in charge of Filing Department have to take the necessary precautions against such possibility.

Suspended Files

Suspended files are a modification of the vertical method of filing. Under this method folders are suspended on a metal frame which is fitted inside the filing drawer. Folders themselves are fitted with metal bars to enable them to remain in suspended position. Sometimes the top metal bar of each file carries a movable index-title tab.

Chief merit of the suspended files is that sagging of files in the drawers is avoided. In case of ordinary folders. There is every chance that any of them may go below the other. Under this system folders do not lie on the bottom at all and hence can be moved freely backward or forward. It also enjoys all the advantages of the vertical system.

14

Relevance of Gandhian Technology in Modern Business Management

In recent year there has been, in the modern business management an increasing awareness of the need to restructure social values with a view to providing greater happiness to the people. Affluent countries are recognizing that mere prosperity is not enough and that man does not live by bread alone. It is no mere coincidence that suicide and divorce rates are higher in such countries and, increasingly, the younger generation are seeking a new framework of society which would provide greater happiness to the individual.

Simultaneously, in the developing countries also, there is increasing recognition that the social and cultural values of these countries are not necessarily in conflict with modern business management and hence need not be discarded in favour of the western system of business management. In many developing countries people are groping for a new order of business management which would harmonise the traditional values of their countries with the compulsions of modern management. It is felt that it should be possible to reorganize their countries' management system in the framework of the values inherited from the past and not switch over completely to western business management.

It is in this context that there has been a greater awareness of the relevance of the principles and teachings of Mahatma Gandhi. Whereas a few decade ago, it was the fashion to regard him as a well intentioned but somewhat eccentric individual unsuited to modern times, it is now being realised that much of what he stood for and preached during his life time has a relevance for modern business management. With increasing urbanization and consequently greater occurrence of slums in cities, pollution of the countryside, wastage of natural resources and greater authoritarianism in political affairs, it is being recognized that the framework of values which Gandhiji had stood for would prove to be an alternative model for modern business management. Particularly in the less affluent countries of Asia and Africa, Gandhiji's insistence on restriction of wants and the need for providing a livelihood to all sections of the population has struck a responsive chord in countries where providing adequate employment opportunities has proved to be the biggest problem in recent years.

It is always not possible to visualise clearly the contours of the new order. Western management thinkers have been trying to picture in many words what a new system of management should be, which would maximise opportunities for the individual to grow. Perhaps, one of the best descriptions of such an order has been given by the famous management thinker, in the following words : "I imagine a world within which machines should function solely for Man's benefit, turning out those goods which are necessary for his well being, relieving him of the necessity for heavy physical labour and dull routine and meaningless activity well-clothed and well-housed. Man in this world lives in balance with his environment, nourished by nature, in harmony with the myriads of other life forms that are beneficial to him. He treats his land wisely, halts erosion and over-cropping and returns all organic matter from the soil from which it has sprung. He lives efficiently and yet minimises artificiality. It is not over crowded world; people can, if they wish, isolate themselves in the silence of a mountain top, or they can walk through primeval forests or across wooded plains. In the world of my imagination, there is organization but it is as decentralised as possible compatible with the requirements for survival. There is a world government but is exists solely for the purpose of preventing war and stabilising population and irrevocably restricted. The government exists for man rather than man for the government. In the world of my imagination, the various regions are self-sufficient and the people are free to govern themselves as they choose and to establish their own cultural patterns. All individuals have a voice in the government and individuals can move about when and where they please. It is a world where man's creativity is blended with the creativity of nature and where a moderate degree of organization is blended with a moderate degree of anarchy. Is such a world impossible of realisation ? Perhaps it is, but who amongst us can really say. At least if we try to create such a world there is a chance that we will succeed. But if we let the present trend continue, it is all too clear that we will lose for ever those qualities of mind and spirit which distinguish the human being from the automation."

Again, new technology has been put forward as an alternative for a sane and rational business management. It is a technology "which places people before government, men before machines, villages before cities, welfare before growth, small before big, practice before theory, quality before quantity, craftsmanship before expertise, and decentralized living, to dictatorship. This is a technology that has no use for conventional ideologies which all suffer from the same defects whether it is capitalism of the USA, socialism of Scandinavia, the welfare state of U.K. or the communism of China.... they are all anti-man and pro-system; in all of them the system is greater than the man. But the crucial questions of course is whether this new technology is 'genuinely viable'. Are these new communities to be seen as crusading enterprises likely to find answers to the problems a society based on science and technology has created by its own foolhardiness? Or are they merely freak-outs for those with the inclination or financial resources to live in this way, of no relevance to any one outside."

The new priorities implicit in a system of management such as the above brings us very close to the Gandhian thesis of decentralised living in rural communities which are self-sufficient and which are almost independent of each other for meeting their basic needs. What one may ask is the basic philosophy of Gandhiji which would be a guide for present business management.

A generation that has suffered the trauma of Two World Wars, the rise and fall of dictators and false gods, the decline of imperialism and colonialism and the extreme, almost absurd, limits to which a machine civilization can go, is better able to appreciate the dangers against which Gandhiji has warned seven decades ago. What might have seemed then as being unduly pessimistic no longer appears so; what seemed then as the mere eccentricity of an individual today appears to many as a surer guide to sane living. It is not merely the old and the wise that see the Gandhian alternative as perhaps the only one if civilisation is to survive; many of the young are also breaking away from the values and mores which an industrial society and culture has forced on modern management.

Having said this, let it not be misunderstood that today's management accept—all that Gandhiji had said or written; quite obviously, the conditions under which he wrote were vastly different and it would be unreasonable to expect that what he had stated then should be accepted in today; he himself would be the first to deny for himself such universal validity. He was only too well aware that in a life span stretching over nearly eight decades, or which half was spent in unceasing service in two continents, one could expect the sort of 'consistency' which we lesser mortals are always straining to attain; Gandhiji had approvingly quoted Emerson, the famed American philosopher, who had said that such consistency was merely the 'hobgoblin of individuals'. "In my search after truth", Gandhiji had once written, "I have discarded many ideas and learnt many new things." He therefore made it clear that he was "not at all concerned with appearing to be consistent" and advised his leaders with that rare courage typical of him that if any body finds any inconsistency between any two writings of him "if he has still faith in my sanity, he would do well to choose the latter of the two on the same subject."

Indeed, Gandhiji's views on machinery, as on much else, changed significantly over the years; the man who regarded all machinery as 'satanic' was later willing to accept "intelligent exceptions" and a considerable degree of industrialization provided it was for the good of the people. The man who wrote once that "it is the machine that has impoverished India" and compared it to a 'snake hole' later said categorically that he was "aiming not at the eradication of all machines but only on their limitation." He made it clear that he was not against machinery as such but only on their indiscriminate use; when critics accused him of being against all machinery, he countered by the argument that his own body was a delicate piece of machinery. He went further to say that he would "favour the use of the most elaborate machines if thereby India's pauperism and resulting idleness can be avoided." He was therefore not against machines per se but on its side aspects, particularly in throwing people out of employment and in the 'dehumanisation' of attitudes. "How can country," he once asked with his impeccable logic "afford to have a machine which will displace the labour of crores of living machines."

One needs to remember that Gandhiji's contacts with the 'machine' civilisation both in South Africa and India were none too happy. In the former, he had led his unarmed people against a government which used the tools of that civilisation to suppress them. He had pitted the 'moral force' of his movement against the 'machine force' of the government; if he had emerged victorious, even partially, it was indeed a significant success—but one should not wonder if his mind reacted rather angrily to what the machine—allied to a powerful government—could do. In India too, he found the same phenomenon, of a vast country of millions ruled by a microscopic minority of 'whites'—because they had the resources of machine civilisation at their disposal which the Indians did not. He realised that if it were to be a contest of machine power, his countrymen would loss—even though numerically they were many times more. It was the moral force that he wanted to use in which one individual was pitted against the other; in such a fight, it was the individual that counted not as part of a group but merely as himself. The result of such a contest would then depend upon the moral strength of the individual, which would not place any special disadvantage on his countrymen.

It was a revolutionary tract which seeks to set out the framework of a new management theory which is to be founded not a conventional economic doctrine but on ethical and moral considerations. It is the blue print for a 'New Way of Life' in which ethics would replace economics and love replace greed, and welfare substitute profit. It is a self-contained, internally consistent doctrine which, given the assumptions with which Gandhiji started, moves with an irresistible logic of its own.

There is a common thread that runs through Gandhiji's philosophy—and if one may describe it by a single word—it is humanism. Gandhiji saw man as a pitiful creature ground down by the instruments which he himself had created. Like Frankenstein, they were becoming too big for him and he wanted to halt the process before it was too late. He wanted to restore to man the dignity due to him as an individual—and which was denied by the false values in a society increasingly dominated by the machine—and hence his repugnance to the machine.

It was an instinctive reaction to the political conditions which Gandhiji had experienced in South Africa and India and it arose out of his innate faith in man. Man was a reflection of the Divine Being, and had a greater and nobler purpose in life. He rejected the Jeans hypothesis that man was born out of an accidental assembly of chemicals; intuitively he regarded such a view as a denial of higher purpose in the creation and evolution of man. If the instruments of Civilisation did not make it possible for man to realise that purpose, he had no option but to destroy such instruments.

Specific Features of the Gandhian Business Management

Scale: Gandhiji was against increasing the scale of industrial operations to make more profits or to bring down the cost of production. While the latter objective might apparently seem desirable, Gandhiji was aware of the fact that increased production by itself would only add to the profits of manufacturers or middlemen unless coupled with proper distribution. Large scale industrialization has, in fact, not solved any of the problems which industrial growth was expected to do; in the developing countries, provision of employment opportunities has always been one of the major bottlenecks and yet large scale industry has hardly provided even 10 per cent of the jobs for new entrants to the labour force. In fact, due to the fact that much of it is also capital intensive, large scale industry has become a drain on the capital resources of any country and, in this context, the emphasis on small and rural industry which Gandhiji had laid down seems to be particularly relevant at the present moment.

It is also not always correct to speak of large scale operations being intrinsically more viable as this would depend on the environment in which the industry operates, the scale of wages as well as the markets which they are intended to serve. In countries such as India where, although the population is large, the purchasing power of the people is very low, demand for most products is generally at a low level. It would seem more desirable to envisage a large number of small production units scattered all over the country avoiding transportation loads and spreading much more widely the effects of industrialization than to set up one or two large scale units in one corner of the country with hardly any impact on the rest of the country. This is in fact the reason why large industry has developed a locational prejudice in favour of large towns and metropolises where infrastructure has been readymade for them at great cost. No amount of incentives to move to less developed areas seem to have much effect in persuading them to do so.

Thus, the scale of operations has a far greater social importance than the purely economical and technological aspects of it. To make the small scale industrial operations economical, it is necessary that we should devise a technology which would make small operations viable in themselves and not necessarily depend upon mass production devices which the West has so far developed to suit its own requirements. What is really required is a greater application of modern scientific techniques to the development of small volume production which so far has not been done in the developing countries. This is indeed a challenging task before the scientists and technologists of these countries to apply modern scientific principles which would result in technological devices that make small volume production intrinsically viable.

Modernization

This does not however mean that such technology should necessarily be obsolete or out of date. It may well be that such a low cast technology will require some of the most modern scientific principles which are currently being through of. It is well-known that considerable thought is being given to making the lowly bullock cart more efficient and any one who has dealt with such problems will readily realise that simple as it may sound, such problem can indeed be most complex in a technological sense. Thus, in the manufacture of sugar, cement, paper, etc., one does not have to be confined by the experiences of the developed countries which are based on large scale production. It seems possible to think in terms of small units which would be intrinsically viable and cater to the requirements of the developing countries.

It needs to be emphasised, however, that any technological device that is developed would need to have an intrinsic efficiency of its own; otherwise it will never be able to compete on equal terms with the rest of the industry. It was never intended by Gandhiji that either the society or the country should be burdened with a large number of inefficient or wasteful economic processes through the small production units. What is contended is that within the broad guidelines of that thought, it should be possible to develop a technology which would satisfy both the criteria, namely, that of decentralized production on a small scale as well as economic efficiency. Gandhiji's own attitude to this problem was well typified by his announcement of a prize for Rs. one lakh in 1927 for improvements to the traditional charkha (spinning wheel). Significantly, the prize was won only after his death in 1950 when the Amber Charkha was developed and since then there has been rapid advancement in the technology of the spinning wheel.

A point that needs to be made is that modern technology particularly in electronics and communication has made possible the realisation of the Gandhian 'utopia' of efficient production units clothing the countryside instead of handling together in urban conglomerations. Truly, the Gandhian vision of decentralised rural communities operating industrial units at a high level of efficiency is no longer a pipe dream but one which is capable of realisation. But such industries would need to be relevant to the countryside and have a direct linkage with it; otherwise, they would remain isolated and outside entities without any organic relationship with the environment.

Relevance

This is not merely in respect of the product but also the tools of production. It is easy enough, given a certain amount of foreign exchange to import the latest equipment and machinery but this would hardly make any impact on the local artisan or the worker as he will be unable to make full use of it. It is a frequent sight in most establishments in India to seen some of the latest equipment imported from abroad being hardly utilised or remaining idle for want of critical spares. Japan is an example of a country where, in spite of advanced concepts of proudction, machines are used which many Western observers would consider as obsolete. However, the Japanese themselves seem to work with these machines with great effectiveness and quite often, the workers are encouraged to improve on the performance of such machinery. The technology that is likely to be most effective in a country like India, is one that is a little ahead of present day practice but not too far ahead to be out of place. Relevance of equipment with local skills is therefore an important factor in the development of such a technology.

The unitisation of existing resources is an important parameter in any technology if it is to be successful. The tropics in which most of the developing countries are located have abundant reserves of natural resources, but these would need to be conserved and worked carefully. There is increased awareness of the fact that these natural resources constitute a precious legacy which the present generation cannot afford to waste without getting maximum impact out of them. Again there are certain areas like utilisation of solar energy which the developing countries have in abundance but have hardly made any use so far. It seems therefore necessary that a major scientific and technological effort should be devoted largely to the unitisation of resources that are available in them, and not geared to the resource pattern of the developed countries.

Emphasis on Human Values

The use of labour saving machinery which the West had to take up because of its lack of manpower is not relevant in the developing countries where manpower is available in abundance. What is needed is to use it productively and to train it for useful purposes. But much of the effort in the developing countries seems to be based on a repetition of the Western experience which regards machines as being more easily managed than men. The Chinese experience and, to a lesser extent, the Indian experience in harnessing manpower need to be studied carefully so that the full utilisation of the human resource available in these countries could well set an example for the developing countries. What is needed is an optimum 'man-machine mix' and not necessarily machine intensive or labour intensive operations. Every industry and in fact every operation has its own optimum mix and its is necessary to find the right mix in the socio-economic conditions obtaining in each country, so as to be most effective.

One of the cardinal facets of Gandhian management theory is its emphasis on human values and the dignity attached to the worker. At one time, it was considered tacitly, if not explicitly, in the western technological framework that man was subordinate to the machine; but even in the West it is now being recognised that any meaningful effort can be obtained from the worker, when he understand the nature of his work. While necessarily, as industrialisation proceeds, the human element has to be subordinated to some extent, it need not completely disappear and particularly in countries like India where the tempo of living is still slow, emphasis on human values is still strong. It should be possible to provide the framework in which workers can produce without necessarily losing the human values of society.

Distributive Aspect

An important feature of the Gandhian management was the distributive aspect which was fundamental to his approach. While western economic thinking was largely based on increased production leaving distribution to take care of itself, Gandhiji had the vision to see the evil effects of concentrated production without the necessary distributive justice. It was at one time considered fashionable to say that what was needed was greater production and that distribution could be left to the market forces. But monopolies and increased concentration of economic power in the hands of a few groups are a danger to democratic society and it seems necessary to build into the pattern of economic growth the necessary checks which would provide for a humane distribution even before production increased to a points where it cannot be controlled. Relevance to the Problems of Today:

Today, as we look back almost 50 years one wonders how close it is to the central issues that now dominate our thinking.

Perhaps, no other problem worries the planners and policy makers of most development countries as the explosive one of finding suitable employment to their growing populations. Employments —meaningful or otherwise—has become the one over-riding concern of all government and many feel unstable and threatened, with employment opportunities unequal to the increasing numbers.

It is this aspect, more than anything else, that bothered Gandhiji in relation to the machine. Again and again, he made it clear in his later writing that it was not the machine that he was against but its impact on people. Nor was he alone in this apprehension; even so confirmed a believer in industrialisation as Jawarharlal Nehru was conscious of the intrinsic logic of Ghadhiji's view points in the Indian context. Writing in the Discovery of India, he says:

> "Foolish comparisons are made between manpower and machine power. Of course, a big machine can do the work of thousand or ten thousand persons. But if those ten thousand sit idly by or starve, the introduction of the machine is not a social gain."

But Gandhiji had a solution for the dilemma: he wanted certain types of machines to be used – those "which do not deprive men the opportunity to labour, but which helps the individual and adds to his efficiency and which men can handle at will without being its slave." He was even willing to use electricity in every home so that the villagers can ply their implements and tools with the help of electric power. From the seemingly rigid and doctrinnaire stand on machines he took in Hind Swaraj, he relented in later years to admit of 'good' machines that help human beings. But "the supreme consideration is the men. The machine should not make atrophied the limbs of men. The saving of labour of the individual should be the object, and honest humanitarian consideration, and not greed, the motive."

This is indeed very close to what Prof. Nobert Wiener, the famous mathematician of MIT whose work in cybernetics founded the control systems that ultimately helped to land man on the moon. In a book, significantly entitled The Human Use of Human Beings, he writes:

"The factory system started as a means of introducing

> discipline into the highly undisciplined home industry of the industrial workers and of keeping the standards of production. If the fractional horse-power motor had been available from the start, and could have increased the production of cottage workers, it is highly probable that a large part of the organization and discipline needed for successful large scale production would have been imposed on such home industries as spinning and weaving."

Today, not only the fractional horsepower motor but a whole host of systems and telecommunication facilities are available that make possible for an individual to operate efficiently from his own home. Large corporate organizations, even in the USA, are now learning that it is no longer necessary for them to operate from crowded metropolitan cities and that they can control their vast national and even overseas operations from the relatively secluded atmosphere of small towns. Multi-nationals such as NCR and others are now moving away from Chicago and Detroit to smaller villages; as Time, the prestigious American weekly, put it: "Urbanity is being delinked from urban living." Thus the Gandhian ideal of converting every home into a productive unit so that the villager can live with his family while engaged in his daily work is no longer a pipe dream but one which is possible and practicable leading, as Gandhiji put it, not to mass production but "production by the masses."

And even in an economic sense, it is the only feasible proposition; today the cost of providing a single work place is being pushed relentlessly upward; a steel plant which costs Rs. 1000 crore can provide no more employment than for 5000 persons which would mean that Rs. 20 lakhs is to be spent on capital assets for every job created. Even if one takes less capital-intensive schemes, the cost in the organized sector for every job created is not less than Rs. one lakh. If 100 million persons who will enter the labour force in the next ten years are to be catered to, the investment required for this purpose alone will be an astronomical figure of Rs. 10,000 billion—clearly beyond there sources of India by any stretch of imagination. At the other end of the spectrum, one can create jobs in the cottage and small industries at Rs. 1000-5000 per person employed, so that the money required is reduced by 20-100 times bringing it well within the realms of possibility.

Those who criticise Gandhiji's ideas of village industries as being outmoded or backward may well pause to think whether, indeed, there is in the resource constraints operating in the country today, any practical alternative to his dream of villages humming with the music of the spinning wheel—which to him was a symbol of the ancient crafts that had once flourished in the country but had now decayed due to apathy and stagnation. It is indeed significant that a leading economist of the Third World—Mahbud-ul Haque (now with the World Bank)—has been advocating treating labour itself as part of the capital stock of a country: "It is only if we proceed from the goal of full employment with people doing something useful even with little doses of capital and organization, that we can eradicate some of the worst forms of poverty."

Gandhiji himself had no illusion about the spinning wheel; he was quite clear in his mind as to what it can do and what is expected of it. In a language that is clear and unambiguous he wrote:

> "The sole claim advanced on its behalf is that it alone offers an immediate, practicable and permanent solution to that problem of problems that confronts India, *viz.*, the enforced idleness for nearly six months in the year of an overwhelming majority of Indian population, owing to lack of supplementary occupation to agriculture and chronic starvation of the masses that results therefrom. I would favour of the most elaborate machinery if thereby India's pauperism and resulting idleness be avoided. I have suggested hand spinning as the only ready means of driving away penury and making famine of work and wealth impossible."

Now wonder that the noted British economist G.D.H. Cole remarked: "Gandhiji's campaign for the development of hand-made cloth industry is no mere fad of a romantic eager to revive the past but a practical attempt to relive the poverty and uplift the standard of the Indian village." The spinning wheel was only one example of what can be done; today, modern science and technology makes it possible to think of many other rural activities which can be revived and made efficient and viable. Bertrand Russell, the eminent mathematician, philosopher and humanist points out:

> "Electricity and motor transport have made small units of industry not only economically possible but even desirable. When a rural industry flourishes, it should be gradually mechanised through electricity but left in small units. India for example is traditionally a land of village communities. It would be a tragedy if this traditional way of life were to be suddenly and violently exchanged for the greater evils of urban industrialisation. The rivers of the Himalayas should provide all the hydro-electric power that is needed for the gradual mechanisation of the village industries of India and for the immeasurable improvement of physical well being without either the obvious disaster of industrial slums or the more subtle loss and degradation when age old traditions are too rudely broken."

Now was Gandhiji contrary to popular misimpression, averse to the gradual mechanisation of the rural industry. He did not want its technology to be frozen at the low level into which it had sunk; he wanted to upgrade it so that it can bring more earning to those who participate in it. Today's version of the spinning wheel with six spindles is a far cry from the comparatively crude model of the twenties—and provides at least four times the wages then earned. But his main insistence was that such production should be decentralised and carried on, if possible in one's own home rather than in the impersonal surroundings of a factory.

Surprisingly, Henry Ford, whose Model-T car revolutionised the automobile industry also believed in decentralised village units: pragmatically, he found it costs less to produce in small units:

> "Wherever it is possible, a policy of decentralisation ought to be adopted. We would need instead of mammoth flour mills, a multitude of smaller units distributed through all the sections where grain is grown—our communities ought to be more complete in themselves. They ought not to be unnecessarily dependent on railway transportation—out of what they produce, they should supply their own needs and ship the surplus."

These are words which Gandhiji would have endorsed wholeheartedly—it could seems if the father of 'mass production' and the prophet of 'production by masses' were not so widely different in their views after all.

Economic Equality

Ultimately, Gandhiji wanted to elevate the poor and the oppressed so that they could walk in dignity. "Economic equality", he wrote "is the master key to non-violent independence. It means the levelling down of a few rich in whose hands is concentrated the bulk of the nation's wealth on the one hand and a levelling up of the semi-starved naked millions on the other. A non-violent system of government is clearly an impossibility so long as the wide gulf between the rich and hungry million persists"—a fact widely accepted today. Even on the industrial scene, it is recognised that the dichotomy that now exists between the prosperous West and the hungry Third World cannot persist for long and that prosperity, like peace, is indivisible.

But Gandhiji had no use for high sounding platitudes. "To him", wrote Gunnar Myrdal, the Swedish sociologist, "development meant people everywhere in the country and not least in the village where most of the people live—Gandhi was certainly a planner but his planning was all embracing. It is only in the latest years that we have more generally come back to Gandhian ideas whenever economists have been moved to press for what Gandhiji was all the time preaching. If Indian planning has not been more successful than it has actually been, the main explanation is that they have not kept so close, as they should, to the fundamental of the teachings of the Father of the Nation."

Jan Tinberge, the Nobel-prize winning Dutch Economist, endorses the Gandhian approach to planning thus:

> "It will have to be realised that India's problems can only be solved by certain types of idealism on the side of its leading personalities to be understood in a wide sense; an idealism based, perhaps, on the Gandhian principles of simplicity and austerity." Today, the nation is going through a trauma in trying to practise many of the things Gandhiji had talked about in his life time so that luxury and ostentation are curbed and the poor can truly inherit the earth.

Implementation Aspects of Gandhian Thought

More than even the approach which Gandhiji preached during his life time, it was the fact that he tried to implement most of them that had the most impact on his countrymen. In fact, it is now being recognised that implementation is a key failure of much of the planning of the developing countries. Grandiose schemes are worked out meticulously on paper but often fail miserably in the field. What seems to be required is a combination of attention to detail as well as a realistic appraisal of the resources, both human and material. In this respect Gandhiji was a pragmatist who took as his motto the famous hymn of Cardinal Newman "One step enough for me". It is in this he differed from most of his contemporaries who came out with much more spectacular schemes for winning the freedom of India. But it was Gandhiji's conviction that only by developing the inner strength of the Indian people could freedom be achieved and retained.

Dignity of Manual Labour

One of the key points which Gandhiji emphasised during his life time was the dignity of manual labour. While many people paid lip-sympathy for this concept, it was only Gandhiji that really put it into practice. In a traditional society which placed greater emphasis on book learning rather than on labour. Gandhiji, taking the concept of John Ruskin, constantly emphasised the need for action. Ruskin's book Unto the Last gripped Gandhiji's imagination during a train trip to Durban and he saw clearly "that if mankind were to progress and reach the ideal of equality and brotherhood, it will have to adopt and act on the principle of 'unto the last'. It must take along with it even the sick, the halt and the lame. But in the machine age these have no place."

Experimentation

Gandhiji never took any statement on its face value unless he had experimented it himself and found it to be true. In this aspect, he revealed a true scientific approach very different from the traditional legacy of India whose forte was speculative thought which relied more on intuition rather than experiment. In fact,

Gandhiji was the experimenter par excellence: he experimented with everything, himself, his wife, his collegues, and in fact with the freedom of 400 million Indians. He tried a variety of methods in various fields: health, medicine, prohibition, untouchability, political freedom, sexual countinence.... all these formed the subject matters of his experiments. What is important, however, is the approach he followed to solve the problems facing the country. It was neither adhoc nor bookish: it was based on his own personal experience and out of the deep conviction that he had formed in all such matters.

Attention of Detail

Here, again, Gandhiji was different from most of his contemporaries. While all of them preferred to pay attention to the broader aspects of India's freedom, Gandhiji looked upon that freedom as consisting of a number of myriad details which contributed ultimately to the success of the entire programme. It was this meticulous approach and attention to detail that really made his campaigns successful. One could easily miss such small points in a programme which was ultimately destined to change the history of mankind. But Gandhiji considered them as important as the end itself, because he believed that it was the means that fashioned these ends.

Individual—The Unit of Planning:

Ultimately Gandhiji saw the freedom of the country in terms of the freedom of the individual. To him, the individual mattered much and his attitude towards machinery and much else is based on his great faith on the dignity of the individual. Man, he said, is the supreme consideration and everything else is subordinate to it. The freedom of India was not an abstract entity, as it was for Pandit Jawaharlal Nehru, but for providing bread, to give a good life to the lowest and the poorest of the Indian people. He wanted 'to wipe the tear from every eye' and although he could not achieve this fully, it was indeed a grand vision. Again and again, he warned the country against possible consequences if the individual were not given his due place. He saw a crowd is a collection of individuals unlike Pandit Nehru who saw individuals as part of the crowd. It was his faith in the individual born out of his basic traditional background as well as his upbringing in the Victorian era that ultimately marked him apart from all of his contemporaries. The talisman that Gandhiji given many years back—whether the step we are to take would help the poorest Indian we know—is as valid today as when he gave it many years back. One wonders in the light of that test, how many of the schemes and projects which today are taken up will really pass that test.

Index